Bart Starr

Bart Starr

When Leadership Mattered

David Claerbaut

TAYLOR TRADE PUBLISHING
Dallas   Lanham   Boulder   New York   Toronto   Oxford

Published by Taylor Trade Publishing
An imprint of The Rowman & Littlefield Publishing Group, Inc.
4501 Forbes Boulevard, Suite 200
Lanham, MD 20706

Distributed by NATIONAL BOOK NETWORK

Library of Congress Cataloging-in-Publication Data
Claerbaut, David.
    Bart Starr : when leadership mattered / David Claerbaut.—1st Taylor Trade pub. ed.
    p.   cm.
    Includes bibliographical references and index.
    ISBN 1-58979-117-7 (cloth : alk. paper)
    1. Starr, Bart.   2. Football players—United States—Biography.   I. Title.
    GV939.S73C53   2004
    796.332'092—dc22   2004008079

∞ ™ The paper used in this publication meets the minimum requirements of American National Standard for Information Sciences—Permanence of Paper for Printed Library Materials, ANSI/NISO Z39.48-1992.

Manufactured in the United States of America.

To my "brother," Ivan Eernisse, my favorite Packer fan

CONTENTS

ACKNOWLEDGMENTS

I want to thank the Green Bay Packer organization for the their assistance in researching this book.

CHAPTER 1

Nothing Has Happened since the Sixties

I T I S O F T E N said that, "Nothing has happened since the sixties. Nothing." Virtually every social force leading into the new millennium has its genesis in the 1960s.

In electoral politics, the age of television and big money arrived in 1960 when John F. Kennedy used both to put away Richard Nixon in the closest presidential campaign in American history. With Kennedy, the heavy, staid air of the fifties began evaporating and was replaced with a vigorous, youthful optimism. In addition, the end of the aging and static Dwight Eisenhower's administration and the entrance of JFK signaled the beginning of the president-as-celebrity syndrome.

On the darker side, the specter of nuclear war developed realistic contours in that decade. The escalating Cold War, the arms race, and the Cuban missile crisis moved the thought of mass annihilation from science fiction into the daily newspapers, and into the mind of the American citizen. High school students gave speeches on the threats of Communism, the danger of nuclear testing, and the peril of stockpiling such weapons. Families, in preparation for a nuclear world war, built bomb shelters stocked with food in their basements. Today, the Cold War is over, but terrorism brings with it new, daily fears of mass destruction right in one's own country.

An atmosphere of continuous change, now a constant, has its roots in the sixties. (Ozzie and) Harriet Nelson and (Ward and) June Cleaver notwithstanding, the role of women was about to be altered radically.

Many date the onset of that change to the publication of Betty Friedan's *The Feminine Mystique* in 1963. Friedan recast the word *woman*, defining it in social and political rather than biological terms. The stage was set for mass education and professionalization of what once was culturally regarded as a domestic gender.

Civil rights also moved on to the main stage of the nation in the sixties. Martin Luther King, who mesmerized the nation with his "I Have a Dream" speech in 1963, led marches, sit-ins, and other non-violent challenges to discrimination. An author, speaker, and one-man political force, the Nobel Prize–winning King became a political icon during the decade. Despite his commitment to peaceful social change, violence simmered under the surface. Other, more militant orators, H. Rap Brown, Stokeley Carmichael, and Eldredge Cleaver among them stirred the angry passions of the victims of racism. Cities burned, confrontations with the police became routine, and lives were lost, as blacks became more strident. King himself, the apostle of non-violence, was dead by an assassin's bullet by 1968. He was just 39 years old. The era of the passive minority was over, and civil rights would never again be a back-shelf issue in American life.

Many historians also mark the sixties as the point at which America lost its innocence. Beginning with the unforgettable mid-day event in Dallas on November 22, 1963—the assassination of President Kennedy—violence, disillusionment, and alienation became visible on the national stage. Before the end of the decade Malcolm X; Medgar Evers; Martin Luther King; and JFK's brother, Robert, would also be murdered.

Arts and leisure reflected the instability of the times. In pop music, the fifties crooners gave way to hard rockers, followed by a British invasion led by the Beatles and then a psychedelic era. The decade began with cigarettes and beer and ended with marijuana and LSD. Sexual mores changed as Hugh Hefner became a pop philosopher. Skirts went up and sexual prohibitions went down. By the end of the sixties, sex, drugs, and rock and roll became a lifestyle for many youths.

So also was protest. Throughout the decade an increasingly unpopular war in Southeast Asia was spilling the blood and draining the spirit of the country. Initially viewed as a heroic and necessary stand against the expansion of Communism, by the late sixties, the Vietnam conflict became regarded by many as a civil war in a nation thousands of miles away, one in which the United States should not be involved. So intense was the resistance to the war, that students burned draft cards, fled to Canada, and openly protested on the streets and university campuses. The word *disorder* became a major part of the American vocabulary and a seemingly omnipotent political figure, President Lyndon Baines Johnson, Kennedy's successor, was all but driven out of office. Johnson, who in 1964 scored the greatest electoral triumph in American history, chose not to run for re-election four years later.

Even Americans' favorite avenue of escape, the toy department of the culture—sports—was not immune to high-speed shifts in the society. Sport changed forever in the sixties. Slow-moving baseball, long the only big-league sport, gave way to quick-breaking professional football as the sport of choice for many fans. It remains the preeminent spectator sport. Meanwhile, hockey and basketball were gaining momentum. College football and basketball reflected the changing politics of the sixties as black players became more prominent and vocal. The large halo-like Afro was more than a hairstyle. It was a political statement, as were the raised fists of John Carlos and Tommy Smith in the 1968 Olympics. Old, authoritarian coaches and baseball managers began to appear anachronistic and fell into disfavor, being replaced by younger, more democratic mentors.

Focus on the individual, though always a part of sports—particularly baseball with its myriad statistics—reached its zenith in this decade. In 1961, Roger Maris, reluctant with his celebrity, hit 61 home runs, eclipsing Babe Ruth's 34-year single-season standard of 60. Lew Alcindor (later Kareem Abdul-Jabbar) was a proclaimed a near one-man gang in driving UCLA basketball to the pinnacle of college hoops. Roger Staubach and, later, O.J. Simpson became larger-than-life college gridiron heroes. Wilt Chamberlain, a veritable behemoth, demolished every meaningful record in the NBA. Brusque, foreboding Jim Brown began dominating NFL defenses. It was more than the feats of these athletic icons that characterized the decade; it was also the celebrity they enjoyed, as the new cultural giant—the media—became the force that enlarged them. The cult of the individual, however, extended beyond a focus on a player's on-the-field exploits. From a self-aggrandizing standpoint, Joe Namath—loud, arrogant, and hedonistic—symbolized the new athlete. Chamberlain also radiated a self-centered aura with his outspoken demeanor. Chamberlain, Namath, and others, however, were trumped by Louisville's young and brash Cassius Clay, who changed his name to Muhammad Ali, refused induction into the military, and declared himself "The Greatest," an unthinkable utterance in decades past. Were that not enough, sports reporting evolved into social commentary with the advent of Howard Cosell—another individual who became larger than the estimable contribution he made to sport.

In a very real sense, then, nothing has really happened since the sixties. Perhaps because it was such a turbulent decade, one giving birth to so much of the culture extant in the new millennium, there remains an enduring fascination with the team of that decade, the Green Bay Packers. The Packers, like the cultural upheavals of the sixties, are also enduring symbols. They are the first modern dynasty in the wildly popular world of professional football. They are the yardstick against which every would-be football giant is measured. And yet, as they continue to tower over the wrecks of time in all of sport, they are a paradox. They were a team coached by a man with old-fashioned, non-sixties beliefs and virtues, one in which the individual was forever subjugated to the concept and identity of the team.

Perhaps that is why they were distinct. They stood as an immutable, invincible bulwark against this backdrop of exciting, frightening, and gurgling change that engulfed the decade in which they dominated. Indeed the team represented the ultimate paradox. On one hand, it enjoyed national celebrity. Not only were many of their games televised by the CBS network, its major figures were lionized, subjects of interviews and features in newspapers and magazines coast to coast. A number wrote best-selling books. They were the Goliaths of the gridiron, the New York Yankees of the nation's favorite sport. They were a genuine dynasty.

On the other hand, they were the ultimate in provinciality. Amid a nation undergoing the spasms of urbanization, they were the *Green Bay* Packers, owned by their community, a town of little more than 50,000 residents nestled in the icy regions of Wisconsin's Fox River Valley. As opposed to the Bears, Lions, and Giants, the team was named for the Indian Packing Company, its original sponsor in 1919. The players were visible in the local community, their wives shopped in the local grocery stores, and their children attended the community's schools. A night on the town more commonly meant a jaunt to Sheboygan or Milwaukee rather than New York or Chicago. Similarly, speaking engagements were more often at nearby high school sports banquets in Chilton, New Holstein, or Kiel, rather than at major events in Chicago, Los Angeles, or mid-town Manhattan.

This provincial flavor added to their image of stability. Expansion teams may be added, new leagues like the AFL formed, and instant replay added to television technology, but the Packers would always be in Green Bay where a handshake was a contract and the team belonged to the community. And while the winds of change shook the moorings of American culture, the Packers were the symbol of enduring excellence. For the first eight years of the decade, the Packers turned in eight winning seasons. They won six conference or divisional championships and five NFL titles, including the first two Super Bowls. Green Bay played in ten post-season games during the decade. Their first one was in Philadelphia, in the inaugural year of the decade, against the Eagles. The Packers pounded their opponents, racking up a 22-13 advantage in first downs and outgaining the Eagles by nearly 200 yards. They lost, 17-13. After the game, Vince Lombardi, having closed the books on just his second season as coach in this Wisconsin community, addressed the team. "Perhaps you didn't realize you could have won this game," he stated. "We're men and we will never let this happen again. We will never be defeated in a championship game again." His words proved prophetic. The Packers won the last nine post-season games in a row. Their overall sixties record was an eye-popping 91-25-4, an almost unthinkable mark in a league designed for parity.

The Green Bay Packers—from their small-town identity to their conservative style—stood with the stability of mighty oaks in a nation approaching what journalists called a collective nervous breakdown. No less than eleven players played through the entire '60–'67 championship era. Growing up as I did in tiny Cedar Grove, Wisconsin, the names of those players were as familiar to small-town Wisconsinites as those of their next-door neighbors. Common as the names of the members of those enduring championship squads were, the team comported itself with a near regal air. Lion great Alex Karras referred to it as a "super aloofness." To Nitschke biographer, Edward Gruver, "The Packers had carried themselves during their title days as if they had all been born in some great palace somewhere and that losing wasn't worth considering." "The Packers Rule the World," the words fairly jumped off the cover of an issue of *Sports Illustrated* after one of their five NFL champion seasons, captured the spirit of the times.

Head Coach and General Manager Vince Lombardi, arguably the dominant figure in the history of the National Football League, literally defined the Packers. In near God-like fashion he created the team in his image. Virtually every nuance of the team bore the stamp of this Mount Rushmore human force. Lombardi personified authority, ruling his team with a curious mixture of love and intimidation. Lombardi himself was not a man of the sixties. He was a short, stocky, conservative man who preached the importance of simple values and a single-minded commitment to excellence. In an era of shared power and democratization, Lombardi was not authoritarian. He was autocratic. A powerful orator with an all-consuming passion for achievement, Lombardi—even his name has a potent ring to it—summoned memories of mythic figures from a more romantic past, those of Knute Rockne, Red Blaik, and Amos Alonzo Stagg.

Amid the hurricanes of change, the sixties remained a time in which leadership and responsibility counted. It was a pre-Watergate era, not yet a time in which committees, task forces, and faceless corporate conglomerates would hide behind a veil of anonymity when things went awry. It was a stand-up-and-be-counted era in which responsibility as well as celebrity was the province of the individual, not the bureaucracy. From George Washington to Abraham Lincoln, from FDR to JFK, the nation continued to revere its leaders. Lyndon Johnson, Martin Luther King, Billy Graham, and Robert Kennedy differed in every way but one: They were leaders.

So it also was in sports. Many of the great teams had leaders. People knew who they were and expected them to take command. The Packers were no exception. Ask the fans. Ask the sportswriters. Ask the players. They will tell you that—on the field—the legendary, seemingly all-powerful Green Bay Packers also had a single unquestioned leader. His name was Bart Starr.

CHAPTER 2

A Great Quarterback

THERE WOULD have been no Green Bay Packers as we know them without Vince Lombardi. His impact was incalculable in scope. Consider the bookends of his Packer tenure. In 1958, the year before Lombardi arrived in Green Bay, the team record was a ghastly 1-10-1. He won immediately. His 7-5 log in '59 marked the team's first winning season since the 6-5-1 1947 squad. For Lombardi, however, it was the first of nine consecutive winning campaigns in Green Bay. His regular season Packer record was 89-29-4. Then he left the sidelines. The following year, 1968, the team went 6-7-1. To put Lombardi's tenure in perspective consider this: the Packers' regular season winning percentage under him was .746. It was a puny .308 in the two seasons ('58 and '68), bookending his time on the Green Bay sidelines.

It is also safe to say that there would also have been no Vince Lombardi as we knew him without a 6′1″, 200 pound, blond, blue-eyed quarterback named Bart Starr.

When you look at the names of the eleven players whose time with the Pack spanned all those championship years—Willie Davis, Boyd Dowler, Forrest Gregg, Henry Jordan, Jerry Kramer, Max McGee, Ray Nitschke, Bob Skoronski, Bart Starr, Fuzzy Thurston, and Willie Wood—and then add Paul Hornung and Jim Taylor, you see a team of all-stars. In fact, Starr played with nine Hall-of-Famers and 25 different Pro-Bowl players (receiving 57 selections, an average of better than seven a season for the team) during the 1960–67 glory years. And it is largely because of that star-studded cast that he is often overlooked, regarded as a me-too player (as in, "Player X had a great game and Starr did too").

Yet not one of those other 25 players was indispensable to the success of the team. As important as Hornung and Taylor were (both were league MVPs), for example, the Pack won their last two championships essentially without them. The celebrated Jerry Kramer missed major chunks of time with serious injuries. Most of the other Pro-Bowlers were not pivotal throughout the entire Packer reign. One was. The Packers could not and did not win without Bart Starr. No one knew that better than Vince Lombardi. "Without a good quarterback," he said with typical bluntness, "you just don't operate."(So critical to the team's success was Starr, that by 1962, the fiery mentor changed his focus from one of teaching to creating as calm an atmosphere as possible for him. "By the nature of his position, your quarterback is your number one man," he explained, "and we are the champions and I know that Bart feels that he has the whole burden of our offense on his shoulders and I will have to try to relax him." Kramer humorously referred to Lombardi's special regard for Starr, claiming that although the coach might well include his quarterback with a "That goes for you too, Bart," when he would rage at the squad, it sounded more like "That goes for you too, Bart, honey."

Despite a changing cast, Starr quarterbacked the team throughout Lombardi's entire tenure. In fact, other than linemen Bob Skoronski and Forrest Gregg, only Starr started all the playoff games during the championship era. And he did not simply hand off, pass, and throw an occasional block. He called the plays. He didn't just make audibles from time to time, changing the play brought in from the sidelines, as has pretty much been the case since the 1970s. *Bart Starr called the plays.* There is no higher trust an offensive coach can place in a player than to allow him to call the plays. This would be particularly true for detail-obsessed perfectionist Lombardi, who had been the offensive coordinator for the venerable New York Giant team of the late fifties. By the time Starr took over the controls in Green Bay, the sun was already setting on the era of quarterback play-calling. There were coaches around the league—Paul Brown and Tom Landry among them—that had taken over the task, shuttling plays in from the side-lines. Others, while leaving the bulk of the calls to their quarterbacks, did not hesitate to send in plays on a frequent basis. Lombardi trusted Starr to make the calls. Moreover, it was probably his turning over the offense to his quarterback that sealed their bond. Starr, as polar opposite as he was from Lombardi temperamentally, became the coach's alter ego. "Of all the people on your ballclub—and you are involved with all of them—there is no other with whom you spend as much time as you do with your quarterback," he wrote in his book, *Run to Daylight*. "If this is a game through which you find self-expression—and if it isn't you don't belong in it—then that quarterback is the primary extension of yourself and he is your greatest challenge."

Lombardi had total confidence in his leader. He praised Starr's stability and judgment. "Your quarterback has to be stable, though, and Bart is that," said Lombardi in his book. "Starr is so stable that out of the sixty-five or seventy plays we run in a game I don't send in more than ten. Then he has the right, not in the huddle but on the line, to negate anything I send in." Bart Starr's control was so complete that he was, in effect, the offensive coordinator as well as the chief executive of the offense he directed. As meticulous as Lombardi's preparation was, according to biographer David Maraniss, it was a standing joke among the players that once the game started, Lombardi was the most useless man on field. While Defensive Coordinator Phil Bengtson directed the defense, Starr called the offense. Lombardi did not even bother to wear a headset.

Starr's indispensability was never in doubt. When the Packers took over for the final time in the '67 Ice Bowl against the Dallas Cowboys trailing 17-14, a shivering, frost-bitten Ray Nitschke stood on the side-lines with hope. "We're losing," he thought, "but we have the ball. And we have Starr." Guard Fuzzy Thurston said that every time Starr stepped into the huddle, ten other players believed the team was going to score. "That's just the way he was," said the venerable Green Bay lineman, "the feeling he inspired in everybody." As far as Thurston's counterpart at guard, Jerry Kramer, was concerned, by 1962 Starr had it all. "He had knowledge, skill, confidence, everything, and at twenty-eight, he was the ideal age for a quarterback," Kramer wrote, proclaiming him "the best quarterback in football."

Much has been made of Starr's intellect, his capacity to do surgery on opposing defenses. His knowledge had been nearly total. And to play for Lombardi it had to be. "His I.Q. must be above average," wrote the coach in describing the quarterback's role, "because he must not only be able to absorb the coach's game plan each week but he must also have a thorough knowledge of what everyone does on every play, and he must know the opponent, the qualities and characteristics of each individual on the other team." Not nearly enough has been made of Starr's football acumen. Early on he mastered everything. "At our quarterback meetings," said Lombardi, "even though he was not first-string, he could repeat almost verbatim everything we had discussed the previous three days, and that meant he had a great memory, dedication, and desire." Perhaps the highest honor Lombardi bestowed on his quarterback came, ironically, when he left Green Bay after the 1969 season to coach the Washington Redskins. He asked Starr for his game notes. "He wanted all my game notes," said Starr to Lombardi biographer Maraniss, "all my team game plans for the teams we'd played over the years. I had my own detailed folders, filed by teams in a cabinet, and I gave them to him and he copied them all and sent them back. It was the nicest tribute he ever paid me." In short, the roles were reversed. The teacher was now learning from his most brilliant pupil.

There is no one, single way to determine who is the greatest quarterback in football history. Some say Johnny Unitas, a Starr contemporary, who was the poster child of the Baltimore Colts for a decade. Others point to Joe Montana. Still others cite Dan Marino, John Elway, or more recent Packer great, Brett Favre. The task is muddied by the changing nature of the game. NFL football was once a running game, then one that balanced the pass against the run. In recent years, it has become a passing game. In addition, the pass-blocking rules were sharply liberated in the eighties, giving the air game additional impetus and skewing the meaning of passing statistics. Nevertheless, internet football analyst Allen Barra has this to say on the subject of who is the greatest. "The best quarterback in pro football history isn't Joe Montana or Johnny Unitas or Otto Graham or Dan Marino or John Elway. If by best you mean most likely to win championships, then the man you want in back of your center is Bart Starr." Football is about winning and Bart Starr won. Almost without exception, All-Pro teammate Jerry Kramer states emphatically that Starr proved to be the best quarterback on the field of any NFL game in which he played.

Many would argue with Barra and Kramer for good reason. That, however, is not the point. The issue is that Bart Starr was, without doubt, one of the best ever. Statistical brilliance is rarely associated with Starr. For example, he threw 2,000 fewer passes than Unitas and was outgained by over 16,000 yards. Yet it is in the statistics that much of the case for Starr's greatness can be made. Nearly 30 years ago, football analyst Bud Goode determined that yards per passing attempt was football's premier statistical correlate with winning. Since 1958, only Bill Parcells' 1996 Patriots has played in an NFL championship game even though it allowed more yards per passing attempt than it gained. Over the past two decades, the team that won that simple statistic won 80 percent of the time. Just below yards per attempt in importance is interception percentage.

Bart Starr lapped the field in these two categories throughout the sixties. His career interception percentage is the lowest of any passer in the decade, and his yards per attempt is near the top. His 7.85 yards per toss is better than that of Roger Staubach (7.67), Sonny Jurgensen (7.56), Joe Montana (7.52), and Dan Marino (7.37). Furthermore, Starr stepped up. In the early sixties the Packers were regarded as a running team, featuring Hall-of-Famers Jim Taylor and Paul Hornung. By the middle of the decade, that reputation was more of a stereotype than a reality. In a 14-team league, Green Bay ranked 11th in rushing in 1965, and 13th the following season. Yet, the team won NFL titles in both campaigns with Starr as the league's MVP during the 1966 season. In that year, he fired 14 TD passes against just three interceptions all year! In addition, he averaged 9 yards per throw.

Flamboyant Paul Hornung was often cited as a clutch player. Indeed the multi-threat halfback that Lombardi fashioned after New York great Frank Gifford came up big in some key moments. But the best big-game performer in Green Bay was the team's leader, Bart Starr. In his ten playoff outings, Starr exceeded his regular season yards per attempt and interception percentage numbers. For teammate Jerry Kramer, it was another statistic that popped out. "The average quarterback," he wrote, "in a normal season, has about one pass in twenty intercepted; the truly exceptional quarterback has about one in thirty intercepted; in six NFL championship games, against the finest defenses and under extreme pressure, Bart has thrown 145 passes and had had only one intercepted. That—like Bart himself—is so good, it's almost unbelievable."

"Bart Starr utilized everything God gave him," said teammate and fellow Hall-of-Famer Ray Nitschke. "He rose to the challenge. His best games were in the big games." Here are Starr's startling post-season numbers.

Playoff Games

W	L	Att	Com	Pct	Ydg	Int	Av/Att	TD	Rating
9	1	213	130	61.0	1753	3	8.2	15	104.8

These include six NFL title games (the Pack won five), two playoff games, and two Super Bowl games, the latter in which he completed 29 of 47 passes for 452 yards and three TDs, against just a single interception, being named MVP both times.

Here are his numbers in the six NFL title games (against Philadelphia, New York, Cleveland, Dallas), when it was all on the line.

NFL Title Games

W	L	Att	Com	Pct	Ydg	Int	Av/Att	TD	Rating
5	1	84	145	57.9	1090	1	7.5	11	104.1

Here, then is the Bart Starr resume in capsule:

- Five-time NFL championship quarterback
- Four-time All-Pro
- Four-time Pro Bowl selection
- Three-time NFL passing leader
- Two-time Super Bowl MVP
- One-time NFL MVP

Bart Starr was a great player.

Amazingly, Starr was never a universally acclaimed, main-stage performer. Even in 1966, his league MVP season, Starr's individual brilliance was obscured amid the dominance of a 12-2 Green Bay team, one in which eleven of his teammates were named All-Pro or selected to the Pro Bowl squad. On his own team, he was consistently dwarfed by the magnitude of Lombardi's personality and the attention-grabbing behavior of Paul Hornung. As a quarterback, he played his entire career in the shadow of Johnny U. Starr, however, handled it well. He tells of a letter he received from some of his friends attending a medical seminar in Japan. It came in an envelope addressed simply, "To the Greatest Quarterback in the World." That was it. It bore no name, no city, no state. Amazingly, the envelope arrived at Starr's Green Bay address. When he got home that evening his wife, Cherry, greeted him with, "Hi, honey. The most interesting thing happened today. You received a letter that was obviously intended for Johnny Unitas."

Curiously, this understatement, this lack of recognition, has as much as anything endeared Starr to the Packer faithful. He was everyman, a self-made superstar. He was Mr. Bootstrap, Mr. Work Ethic, an inspiration to every youngster with less than extraordinary athletic gifts who nonetheless yearns to be one of the greats of gridiron. Moreover, Starr was vanilla, straight arrow, the type of young man you want to marry your daughter. He was a nice guy who finished first.

Every Boy Scout can recite the characteristics of a good scout. "A Boy Scout is trustworthy, loyal, helpful, friendly, courteous, kind, obedient, cheerful, thrifty, brave, clean, and reverent." By that definition, Bart Starr was a Boy Scout. But a string of adjectives are really not very revealing. They do not capture the essence of a person. Jerry Kramer, an introspective man who played eleven years with Bart Starr, felt he did not really know him. "I crouched in front of him for perhaps a hundred games, almost touching every time he leaned forward to take the snap from the center," he said in *Distant Replay*. "I saw him respond to pain with courage, and to pressure with poise, and I even heard Bart Starr swear, maybe once or twice in eleven years. And yet I never felt I really got to know Bart Starr. I never felt I got beneath the surface."

Kramer's best sense of the man came while sitting in the den of Starr's home, a room swimming with trophies and other accolades. "The true measure of success," Starr stated with unblinking blue eyes, "is what you've contributed to your community and your nation. I've tried to live a life pleasing to my family and my God." It is hard to question that. Moreover, it is a telling statement. Bart Starr, in contrast to so many others, has lived a purpose-driven life. While many chased after fame, comfort, fun, and ease, Starr has forever remained focused. It is perhaps why he became such a remarkable leader, but also a reason why he is not easily understood. Nonetheless, that mission statement of life, in and of itself, is not the stuff of great self-revelation. Indeed, few do know Bart Starr, because intense self-revelation is not part of his makeup.

The legendary Tom Landry, a person of a similar temperament and openly expressed Christian values, was once accused of being a "plastic man." Now gone, many realize the careful introspection that typified Landry indicates greatness rather than plasticity. "On the surface," noted Kramer, "Bart came as close to perfection as any man I ever met, perfection as a quarterback and as a human being. Bart never said he was perfect, but he did say he tried to be." Kramer was puzzled despite his great respect for Starr. "He was too good to be true, which made me uneasy," he said. "I couldn't help wondering if he always believed what he said, if he ever said what he believed. Sometimes I thought there was no *real* Bart Starr, only the Bart Starr he wanted you to see, the Bart Starr he felt the public expected." The years, however, indicate that Starr was exactly what he said he was about. Unlike so many of us, his walk has consistently matched his talk. He has proven real.

The year after Starr was fired as coach of the Packers—a tenure lasting nine years in which the last three indicated he had gotten the team turned in the right direction—the team organized a reunion for its championship players. The hurt of the dismissal was fresh. Many of the players wondered if Bart would attend. "I don't know if I would have come if I were he," wrote Kramer with admirable honesty.

"If it had been a few years later," Starr told Kramer, "It would have been much easier. But the pain was still fresh and emotionally, I didn't know if I could handle it."

"Of course Bart decided to come to the reunion," chronicled Kramer. "It was the right thing to do."

Bart Starr has often been described as shy. Self-contained is perhaps a more accurate term. "My emotions often ruled me," confessed Kramer. "Bart ruled his." Emotional control is fundamental to understanding who Bart Starr is. It has cost him much yet given him more. It has cost him celebrity while giving him poise. It has meant perhaps fewer close personal relationships, yet greater respect from those with whom he has come in contact. It has meant less jocularity, yet greater purpose and vision. It has made him less of a peer, yet more of a leader.

Emotional control did not come easily for Bart Starr. He learned it early in life, during a difficult, tragedy-stained childhood.

CHAPTER 3

Faith and Will

"I DO NOT believe leaders are born leaders," said basketball legend Bill Russell, one of the few figures in the annals of sport who rivals Starr in being a winner. "Leadership is an acquired skill," he wrote in *Russell Rules*. For no one is that more true than for Bart Starr. It has been said that the child is the father of the man. Once again, for no one is that more true than for Bart Starr. Starr was born in Birmingham, Alabama, on January 9, 1934, five years after the epic crash of the stock market. He was reared in the cauldron of poverty, provincialism, and racism that was the South, hardly a finishing school for nationally recognized leadership. But it was there in that childhood that Bart Starr learned how to deal with pain and adversity.

Both of his parents had rural roots. Starr's mother, the former Lulu Inez Tucker was born in Deatsville, Alabama, eighteen miles from Birmingham where her family moved when she was three. His father, Ben Bryan Starr, was a man of striking, Native American features—high cheekbones (that characterize the physiognomy of his son), square jaw, and very dark hair—owing to his partially Cherokee ancestry. Born in Dadeville, his family was from Anniston, Alabama. Ben Starr was a powerful man, having worked as a blacksmith, mechanic, and welder. He married Lulu Tucker in October of 1932, fifteen months before the birth of Bryan Bartlett (Bart) Starr. Though almost never referred to by his first name, Starr was given his middle name in honor of the obstetrician, Haywood Bartlett, who delivered him. Two years later a younger brother, Hilton, arrived.

The incredible stability Bart was to develop came from the inside. It did not come from a secure sense of place, so typical of life in the thirties. Constantly moving, Starr was deprived of geographical roots. At three, the family moved to Columbia, Tennessee, where Ben worked for the Monsanto Chemical Company. Hardly three years later it was back to Birmingham, where Bart entered the first grade, while Ben supervised prisoner detail work on the highways. It didn't end there. The elder Starr was a member of the National Guard, and his unit was activated at the onset of nation's involvement in World War II. It was the beginning of what would be a career in the military for Ben. The family spent two years in Gainesville, Florida, while Ben was stationed at Fort Blanding. From there it was across the country to Fort Ord, on California's Monterey peninsula, below the Bay area. In 1942, with Bart but eight years old, his father left for the Pacific combat zone. He did not see Ben for four years.

The significance of his father's mission hit home for Bart while sitting in a theater watching a Fox Movietone newsreel that preceded the main attraction, Gene Autry's *Cowboy Serenade*. There he saw a clip of General Douglas MacArthur's dramatic return to the Philippines. More important, however, he noticed a man he thought was his father situated behind the celebrated General at Mindanao. "That looks like Dad behind MacArthur!" he said to his brother. The two sat through the singing cowboy's thespian performance three times before both were convinced. Ben later confirmed the citing, acknowledging that he had been with MacArthur on that occasion.

Upon his return, Ben decided the family had moved enough and decided to settle in a white-frame house on National Avenue back in Montgomery. Despite the oppressive summer heat, Bart enjoyed growing up there. What he did not enjoy was his father's temperament. Ben Starr had always been a hard and demanding man, but the military experience in which he rose to a non-commissioned officer in the Air Force seemed to calcify his personality. Ben drilled discipline into his two sons, along with obedience and respect for one's elders. Ben's efforts were not in vain. "He is the son of a regular Army master sergeant and he grew up on Army posts and air force bases and he still calls me 'sir,'" Lombardi noted years later. "When I first met him he struck me as so polite and so self-effacing that I wondered if maybe he wasn't too nice a boy to be the authoritarian leader that your quarterback must be."

For Starr, Ben's methods were emotionally stifling. "He ran our household as he did his squadron—he was my master sergeant. I was not allowed to express my own views or disagree with him. I never even raised my voice," Starr writes. In short, Bart Starr learned to be self-contained as the son of Ben Starr.

More than respect was at stake, however. There was also fear. "He intimidated me," says Starr.

There was also the pain of rejection. Typical of children on the 1940s, Bart and his brother played the various sports with peers from the middle-class neighborhood. In the absence of Little League baseball and Pop Warner football, the youths improvised in developing playing fields and gridirons. Baseball was the favorite game of the time, truly the national pastime of the forties, and another quiet figure, Joe Di-Maggio, was Bart's hero. When it came to football, however, no holds were barred. The boys played tackle football without helmets or any other gear. Saturday was a special day. It was then that the youngsters held their "championship game" before an imaginary crowd at Hurt Military Academy. The excitement and fierce competition bred a love for football in Bart.

Ben Starr also valued competition, particularly competition ending in victory. "For Dad, it was everything," notes Starr. Unable to play as a youth owing to early employment, Ben Starr lived vicariously through the athletic endeavors of his sons, coaching and playing with them frequently. "Touch or tackle?" Bart asked his father when they played football.

"You can tackle me if you can. I'll do the touching," was Ben's reply.

"My father was my first football coach," Starr told biographer Gene Schoor.

Bart, however, was not Ben's favorite player. It was his much more aggressive younger brother nicknamed Bubba. Ben believed Hilton, not Bart, was the one destined for athletic greatness, and he made no secret of it. "Hilton had more natural ability that I did," said Starr. Moreover, his personality nearly mirrored their father's. "He had more fire in his play, too. My brother was the opposite of me. He was uninhibited—mean and nasty—and he would knock your block off with a tackle. I had to learn that. Hilton just did that naturally. That was the difference in our makeup. And I think my dad saw that." "A natural athlete with a blazing desire and volatile temper," is how Starr described his brother in his autobiography. "Bubba was aggressive, with a mean streak. I was an introvert."

Ben saw it all right. In contrast to the loving, even-handed nature of Lulu, Ben luxuriated in Bubba, lavishing attention on him, as Bart watched in dismay. Ben's words often had a chiding edge. "With your talent, if you had your brother Hilton's guts, you'd be able to make it anywhere," Ben would say. There are fewer more painful experiences for a child than to be regarded as inferior to a sibling, particularly a younger one. It was, in a word, humiliating. Philosopher Friedrich Nietzsche once said that what does not destroy you makes you stronger. Such was the case with Bart. The way he handled it offers a glimpse into the psyche of the man who would eventually excel for perhaps as tough a football taskmaster as ever walked the NFL sidelines. "And it was the greatest thing he could have said to me," said Starr in referring to the unflattering comparisons with Bubba. "It got my fires burning." If nothing else, Bart Starr—early on—had an iron will. A child with lesser resolve would have crumbled under the scourge of Ben's criticism.

He also had spiritual faith. Though often diminished in import in an increasingly secular society, awareness of his Christian mindset is central to understanding Bart Starr. Reared in the Bible belt, the Starrs were practicing Christians. And Bart was more than an obedient churchgoer. Beginning in childhood, he was a believer, something this quiet man has never had difficulty talking about. During his playing career, he often led his team in devotionals. While living in Green Bay, he served on the governing board of his church. "He really is one of the finest Christian gentlemen I have ever known," said Rev. Roger Bourland of the man who practiced a spiritual discipline daily. "Bart had an abiding faith in the Lord, still has an abiding faith in the Lord, and it has been and is still evident in his works both on and off the playing field," wrote biographer Schoor.

"I pray every day and give thanks to God for our blessings," said Starr in a 2001 interview. "I have a wonderful routine that I discovered years ago that is very meaningful to me. I read *The Upper Room Disci-*

plines daily devotions each night. It provides a quiet time in which you can reflect on your blessings. It became a discipline for me many years ago. I really enjoy it. I think if we take time to thank God for our blessings, it keeps us in the proper perspective."

From childhood forward, Starr would have to call on his iron will, fed by his faith that God did all things for a reason, to endure the unintended emotional assault. His faith kept him from despair, and it was richly rewarded. "God gives us unique strengths and assets," he told the *Birmingham Christian Family* in 2001, "He also gives us a great potential for a very strong, positive attitude, which allows us to enhance that talent. Ultimately, it comes back to us, what do we do with that talent? I learned that from my parents, Coach Lombardi, and my wife, Cherry. You see it and you want to perpetuate it."

His will kept him from becoming resigned to a status any less than his potential would permit. As for his experience as the older, yet lesser son, Starr did not let the hurt of the slights show. "I suppressed my feelings," he recalls. "I noticed the attention Bubba received from Dad, resented it, and became determined to prove to my father that I, too, could excel."

Despite their conflicting personalities, the two brothers were inseparable—until one warm, fateful Sunday. Upon returning from church, a group of kids were barefoot, "We were playing 'Hide and Seek' and I heard Hilton say, 'Ouch!'" recalls cousin Juanita Bartlett, "and I saw him pull something out of his foot." He had pierced his heel with a dog bone. An infection set in and the eleven-year-old died of tetanus three days later. "I was devastated," writes Starr sadly. "For two years I felt guilty about resenting the attention that Bubba had received from Dad." He was also lonely. "There was suddenly a big space in my life. I don't think I've ever felt lonelier in my life."

The elder Starrs were wracked by grief and guilt. A week after the shattering incident, Ben left for a tour of duty in Japan. "I will never forget the lonely look of despair on his face and bitterness in his voice when he said good-bye," notes Starr. Thirteen-year-old Bart spent days in his room brooding over the loss of his brother while Lulu anguished in guilt. "My mother felt overwhelming guilt because of the circumstances following the accident," said Starr. "She dearly loved Bubba and was reluctant to bring him in for a tetanus shot, which was a relatively new medical development, but which, it ended up, would have saved his life."

Faith again was key. "It was a very difficult period. Anything less than a strong faith and I do not think you could get through something like that." Not surprisingly, the tragedy has never gone away. Typical of his handling of adversity, the determined Bart turned Hilton's memory into an inspiration. "No, I've never forgotten Hilton," Starr told Schoor. "Many times I've thought of him in a tough game, and set myself, dedicated myself, to do something especially for my kid brother. Maybe it's hard to believe, but I find myself doing just that, dedicating myself to some task for Hilton, even today." For the family, the hole has never been filled. There has been more coping than resolution. "Our family still avoids discussing it," said Starr, "but a vivid memory remains."

Scarred and shaped by the pain, life went on for the Starrs. For Lulu there was the guilt. Bart was entering his teenage years. For Ben, there was but one son left—the second son.

CHAPTER 4

Unlikely Hero

T HE LOSS of Bubba did not bring health to Ben and Bart's relationship. "When my father returned from Japan, I thought our relationship would improve," Starr wrote. "It deteriorated." Bart worried that he could never do enough to satisfy Ben, according to Lombardi biographer Maraniss. Driven as he was, he could win neither his father's love nor respect. Ben, believing Bart lacked the temperament to excel athletically, kept the image of Bubba alive in a painful way, with comments beginning with the words "Your brother would have . . ."

It is doubtful that the demanding father understood the effect he was having on his sensitive son. Such fathers rarely do. And it was not as if Ben was not interested in Bart's development. On the contrary, he spent hours playing baseball with Bart, focusing on improving the youngster's fundamental skills. When Bart was fourteen, his father gave him a prized possession—a baseball glove. Moreover, Montgomery had a minor league team in the South Atlantic League, and Ben took a side job as a ticket taker. He took Bart to almost every game, where he became the ball boy. He would watch the minor league pitching duels, imagining that the great Bob Feller was facing Ted Williams or his hero, Joe DiMaggio.

Starr's adoration for the Yankee Clipper was sealed when he went to visit his Aunt Myrtle in Detroit, and watched Joe D from the Tiger Stadium bleachers. Typical of a fan, Starr believed DiMaggio's miraculous 56-game hitting streak would beget one of 57. "I was sure he would have broken his old record right in front of me," he recalled. "His best years were now behind him, but he never disappointed. Not even a hitless afternoon could quell my enthusiasm; I knew Joe would start a new streak the next day."

It was through baseball that Starr first became aware of the repugnance of racism. Growing up in Montgomery in the forties, Bart lived a totally segregated life. In Detroit, however, he played pickup games on sandlots with black as well as white boys. One day his father decided to observe his son to see how much his baseball skills had sharpened. When Ben, a Southerner of his generation, noticed that the games were integrated he pulled his son off the field instantly, brought him back to his aunt's home, and had young Bart wash and rewash his car in the summer heat as a punishment. "His military career had broadened his viewpoint, but it would be years before he became more open-minded," noted Starr. "Ironically, his greatest progress occurred during his visits to Green Bay—a city with no permanent black residents at that time—when he met such teammates as Willie Davis, Herb Adderley, Elijah Pitts, and Willie Wood."

In the fall, attention turned to football, particularly in Alabama. "I enjoyed playing pickup games," said Starr, "but was not a die-hard fan, mainly because I had yet to see anyone dominate and control a football game." That changed one autumn day at the Montgomery's Crampton Bowl, where the Crimson Tide was playing. Alabama featured a tailback named Harry Gilmer, whose jump pass led to NFL fame, where he spent a long career as a player and coach. "I had found a new hero, a new goal," remembers Starr. "I wanted to throw the football as well as Harry."

His first organized football experience came when he was in eighth grade, for a team sponsored by the local VFW post. "I don't remember much about playing on that team," he recounts. "I remember I was small and I played in the backfield, but I didn't really learn much about how to play the game until I went to junior high school." At Baldwin Junior High School, where he started at wingback, the future NFL great was all bones. "There he was, a scrawny kid who couldn't have weighed more than a hundred and five or ten pounds, with a football uniform hanging loose all over him," recalled childhood friend Bobby Barnes.

The brains and the craftiness were already there, however. "You know, he was a tough little competitor even then," says Barnes.

Bill Moseley, who according to Starr was knowledgeable, upbeat, and a disciple of then-Kentucky coach, Bear Bryant, coached the Sidney Lanier High School football team. Moseley, however, was no more impressed with the quiet teenager than was Ben Starr. "He was one of those silent boys out for the team," Moseley told Schoor, "but that first year of high school he was kind of small for the team and there was nothing about him that made me pay him any special attention." After a few weeks of practice, discouraged at being overlooked, something Starr would become accustomed to, he decided to quit. "I knew I was better than the backup quarterbacks but was already relegated to the junior varsity. Frustrated over the coach's decision, I strolled into our house and told my father I was quitting," he remembers.

The incident provides insight into Bart Starr's personality. Ben Starr's continuous you-don't-measure-up criticisms did not break Starr's will. He could endure the slights. In fact, they seemed to intensify Bart's desire to establish his competence and render meaningless these negative assessments. At the very least, Ben did not deny his son the opportunity to prove him wrong. Later, under Lombardi, the same thing happened. Starr was not defeated by the stinging verbal assaults of the authoritarian mentor. No matter how negatively perceived, Starr was after all, the quarterback. And even when a backup, at least he was out there on the field and in on the meetings with Lombardi and being given an opportunity to demonstrate his competence. The only breaking point for Starr was what he perceived as a total lack of opportunity.

Coach Moseley, by ignoring him, very nearly did break the teenager's spirit. Unlike so many extroverted leaders, Bart Starr is not a person to call attention to himself. Therefore, he had no resources to counter his being overlooked. As certain as Starr was that he was superior to some of the youths positioned ahead of him (and who could doubt him, given his estimable intellect and disinclination toward arrogance?), he could not prove Moseley's less than positive opinion of his football skills incorrect, because he was not being given a chance. Overlooking the skills of one's players is one of the most common failings of coaches in every sport and at every level. It is perhaps most common, however, in football at the high school level. There are simply so many players and so few coaches. When a player is as scrawny physically and as nondescript temperamentally as Starr certainly was, he can become all but invisible—especially when slotted at a position that attracts players with extroversion and dash.

Ben Starr wanted nothing of quitting. "All right, it's your decision. I'm glad you'll be home in the afternoons," he said disingenuously. "I want you to weed the garden and cut the cornstalks. I want the garden cleaned up for fall." Ben knew Bart's dislike of gardening and he received the response he had hoped for. The next day at practice, Bart was the first player on the field and the last one to leave.

Small as he was, Starr demonstrated the will and persistence that would make him an NFL legend. "Forget about passing," his peers would say as Starr attempted to grip the ball with his too-small hands. But he kept throwing and learning, evincing the same studious attention to the intricacies of the game for which he would later be regaled by Lombardi. ("No one on the team is more conscientious and dedicated than Bart Starr," Lombardi once wrote of his quarterback.) In short, his scholarly approach to the game did not have its genesis in his relationship with Lombardi. It had its roots at Sidney Lanier High School. This quest to learn, to understand why, is also—with the benefit of hindsight—one of the early signs of Starr becoming a leader. Bill Russell's first lesson in leadership in his eleven *Russell Rules* is called, "Commitment Begins with Curiosity." "Curiosity is as common as the air we breathe," wrote Russell, "but it is also the oxygen of accomplishment and success." Curiosity is a process that flows from will, according to Russell. "To be really committed, you must always pursue the questions until you get meaningful answers." It is from curiosity that people solve problems and grow. Early on, and in a disciplined, mature way, Bart Starr was curious.

Often people like to view this curiosity and commitment to comprehend, to engage in intense preparation, as Starr's way of compensating for his limited athletic skills. That misses the point entirely. Starr attacked the game as a student because he was highly intelligent and because he found the game intellectually satisfying. "Other players chafed at the repetition and meticulousness of Lombardi, particularly the film watching and classroom lectures over seeming minutiae,"

Starr told Maraniss. "I loved it. I loved the meetings. I never, ever was bored or tired at any meeting we were in with Lombardi. I appreciated what he was trying to teach. He was always raising the bar."

This as much as anything was what Bart Starr loved about football. While under Lombardi, he could look past the bluster and overbearing Ben Starr–like techniques, and develop a vision of success, realizing that it was the residue of careful preparation, the synchronizing of the activities of eleven men as they pursued a common goal. Unlike his peers in high school, girls, popularity, or athletic acclaim did not mesmerize Bart. He loved football intrinsically. "Bart Starr was alert," recalled Moseley. "He was a good listener and he had a good head. All I ever noticed about him in that first year was alertness, and a quiet, positive attitude. I never had to explain a play twice to Bart. He didn't fool around when he was out there playing the game or practicing it. He was all business. I never doubted for a minute that he was always out there, trying. He was on the field to make the team, to play football."

These are charitable reminiscences on Moseley's part, but you have to wonder whether the old coach was indulging in revisionist history, as the attributes he cited were apparently not enough for him to play the quiet boy who had a burning desire to contribute. In fact, it was not until his junior year that Starr's varsity opportunity arrived. When it did, however, it came with a bang.

In the third game of the 1950 season, Lanier High faced one of the strongest teams in the state. Tuscaloosa—led by all-star tackle Hugh Thomas, son of acclaimed University of Alabama coach Frank Thomas—was undefeated in its previous seventeen games. A crowd in excess of 12,000 engulfed Crampton Field. Lanier had its own star in quarterback Don Shannon, whose brilliance as a passer, nifty runner, and effective leadership, kept Starr on the bench. Lanier entered the game 2-0, having blown out Alex City 33-0, and defeated Douthan 14-7.

Starr took his customary spot on the bench, ready to root for Shannon, his pal Bobby Barnes, Don Abernathy, and Jimmy Moore as they ran against the mighty Tuscaloosa defense. Then suddenly Bart Starr's football odyssey took a sharp turn. Don Shannon was lying on the field, having been hit by a gang of Tuscaloosa gridders. He did not get up. His leg was broken.

The bell had tolled for Shannon. It had rung for Bart Starr. If ever his curiosity, his preparedness, would pay off it was in this game. The moment was filled with tension for Moseley, however. He could see his dreams of gridiron success turn into a nightmare of might-have-beens. Here he was in a game that could potentially decide the state championship, and not only was he losing his ace signal-caller, he was about to turn over the offensive reins to a diffident 150-pound scrub.

According to Schoor, Moseley's counsel to Starr hardly exuded the confidence customarily typifying a coach's regard for his field general. "This is your chance," he said. "Don't take any unnecessary chances. Play straight conservative football. Nothing fancy, OK?" To tell Bart Starr to avoid fancy maneuvers seems about as necessary as telling Joe Montana to vacate the pocket should pass protection break down. Nervous as he was, the sweaty-handed Starr knew this was his opportunity to lead. First, however, he had to establish himself with his teammates.

End Nick Germano and back Don Abernathy blurted out suggested plays in the huddle. Starr seized the moment. "Now all you guys stop jabbering," he said tersely. "I'm the guy in charge of the huddle. I'll call the plays. When I want your advice, I'll ask. Just you guys do your job from now on. Is that clear?"

With that he took command, opening with a first down toss to Bobby Barnes, and following with an eight-yard dash by Abernathy. Although Lanier did not score on the drive, the crowd sensed Starr's leadership and came to life. So did his teammates. In the third quarter, Bart broke a scoreless tie carrying the ball into the end zone on an end sweep. Lanier clinched the upset win in the final quarter when Starr delivered a shovel pass to Barnes for a 38-yard touchdown. The final score was 13-0. Crampton was bedlam with Starr the unlikely hero of one of the state's epic high school upsets.

In executing the drive, Starr showed the football world that he had mastered one of Bill Russell's key lessons in leadership. Not only did he have the temerity to establish himself as the man in charge, he showed he could change the flow of the game. Refusing to adopt a victim mentality, he had waited his turn and when it came, turned around the direction of not just this game but his very football life. "Failures and setbacks occur all the time," noted Russell. "Each one of us deals with adversity differently. The swing of our lives from good times to bad and back again is as inevitable as variations in the weather. But in the ways we deal with these variations we define ourselves."

Starr had most certainly defined himself. Moreover, he had demonstrated Russell's belief that anyone can win. Indeed, at the outset of the season, Starr was among the most unlikely of heroes. He was, if anything, regarded as a loser. Yet he practiced Russell's rule of looking for an opportunity to win in any situation. "What I absorbed growing up," noted Russell about the hardscrabble days of his youth, "and in every subsequent phase of my life was an understanding that winning was always a possibility. Don't overlook it." Starr certainly did not overlook his opportunity on that magic day against Tuscaloosa. "He did not let his situation dictate whether he could be a winner," said Russell of K.C. Jones, words that perfectly typify the teenager in Birmingham, "He chose to be a winner even when it seemed he did not have a choice in the matter."

Moseley believed Starr was a winner. The next day he gave Bart the plays for the rest of the season, enjoining the youngster to commit to memory the assignment of every man on every play. Realizing Starr's intellectual acumen he said, "You've got a sixth sense for this game that will make you a fine quarterback, and perhaps some day a fine coach. Now, go on home and work on those plays."

The "curious" Starr mastered the task in three days.

Moseley, ever the thorough taskmaster, tested Starr's memory intensely. He wanted to know how well his accidental quarterback knew the system. Clearly and concisely, Starr detailed the movements of every player on every play. Moseley was not only satisfied; he became a fan of his young quarterback's gridiron gifts.

"Bart Starr was the kind of player I could plan and develop an entire offensive system around," he crowed, demonstrating a 180-degree turn in his evaluation of Starr. "I created an entire series of new plays to take advantage of Bart's particular abilities. He was that good. In fact, he was the smartest young football player, the greatest passer I've ever seen play high school football."

CHAPTER 5

College Bound

S IDNEY LANIER HIGH went undefeated in Bart's junior year
and the awards and accolades accumulated quickly. He could play
both ways, and punt with striking effectiveness. Perhaps more
important, he had demonstrated his leadership skills. Having arrived
as a prep star, Starr expected to receive one of the things he most
craved—his father's approval. He was disappointed. "Surely my individual awards and our team success would please Dad," Starr said,
describing his thoughts at the time. "It may have, but he stepped up
his critiques, second-guessing play calling and criticizing poor passes.
I wanted to improve as badly as he wanted me to, but I needed a
mentor. Coach Moseley led me to him."

In the summer of '51, Moseley arranged to have Kentucky's All-
American quarterback Babe Parilli tutor Starr. It was a transforming
experience for the high school T-man. Initially, Starr was so nervous
he dropped his food tray in the camp's cafeteria line. By the end of the
several-week session, he had solidified his fundamentals and grown in
confidence such that he pictured himself starring as Parilli's successor
for Bear Bryant's Kentucky Wildcats. In his enthusiasm, Starr taped
pictures of Parilli all over his bedroom back in Montgomery.

The 1951 season opened with a rush for Lanier, now captained by
Starr and Barnes. Riding an 11-game winning streak, the team defeated
Alex City and Douthan in their first two games, and followed that with
a 21-6 thrashing of mighty Tuscaloosa—a game in which the now-
celebrated Starr tossed three touchdowns.

The winning streak was ended the following week by an experienced Ramsey squad, 26-6. Undaunted, the team bounced back, defeating Phoenix High and then upsetting powerful Murphy High by a 19-13 count. Starr hit on 11 of his 12 passes in the stirring triumph. Despite these heroics, it was late in November, however, when Starr put himself on the college prospect map, as Lanier traveled to Kentucky to play Manual High School of Louisville. The Kentucky school boasted a vaunted defensive line, and the scouts were curious as to how Starr would stand up to the pressure.

Starr wowed them. Early in the first quarter, he eluded a heavy rush, slipped the grasp of a defender, and lofted a 25-yard scoring strike to his favorite target, Nick Germanos. He continued his brilliance throughout the game and was confronted with scouts and coaches eager to talk to him in the locker room when it was over. By season's end he was named All-State, and All-American, and was recruited by every Southeastern Conference university with the exception of Tennessee.

Although all the tools were not there as yet, there were tools. If anything is overstated in the descriptions of Bart Starr, it is the modest nature of his athletic skills. As an athlete he is regularly described as ordinary, unimpressive, not gifted. You do not become a high school All-American and an NFL Hall of Fame quarterback without at least latent athletic gifts. Though never regarded as extraordinarily skilled, Starr's athleticism, like his personality, is understated.

"He didn't have the tools, not yet," recalled childhood chum Barnes of the skinny junior high Starr, "but playing against him I knew he had plenty of football sense. Maybe that's what drew me to him. I liked him, even in that suit that flopped all over him." But Starr did have raw skills, and Barnes, a tremendous athlete in his youth, observed that early. One day, he and Bart cut a high school class and went on a bird shoot. "We got into this cornfield, with our shotguns, where we had spotted some birds," Barnes told biographer Schoor. "We didn't know whose cornfield it was, and for a while we didn't care."

Starr then spotted a truck coming down the road, likely occupied by a soon-to-be-angry farmer when he saw the boys stomping on his cornfield. The boys broke out into a sprint. "I was the fastest man on the Lanier High School track team," recalled Barnes. "But you should have seen Bart. Here I was, running as fast as I could; and there was Bart, catching up with me, and passing me like a shot. I tell you, that Bart Starr can run. He can run with the best of them."

Perhaps diminishing Starr's athleticism makes his story more romantic. It is, nonetheless, typical of the media's often-unconscious tendency to stereotype the pedestrian-appearing athlete, particularly if the athlete is white. When a black athlete stands out, he is referred to as being "very athletic," something one rarely sees applied to whites. The 6-1 Joe Montana could execute a flat-foot slam dunk as a high school sophomore and was widely sought after as a point guard by college scouts. Yet, few refer to Montana as a great athlete. Much was made of his leadership skills and on-the-field football sense. Conversely, Magic Johnson, though not fast, a comparatively poor shooter, and devoid of jumping ability, is rarely celebrated for his wily basketball intellect as, for example, is his lifelong counterpart, Larry Bird. Bart Starr was brilliant, hard-working, and committed, but he could also throw.

In any case, Starr's first college choice was Kentucky, and why not? Not only did Bear Bryant want him; his hero, Babe Parilli was assisting in the recruiting effort. Life could hardly have been better. From benchwarmer to All-American, Starr now had his pick of colleges, and what's more, he had his first choice. It is one thing for a football-crazy youngster to receive a scholarship offer—an opportunity to continue to do the thing he most loves—to play football and have the university bankroll the college expenses associated with getting a degree. It is another to have the school program that is prominently decorating your bedroom wall offer a football scholarship.

If there is anything that has typified the life of Bart Starr, however, it is that things rarely were as they seemed to be. At least they rarely turned out as planned. As certain as Bart was that he would be playing for the Bear and succeeding the legendary Parilli at Kentucky in the fall, he did not feel the same way the following spring.

The reason is that Bart Starr was in love.

An attractive perky brunette named Cherry Louise Morton, had taken residence in Starr's psyche. For weeks he thought about her, but he had pretty well relegated Ms. Morton to his fantasy life for two very good reasons. One is that he had no confidence in himself as a performer in the dating marketplace. There were no playbooks for that, only highly developed social skills. The other, however, was worse. Cherry Morton was already going with a guy from a wealthy family. Nonetheless, Starr was nothing if not persistent, and he did not or perhaps could not let go of his interest in Morton. He asked his favorite pass receiver Nick Germanos to float the idea of dating him to Cherry. Her answer was both encouraging and terrifying to the nondemonstrative, introverted Starr. "If he wants a date," she told Germanos, "he will have to ask me himself."

Facing the Manual rush earlier in the fall, and facing the Fearsome Foursome of the Rams later in his career, was far easier than his request for a date with Cherry Morton. But he did, and as awkward as he felt, it had a life-changing impact. And he did feel awkward. Starr relates in his biography that at the moment at which he thought they would have their first kiss, he discovered that as he leaned over to approach her she was fast asleep. Initially, it was devastating. Vanilla Bart felt that he may have driven the lively young teenager into a boredom-induced coma. Only later did he find out that her slumber was the result of feeling incredibly relaxed with Starr.

There are few motivations more powerful to a teenager than hanging on to his or her first love. Given that it was not in Starr's nature to parlay his football celebrity—big as it was in a football haven like that of Montgomery, Alabama—into an active social life, it was even more important for him. There was a problem. Cherry Morton had already committed to Auburn, located in the eastern part of Alabama, far away from Lexington, Kentucky. Absence, Bart feared, may not make Cherry's heart grow fonder. Rather, it may invite unwelcome competition. Although Cherry put no pressure on Bart to change his mind, his thoughts moved toward the Crimson Tide. Alabama, located in Tuscaloosa, was a more manageable 130 miles from Auburn.

Besides, the Crimson Tide wanted him as well, and there were points other than proximity to Cherry in its favor. Alabama boasted a powerful and alluring gridiron tradition of its own, with such greats as end Don Hutson, lineman Fred Singleton, tailback Dixie Howell, and passer Harry Gilmer having worn the crimson. He was introduced to Frank Thomas, the revered coach, who had chalked up two national championships, four Southeastern Conferences titles, and five Rose

Bowl wins in his fifteen-year tenure. Thomas, who had turned the reins over to Rod Drew in 1947, was helpful in the recruiting process. He sagely avoided putting unnecessary pressure on the conscientious teenager in his approach to him. Rather than tell Starr what great expectations the Alabama faithful had for the young quarterback, he sold the academic side of the college experience to the honor student "Son, you'll enjoy playing football here, but you'll also get a good education," the famous mentor said. In addition, several of his teammates, Germanos and Barnes, were pointed in the direction of the Tide, and Ben clearly favored seeing his son play in Tuscaloosa rather than Lexington.

So Bart Starr decided to go to Alabama. And it was almost a disaster.

CHAPTER 6

High and Low Tide

THINGS BEGAN rather auspiciously for the freshman Starr at Alabama. Owing to the presence of the Korean War with so many young males in the armed forces, freshman were eligible for varsity play in Bart's first year in Tuscaloosa. Moreover, the 1952 squad figured to be among the nation's best. That was the good news. The bad news was that Coach Drew's offense relied mainly on the Split T, a formation that necessitated that a quarterback be dual threat—able to run as well as he could throw. As such, the Tide's two returning signal callers, Clell Hobson and Bobby Wilson, felt no pressure from the presence of the Lanier High All-American passer that first season.

Starr did manage to earn the number three slot and played enough to gain a varsity letter and some favorable publicity on the Tide's 9-2 powerhouse. Schoor relates that a sports reporter for *The Crimson-White* paper, a weekly university publication, had this to say about Starr early in the season. "Opportunity knocks but once, and Bart Starr, freshman, was not one to fail in opening the door.

"In the Mississippi Southern game Bart Starr proved himself an able quarterback, handling the ball with clock-like precision. The Virginia Tech game proved his worth was not by chance. For the two games his passing percentage is 66 2/3 per cent, completing 8 out of 12 attempts.

"Bart is 18 years old and weighs 170 pounds. He wrapped up All-City honors twice, and he was All-American in his senior year at Lanier

High School. It seems that Bart is all that his last name implies, Star."
He went on to suggest that Starr was potentially another Harry Gilmer.

The seeds of Starr's leadership are evident at the top of the report.
Once again, when the door of opportunity swung open, Bart Starr was
prepared. The incredible discipline, instilled not without a commensu-
rate degree of pain by Ben, paid off for the youngster. It takes discipline
to prepare, particularly when you don't know if you will have any
opportunity at all to demonstrate that preparedness, but—no different
from his junior year at Lanier—Bart Starr was prepared.

The Crimson Tide finished the campaign with authority by demol-
ishing Syracuse 61-6 in the New Year's Day Orange Bowl. The game is
etched in Starr's memory, in part because he was sent into the game
to throw the ball in the blowout. The reason was that receiver Joe
Curtis, was one catch short of the Orange Bowl record for pass recep-
tions. After dropping three straight tosses, Curtis gathered in the
fourth for a touchdown and the record.

Spring brought baseball, a game Bart loved. It also, however, provided time for him to commute to Auburn to see Cherry. Realizing he
had a good chance at making varsity, Ben, along with Bart's uncle
Hilton Battle, kept the phone lines warm urging him to give what was
then the nation's only real major sport a go. Unfortunately for them,
love conquered curveballs and Bart made frequent pilgrimages to Auburn. "I can't believe you're going to drive to Auburn to see some
girl," Starr remembers Uncle Hilton remonstrating. "You'd be better
off chasing fly balls."

Once again, the fact that Starr had a real shot at playing varsity
baseball as a freshman at a major university, after lettering at the demanding quarterback position on a 9-2 national football powerhouse,
lays waste to the myth of Starr's sub-par athleticism. Starr was understated rather than flashy, conservative rather than flamboyant. He was,
it appears, not devoid of considerable athletic prowess.

Things could hardly have looked much better than they did in 1953.
Bart Starr—proudly wearing #10 for the Tide—was mighty Alabama's
main man at quarterback as well as a member of the starting defensive
backfield. The Tide rolled to a 6-2-2 championship season. Comparisons with Harry Gilmer were no longer exaggerations, as Starr's 870
yards came within 80 of Gilmer's 1945 mark, and this despite Bart

missing one game due to injury. He hit on 59 of 119 attempts including eight TD strikes. Against Georgia, Bart threw for three TDs in a 33-12 win, and 'Bama fans took note of his marksmanship.

"Starr's the greatest passer in Tide history," was the word around Tuscaloosa, "better than Harry Gilmer." But there was more. Coach Drew discovered Starr's punting prowess and was rewarded with Bart's 41.4 yards per punt average, good for second in the nation. Who was number one? It is a wonderful trivia question. Starr finished second to the man who would be his backup in Green Bay, Georgia's Zeke Bratkowski.

The Tide's reward for the banner '54 campaign was a date with Rice in the Cotton Bowl in Dallas, Texas. The Owls were led by All-Everything running back, Dickie Moegle. And Moegle did not disappoint; Rice trounced Alabama 28-3 with the help of two Starr interceptions. Despite Moegle's brilliance, the most memorable play of the game was turned in by the Tide's #42, Tommy Lewis. With Rice all but sealed on their 5-yard line, Moegle circled right end. Just as Starr was ready to bring him down, he was obliterated by a block, and with that, Moegle was off down the sideline with only the end zone in sight. That is until Lewis impulsively decided to leave the Tide bench and nail him to the turf in midfield. It was a win-win caper. Moegle was awarded a touchdown, while Lewis, because of the caper, made an appearance as a guest on the *Ed Sullivan Show*. The story, however, gets crazier. Later in life Lewis served as an assistant football coach at Huntsville High in Huntsville, Alabama. During a game against of all schools, Sidney Lanier, a Lanier back broke loose for what appeared a certain touchdown. As he passed the 50, a player jumped off the Huntsville bench and leveled him. And, oh yes, he wore number 42.

"Bart, for the first time in my life, I knew exactly how to console someone," Lewis told Starr later.

"Tommy," said Starr, "you coached the boy well."

Despite the Cotton Bowl defeat, Starr, only a sophomore, was a celebrity. He was riding high and looking forward to his junior year at one of the most football-centered universities in the land.

He did have concerns. The long distance nature of his relationship with Cherry was wearing on Starr. She had left Auburn and moved with her parents to Jackson, Mississippi. Bart borrowed Bobby Barnes's slick Mercury coupe whenever he could to make the commute. Marriage was on both Bart and Cherry's minds, but they were concerned about the football fall-out that such a union might have on Starr's career at 'Bama. Football coaches had little regard for lovestruck gridders who did not have football front and center in their minds. Even worse, scholarships had been known to be revoked in the cases of such distracted players.

When Cherry visited Bart in Tuscaloosa in May of 1954, they tossed their concern to the winds and eloped on impulse. Clearly, Bart was in love because impulsive is one of the least likely words anyone uses to describe the demeanor of the ever-prepared, always rational Starr. In any case, the two dashed off to Columbus, Mississippi, with best man Nick Germanos to make the union official. All parties vowed secrecy to minimize any risks.

Mum continued to be the word that summer when Bart returned to Tuscaloosa, while Cherry began working in a clerical role in Jackson. The two did not see one another again until late July. Deceit, however, is not one of Starr's cardinal characteristics. He unwittingly addressed a letter to "Mrs. Bart Starr," only to have Cherry's mother remark at the presumptuous nature of such a reference. "You'd think the boy was married to you," she said.

"Well, he is," was Cherry's brief but emotional response.

All was well in the Morton household when the news broke. Cherry's parents were elated. The Mortons' mood was not matched by that of Lulu and Ben Starr. Lulu called and suggested that the newlyweds join them to meet with the family pastor. Assuming the rendezvous was about marriage counseling, the happy couple complied. It wasn't. "I want everyone to know," announced the usually loving and caring Lulu, "that I'm going to have this marriage annulled if I have to take it all the way to the Supreme Court."

She didn't, and the couple headed to Tuscaloosa with Bart's parents understandably concerned about how he would be able to support a wife while laboring on the gridiron and in the classroom. Life was humble for the pair, as they resided in a $15 a month apartment, complete with a weed growing through the floorboards of the living room and bedroom suite. Nonetheless, the couple was together, happy, and looking forward to a blowing-the-doors-off Alabama football future for Bart

And football-wise, that is as good as it got.

Bart Starr was never a consistently starting quarterback for the Alabama Crimson Tide again.

In the summer of 1954 he felt a sharp pain in his back while practicing his punting. Thinking it was nothing he continued to practice that day and the next, despite being scarcely able to lift his leg above his waist. He also found throwing passes difficult to the extent that eventually even gripping the ball was a challenge. X-rays were taken and it was determined that he had thrown his sacroiliac out. When he asked the physician what he could do about it, he received the worst news an eager football player can receive. He would have to rest it.

"You mean I can't play football?" asked the troubled junior.

"I wouldn't think so," was the reply. "It's going to hurt every time you move. The more you move the more it will hurt."

Starr's will sprung into action and he tried to play through the pain, but to no avail. The more he threw the more pain he experienced until he could hardly raise his arms. Rest was what was prescribed, and rest was what it would be. The 1954 season was pretty much toast. Although he did eventually recover, Starr played only sparingly during the disappointing 4-5-2 campaign's final month. His statistics show it. He threw only 41 passes, completing 24.

The 4-5-2 season proved a loser in more ways than one for Drew. He resigned amid pressure despite going 20-10-5 over the past three seasons. Drew's loss was not at all Starr's gain. The school summoned J. B. Whitworth from Oklahoma A&M (later Oklahoma State) to direct the Tide's football fortunes. Incredibly, Whitworth, a former star lineman at Alabama, was hired off a losing season at A&M to replace a coach who had won nearly two-thirds of his games. Full of bravado, Whitworth made his impact felt quickly. Publicly expecting a rapid turnaround, the new mentor decided to take a broom to the Tide's football operation. With the exception of two seniors, Whitworth would flush the toilet and begin with a whole new starting lineup.

"They've grown accustomed to losing," said the new coach, who himself had come off a losing year. "It was a losing team last year, and they probably think they're going to be a losing team this year," he declared about a group of players who had won over 60 percent of their games and been to two bowls over the previous three seasons.

No matter, youth would be served. "We're going to start the season with a squad of sophomores and juniors," said the decisive new coach. Whitworth's "logic" was simply bizarre. It strained the credulity of a rational person, to paraphrase Howard Cosell. Moreover, any hope Starr had for a return to the limelight in his senior season was dashed when Whitworth installed the Oklahoma Split T offense, one that emphasized a quarterback's running skills over his passing acumen. And Whitworth was obsessed with the Sooners. "This is what they're doing at Oklahoma," prefaced virtually every Whitworth phrase, says Starr in his autobiography.

It was Sidney Lanier High revisited for Starr, only in reverse. In high school Starr had been ignored until, by the grace of God, he had an opportunity to prove himself in a pivotal game. At Alabama, however, he had proven himself first, and then been ignored. It was devastating. "I was psychologically demoralized and I didn't fare much better physically," Starr wrote in summarizing his final season's experience. "That fall, I severely sprained an ankle and could no longer punt."

As for Whitworth, he turned the program around all right. He lost all ten games.

About the only time Starr and the seniors got on the field was when the game appeared irretrievably lost. It happened enough that Starr did manage to complete 55 of 96 passes for 587 yards in limited duty. Starr counted the year a washout. "It was depressing," he told Schoor, "I began to lose confidence in myself." Moreover, when Whitworth did put him in, he couldn't recapture the command he had possessed the years before. "When I'd get on the field," Starr recalled, "I just wasn't the kind of quarterback I should have been, the kind of leader I'd been as a junior, sophomore, a freshman." What happened to Starr's psyche is common in the world of sport. Confidence thrives on success, and once success wanes, internal questions arise. It happens to the best, even the coaches. Bill Parcells said that a coach can win for a long time, but once the losses mount he does not call up the many memories of triumph. Instead, he wonders if he will ever win another game.

"My senior year was a disaster," was Bart's succinct summation of the 1955 campaign.

It was a curious comedown for Bart. From rising star on the national scene to scrub on a winless 'Bama squad, a once-shimmering future in the NFL now appeared to be a nothing more than a cruel mirage. It was good that Starr was a Dean's list academic performer, because it seemed certain he would now have to carve out a professional career that most assuredly would not take place on the gridiron.

CHAPTER 7

Character Triumphs

B Y N O W , Starr had most of the ingredients that would set him apart as a leader. He possessed the will, the curiosity, the intelligence, the poise, the discipline, the commitment to preparation, and sufficient natural skills in his area of expertise—football—to be a topflight NFL quarterback. Yet, when the young man left Tuscaloosa, no reasonable person expected this honor student to make a dollar playing a down of professional football. J.B. Whitworth's folly ended all that.

Fortunately for Starr, Whitworth's ignorance was countervailed by another coach's wisdom. Alabama Head Basketball Coach Johnny Dee liked Starr. The former Notre Dame great, and later highly successful Irish coach, all but openly questioned his colleague Whitworth's disregard for Starr. The young man had shown tremendous self-control, tremendous character in quietly making the best of an incredibly mismanaged situation. As much as he had burned inwardly, chafing at the injustice of sitting on the bench of a 10-game loser, Starr had maintained his dignity and self-respect, enduring the debacle with class.

He had also held on to his dream.

Having developed a friendship with Dee over the past several seasons, in part by watching the aggressive mentor's basketball practices in the winter, Bart visited him in his office to discuss what future if any he might have in football. Dee was very willing to help him. "The first thing we must do is get you in the Blue-Gray game," he said. "It shouldn't be too hard for a kid from Alabama." The game would be played at familiar Crampton Bowl in Montgomery.

Getting into the Blue-Gray game represented a potentially huge opportunity. This was 1955—before BLESTO, scouting combines, try-out camps, and armies of paid super-scouts scouring the country for football talent. For a player like Starr, who had slipped well below the national radar screen during the past two seasons, strutting his stuff on television was one of the only ways to get back on the board. Moreover, the Blue-Gray game was truly an All-Star classic, one of a very few televised post-season gridiron events, and pro scouts would be there. He was excited.

One day during practice, Charley Winner, a Baltimore Colts assistant asked Starr, "Can you play defense?"

Starr had a ready answer. "Coach, I'll play anywhere. I just want a chance." Lacking great sprinter speed, Bart had learned to use his intelligence, aggressiveness, and fundamentally solid tackling technique to make it in the defensive backfield.

What appeared to be a wonderful opportunity proved to be yet another painful experience. Paul Dietzel, the celebrated mentor at powerful LSU, coached the Gray. Earlier in his career, Dietzel attempted to recruit Starr for Bear Bryant at Kentucky. In this game, he let Starr rot on the bench. "As I sat on the bench in front of my hometown friends," wrote Starr, "I couldn't help but believe he was holding my decision to play for Alabama against me. The only other quarterback on the Gray squad, Bob Hardy of Kentucky, played virtually the entire game despite having a sore arm."

Bitter, embarrassed, and in despair, Starr wept after the game. Incredible as it seems, this High School All-American and NFL Hall-of-Fame quarterback-to-be was deemed not good enough to play for an 0-10 college team or to share duties with a sore-armed, and all-but-anonymous Kentucky quarterback in a college all-star exhibition game.

Bart Starr was now hopeless. The high school All-American, the quarterback Bill Moseley called the greatest high school passer he had ever seen, was staring at the premature end of his career. Just two years previous, it was certain that Starr's football reputation would only enlarge has he led the Crimson Tide to ever greater heights. As much as Starr loved playing and studying the game, he wanted to extend his career and play pro football. Now, however, held back by injury and a trashed by a gross coaching miscalculation, his gridiron dreams were aborted.

Often character and will are overlooked. This time, for Bart Starr, they triumphed. "The basketball coach thought he had the qualities and the leadership, and he could throw the ball," recalls teammate Albert Elmore. Dee knew two key members of the Green Bay Packer organization—Jack Vainisi, the player personnel director, and an assistant coach named Lou Rymkus. He contacted Vainisi and, according to Schoor, lauded Starr as a prospect. "He's got all the essentials and would make a fine quarterback," Dee claimed. "He's a great passer, a fine kicker, and commands respect from all of his teammates. He's also a very bright young man, an A student. I think he would be fine Green Bay quarterback prospect."

Dee's regard for character foreshadowed that of Vince Lombardi's. According to the man who was perhaps football's greatest coach, will was merely character in action. Quality character in action was, for Lombardi, among the most important attributes in society. "The character, rather than education," he said in his speeches, "is man's greatest need and man's greatest safeguard, because character is higher than intellect." Starr, however, had both character and intellect and that Dee observed these qualities in him was a godsend for Starr.

It is important to keep in mind that this was an essentially pre-TV era. Unless you played for Notre Dame or starred for some other national powerhouse, you were almost certainly destined to the same fate as that of Starr at the beginning of his high school career. You would be ignored. Networking was perhaps the most powerful factor in finding talent at that time. Coaches, fans, parents, friends, professional cronies, and others would alert a personnel man to a prospect off the national radar, and Bart Starr most certainly was not on the national screen. This was how the "finds" were often found. In fact, as late as the 1960s, the Dallas Cowboys superscout, Gil Brandt, gained huge prominence for his capacity to find gridiron diamonds in the rough of small colleges and unpublicized programs.

Vainisi responded. He told Dee he would send Rymkus down to look at Starr. Jack Vainisi decided to take a chance on Bart Starr, though not a big one. He drafted the Alabamian in the 17th round of the 1956 draft, making Bart the 199th player to be selected.

President John F. Kennedy once said that success has many fathers, while failure is an orphan. Success may indeed have many fathers, but when one of them is Vince Lombardi, the other fathers will likely be anonymous. Few figures have contributed more and received less credit for the success that was the Green Bay Packers than one Jack Vainisi. Vainisi grew up in Chicago's Catholic north side, the crucible of Chicago Bears football. In fact, Jack was a schoolmate of Mugsy Halas, George Halas' son, and went to St. Hillary's grade school where members of the Bears would stop by and assist the priest in coaching the eighth grade team. Vainisi's father operated Tony's Fine Foods, a grocery and delicatessen at which Bears' players hung out and Jack's mother cooked gargantuan Italian meals for members of the team.

An All-Chicagoland lineman at St. George High School, Vainisi was accorded the highest honor any prep gridder could receive. He was recruited by Notre Dame. After a single season with the Irish under Hugh Devore, Jack was drafted into the army and stationed in Japan. After returning from the military he finished his degree at Notre Dame, though no longer playing football due to physical problems. That, however, did not mean Jack Vainisi was finished with football. He loved the game, and if he couldn't play he wanted to get into the administrative—front office—end of the game. He did so as a scout in 1950, when Gene Ronzani became the Green Bay Packer head coach and Devore his top assistant. No one worked harder at his job than Jack Vainisi. He developed contacts with myriad high school, college, and professional coaches as he scoured the nation for talent. Well ahead of his time, Vainisi catalogued his scouting reports in thick, blue canvas, three-ringed notebooks. He evaluated and coded the statistics of nearly four thousand players.

After years in the football wilderness, it was Vainisi who pushed the organization to hire fellow Italian American Vince Lombardi after the 1958 season. Vainisi knew Lombardi, who was then the offensive coordinator for the New York Giants, and Lombardi regarded him highly—so highly that he told the Packer brass that he would not have considered their offer had Vainisi not been in their employ. Conversely, Vainisi urged Lombardi to demand complete control of the football operation as a condition of acceptance, fearing that petty barriers and interference might otherwise waylay the new coach. According to Maraniss, Vainisi had little use for members of the Packer board of directors, seeing them as both small-minded and elitist. Moreover, their attitudes of superiority toward Italians, evidenced by such references as "there's the Italian Mafia," when they might see Lombardi and Vainisi together, were less than respectful.

As central to the Packers' success as Lombardi was, it was Vainisi, the team's scout and personnel man throughout the fifties, who was the architect of the great Packer teams. It was his efforts and recommendations that got Dave Hanner back in 1952 and then went on to garner no less than seven Hall of Famers. In brief, Vainisi put together virtually the entire corps of the great teams of the Lombardi era.

In any case, the story of Jack Vainisi does not have a happy ending. After years of emotional and physical investment in the Packers' football success, Jack Vainisi, with his wife pregnant and with two young daughters, died just before the team won its first title of any kind. On the Sunday after Thanksgiving in 1960, just after returning from mass, he collapsed in his bathroom. Jack Vainisi was only 33 years old. He had suffered from rheumatic fever, a condition that had damaged his heart, something that he had discovered after returning from Japan, after having been misdiagnosed as suffering from scarlet fever. Though but a footnote in Green Bay history, there would be no Packers without Lombardi nor would there be a Bart Starr without Jack Vainisi.

As for Starr, though also courted by Hamilton of Canadian Football League, Green Bay was the only choice. He couldn't picture himself playing in the ice and snow of Canada he said later, certainly tongue-in-cheek. Packer assistant coach, Ray "Scooter" McLean was dispatched to Tuscaloosa to sign Starr. The Packers offered him $6,500, less than what the Tigercats of the CFL were willing to spend. Starr asked for an additional thousand, hoping to use the money to pay some medical expenses incurred when his wife had suffered a miscarriage. McLean called Green Bay for approval and Starr signed. The thousand dollars he received upon signing did not turn out to be a signing bonus, however. It was deducted from the $6,500 figure initially quoted.

Nonetheless, Starr was elated. All he wanted was a chance. Faith and will would carry him the rest of the way.

CHAPTER 8

Humble Beginnings

WHEN THE PACKER pre-season camp of 1956 began, Bart Starr was, as always, prepared to make the most of his opportunity.

Upon graduating from Alabama, he received the Air Force ROTC commission. He saluted Ben, who returned the salute, and then gave his father the traditional first dollar. After viewing Bart's lieutenant bars, Ben stayed firmly in character. "You might outrank me," the family patriarch acknowledged, "but I'm still the boss." He did, however, give his son a bear hug. But Starr was not thinking about the service, he was thinking about quarterbacking in the NFL. "I was committed that I was going to do whatever it took to make that team," he says. To ready himself, he worked intensely on his passing skills. "Johnny Dee helped again by securing three footballs for me," recounts Bart in his autobiography, "something the football coaches had been unwilling to do."

From there he started throwing. For a month he fired footballs through a tire. The pigskins, he claims, became so battered that they eventually looked like the round footballs of the thirties. The faithful Cherry encouraged him every step of the way, retrieving his tosses and cheering him on. Moved by her energy and dedication, he finally asked his wife how she could persist so cheerfully. "I checked my weight this morning," she said, "and discovered that I had lost five pounds!"

Though he had not even made the team, another seed of leadership was evident in Starr. He was practicing another of Russell's lessons of leadership. He was developing craftsmanship. "Success," wrote Russell, "is a result of consistent practice of winning skills and actions. There is nothing miraculous about the process. There is no luck involved. Amateurs hope, professionals work." Indeed, *luck, chance,* and *accident* are words rarely used by Russell or Starr.

Starr needed every scintilla of preparation if he was to become a professional. He had played little for two years and would be battling players with NFL experience for a spot on the Packer roster. When not practicing his throws, he devoured every bit of information he could find on the Green Bay Packers. He studied game reports and statistics from the previous, 1955, season, one in which the team had split its twelve games. Moreover, he looked for material on veteran quarterback Tobin Rote, who came to Green Bay from Rice in 1950, having played under Ronzani and his successor, current coach Lisle "Liz" Blackbourn.

In the 1950s if a youngster was a multi-sport star with baseball among his athletic specialties, there was simply no choice to be made when he chose a professional career. It would be the summer game, truly the national pastime. That, of course, is no longer the case. Big dollars (much larger than $6,500 a year) are available in football, basketball, and hockey (as well as other sports), and so baseball no longer has a corner on the superstar market. Stated another way, when Starr set out to seek his professional fortune in 1956, the NFL was not big league. It was professional football all right, but professional football was not a genuinely big league sport—college football was. Furthermore, if the NFL was a second-class professional entity, its Green Bay entry was not even on the chart.

And Bart Starr found that out within minutes of setting foot on Wisconsin soil, something he recounts with humor in his autobiography. Although training camp was held in Stevens Point, Wisconsin, Starr went to Green Bay first. Upon arrival, he was squired to the Northland Hotel by Tom Miller, a Packer executive. Meals were provided not by a catering service, but by the YMCA cafeteria across from the hotel. Workouts were held not in a giant stadium, but rather at Green Bay East High School, where—believe it or not—the NFL Packers played their home games.

Those were the high points. From there things got worse. The Packer dressing room consisted of thirty-three lockers arranged sardine style, and located in a room no larger than Ben Starr's garage in

Montgomery. Moreover, the team did not use the resources it may have saved on its players to roll out red carpets for the rest of its employees. The Packer offices, occupying a two-story building across from the Downtowner Motel, were so small the coaches had to use a side door to enter the dwelling.

Equipment, always a concern to those engaging in the violent world of professional football, came from a shed proximal to the practice field. Gary Knafelc, an end who joined the Packers by way of Colorado in 1954, and later a Starr roommate, described the quality of the gear succinctly. "I had better stuff than that in high school," he said. Knafelc was not exaggerating. The end had his father send him the pads he wore in the College All-Star Game, using them throughout his rookie season.

The training room contained what was euphemistically referred to as a whirlpool, but was actually little more than a tub with a rusty pipe. A makeshift Jacuzzi took up half of the room. Because the remaining space was the size of a phone booth, players lined up outside the door waiting for their turn to be taped.

And Starr loved it. "Nonetheless," he notes, "the inconveniences failed to diminish my exhilaration over the opportunity to play in the National Football League."

"I thought Green Bay was the end of the world," said Hoosier Bob Skoronski who, along with fellow rookies Jack Losch and Forrest Gregg, played in the College All-Star Game in Chicago's Soldier Field. "Then on the way up here, I wondered, 'Where are we going now?' There isn't even a building next to the runway at the airport. What if someone had to use the facilities?" For Starr, after four days of rookie practice, it was off to pre-season camp at Steven Point, even smaller than the metropolis of Green Bay's population of 50,000.

No dilapidated facility, or inconvenience was of the slightest concern to the determined Bart Starr. He was competing with three other quarterbacks—two rookies and second-year man Paul Held—for the lone backup position. Veteran Tobin Rote was "The Man" for the Pack when it came to directing the team on the field. "I was clearly the least physically gifted," notes Starr, with typical humility. One could believe he was even more correct on his second point, however. "I was also the best prepared." He had paid his craftsman dues throwing at that tire and digesting every available Packer tidbit just a few months earlier.

Wearing #42, the quiet, unassuming rookie must have stood out amid the colorful and zany cast of characters that were the 1956 Green Bay Packers. According to Starr, it was a talented group that, though intense and competitive, never permitted the outcome of a game to interfere with their activities off the gridiron. Tobin Rote ran the team—not merely on the field. He ran the team. That Liz Blackbourn (10-14 in his first two seasons) was a solid gridiron name in Packerland, having coached at Milwaukee's Marquette University, meant nothing to the man from Rice. In one pre-season game, Blackbourn sent a substitute into the Green Bay huddle, only to have Rote wave him back to the sidelines, much to the amazement of the compliant Starr.

Rote did, however, take a liking to the rookie from Alabama. The fiercely competitive, powerful 6-3, 210-pound Rote told Starr to strengthen his arm. "Your arm isn't strong enough and you won't last long if you don't improve," he counseled the rookie. "You don't have to throw the ball seventy-five yards, but you must put enough zip on it to make the defense respect you. If they don't, the opposing defensive backs will eat your receivers alive." Starr went to work immediately, turning his fly ball passes into line drives. He studied pass patterns, consumed films of opponents, and slowly watched his confidence increase.

Rote's wisdom was fed by his hunger to play, even in the pre-season. There were plays in which the sturdy leader was flattened—knocked out—by a blind-side shot, only to re-enter the huddle on the next play. "Tobin was a very tough guy," Starr told football writer Tex Maule. "He had his own style, which wasn't at all like mine, and he was set in it, but he was thoughtful and helpful with me and he gave me some very useful tips." It was Rote's toughness that particularly impressed Starr. "He was rugged," Starr recalled. "He took some shots that might have put a lot of guys out of action and came right back on the next play and acted as if nothing had happened."

Starr discerned a subtle aspect of Rote's leadership. "He didn't let the punishment affect the way he threw the ball, and that's something else I learned from him," Starr told Maule. "If you start flinching after you've been hit hard a few times, you're through, because everyone in the league will know it and they'll come after you even harder."

Rote's counsel to Starr, however, extended to the physical aspects of the game. "It's give and take," he said to the rookie. "Try to relax and roll with the tackle when those big linemen hit you. Don't try to fight them off. You're a quarterback; not a fullback. You won't get hurt if you learn to fall." He also advised Starr to be patient in the pocket, telling him to hold onto the ball until a receiver is ready to break open, and when unable to spot a receiver, simply to hold the ball rather than risk an interception with a desperate throw. That Rote took a liking to Starr was not at all typical in a day in which hazing rookies was as common an activity among veterans as reviewing plays. Nonetheless, he must have been insightful and perhaps sensitive enough to see Starr for what he really was: a young athlete eager to learn and who would render to a veteran of Rote's stature the respect he commanded.

Rote was joined in the backfield by veteran fullback Howie Ferguson and the elusive halfback Al Carmichael, the latter having set an NFL kickoff return record of 106 yards. The center was All-Pro Jim Ringo, who had a little payback on his mind when he saw the callow rookie.

One day, Rote had Starr take over the holding chores for the place-kickers. Ringo shot three straight impossible-to-catch snaps to Starr. Realizing Ringo was among the most expert snappers in the NFL, Starr was baffled. After several more, Ringo looked at Bart. "Starr, I'll never forget that Orange Bowl game," he said with a sly grin. Ringo had been on the opposite end of that 61-6 Alabama annihilation of Syracuse in Starr's freshman year.

Starr held the great Billy Howton in particularly high regard. In one scrimmage, Starr nailed Howton with a perfect dart, only to see the glue-fingered pass grabber drop it. Rather than ignore the miscue, because it came on a pass from a nondescript rookie, Howton said, "Rook, that was a fine pass. I'll never drop another one." Howton's commitment to excellence left a lasting impression on Starr. "His unwillingness to accept anything less than perfection exemplified the attitude of a true professional," Starr stated.

Pranks were everywhere. Jim Ringo, deciding to force teammate Carmichael to miss a mandatory team meeting, taped Carmichael's door shut while he was napping. To secure the door, Ringo wrapped the end of the tape around another doorknob across the hall. Once awakened, a frantic Carmichael found himself trapped in his room and facing a fine. One day, Paul Held observed the hairy defensive lineman John Martinkovic sitting bare-chested on the training table. As Held walked by, he feigned a slip, reached out, and slapped the strip of training tape in his hands across the hairy Martinkovic. "Oops, sorry," said the prankster, as he proceeded to rip the tape along with a liberal supply of hair follicles from the chest of the pained teammate. Martinkovic was prepared, however. Quickly he situated the giant chaw of chewing tobacco in his mouth such that he was able to emit a stream of effluent between Held's eyes.

In addition to these characters, the team included perhaps the quintessentially opposite personality to the polite, "yes, sir" Starr: Richard Afflis. Afflis is much better known by his professional wrestling nickname, Dick the Bruiser. On one occasion, Afflis indulged in a beer-can crushing contest with teammate, Jerry Helluin, also a defensive lineman. With stylistic variety typical of NBA Slam Dunk contests, the two men demolished the beer cans. Finally, Afflis took his game to a new level. He mashed the can against his nose with such force that blood literally poured down his face.

"What do you think of that?" he asked in a challenging tone.

"You win," said Helluin.

It was open season on everyone, including Coach Blackbourn. One morning, kicker Fred Cone filled a glass of orange juice with the contents of a saltshaker and placed it in front of an empty seat at breakfast. Blackbourn took the vacant spot a bit later. Apparently rather thirsty, the head mentor elected to guzzle down the orange juice rather than sip it slowly. "He tossed it down in one gulp," notes Starr, "and his eyes crossed as he reached for this throat with his left hand."

It is safe to say that Starr was far more of an observer than a participant in these memorable high jinks. Starr wanted to make the team. He dreaded the possible knock on the door from the "Turk," the assistant coach who with an "I'm sorry," would summon the player to the painful meeting at which he would receive his release from the team, likely ending his professional football career. The mantra rarely changed. The player would be told that he had worked hard, had talent, and was appreciated by the coaching staff for his efforts. Nonetheless, it being a numbers game, the team could not carry every player it might want to keep and so he was to be one of the odd men out.

The whole experience had a bogeyman quality in NFL pre-season camps. Superstition dictated that players not refer to the assistant coach by his actual name. He was simply called the Turk. Nor did they mention the name of a recently released would-be teammate. All associations with football death were to be avoided. The focus was always on surviving.

Starr's early performance in team scrimmages was sufficiently impressive to warrant playing time in the exhibition games. "Although I lacked professional experience," he notes, "I had both confidence in myself and an excellent role model in Tobin." Obsessed with perfection and excessively concerned with his mistakes, Starr nonetheless survived the early cuts. The other two rookies were let go, leaving Starr and Held in quest of the cherished understudy role. The competition went down to the checkered flag at the end of run, with Held being released after the final pre-season game. "I was never sure I had made the club," Starr said, "not in that first year, until the final cuts were announced. It was quite an experience."

When he got the word that he made the cut, Starr was understandably euphoric, given the long shot he was coming out of mothballs from Alabama. "It was one of the happiest days of my life."

Be it ever so humble, Bart Starr was an NFL quarterback.

And humble it was, as Starr threw only 44 passes (completing 24, with two going for touchdowns and three into the interception category) for a modest 325 yards on a team that closed the books a puny 4-8-0. As Starr pointed out, the 1956 Packer team had no shortage of ability. In addition to Skoronski and Gregg, cornerstones in the dominating Lombardi juggernaut of the sixties, the squad included Ringo, Knafelc, Hanner, Rote, and Martinkovic, along with linebackers Roger Zatkoff, Bill Forester, Tom Bettis, and Dereal Teteak, and one-eyed All-Pro safety Bobby Dillon. Starr summarized the team succinctly. "Although there was an abundance of talent," he stated, "the Packers lacked coaching leadership and had become accustomed to losing." As for his own performance, "I wasn't that good," acknowledged the rookie, "but I wasn't too bad."

Despite his son's new professional status, Ben Starr was not yet ready to luxuriate in Bart's success, at least not in his presence. When the elder Starrs arrived for a visit during the season for a game against San Francisco, Ben did not enthuse over his son's having made an NFL roster at this most important of positions. In fact, he did not center his post-game conversation on football at all. Instead he took a ride in the country to look at the quality farm land. At one point, he asked his son to stop the car. Ben walked into a nearby field, and scooped up a handful of dirt. Holding it in his outstretched hands he allowed the dirt to fall through his fingers and back on the earth. "Son, the good Lord knew what he was doing," Ben said. "If he had blessed us with such fine soil in Alabama, there wouldn't be anyone living up here."

CHAPTER 9

Illusion

B

Y THE END of the 1956 season Liz Blackbourn was impressed with his rookie signal caller. By endless study and film watching, Starr had mastered every play in the Packer playbook, familiarized himself with strategies used by opponents, and could concoct offense tactics on his own. Once again, however, people were not at all sold on Bart Starr. For Blackbourn the question was his arm.

For Bart, however, the issue was military duty. Bearing the ROTC commission, he was called to active duty January 3, 1957, and assigned to the Eglin base near Panama City, Florida. The good news for Starr was that service football was big at that time, and with Zeke Bratkowski finishing his hitch at Eglin, it appeared Starr would be the man under the center. It wasn't to be. During his physical it became apparent that he had a back problem and upon further examination by an orthopedic physician a final decision as to his fitness to serve was postponed. Later, the general in command would not sign the medical waiver necessary for Starr's remaining on active duty and so the second-year Packer received his discharge six weeks later.

Military lifer Ben was light-hearted about the matter, even having fun with Bart. "Son, I didn't think you would make a career of it," he said on the phone to the apprehensive and somewhat embarrassed young man, "but don't you think two months is a little ridiculous?" Having endured a little ribbing, Bart and Cherry eagerly headed back to Green Bay in May, hoping to settle there. "We looked forward to raising our family in a safe, quiet town with traditional values," he wrote. "Despite the severe winters, northeastern Wisconsin was a recreational paradise."

Leadership inevitably emerges—often in less than demonstrative ways. Such was the case in Starr's relationship with Nate Borden. Drafted in 1955 out of Indiana, Borden was the Packers' only black player, and Nate never had the luxury of forgetting about it. Not only could he not find housing within the city limits, he was rejected by a number of his own white teammates. When Borden tried to stay in a motel just outside of Green Bay, one at which a number of Packers were staying, his "teammates" firmly told the motel manager that accommodating Borden meant losing their business. Typically, the manager chose a buck over principle and Borden was left to put his family in what amounted to a near shanty.

Many of the racist Packers hailed from the South. One Southerner, however, did not join in the bigotry. That was Bart Starr. He and Cherry called Borden and invited him to dine with them. From that day forward, Borden and his family were frequent guests in the Starrs' rented residence.

This little anecdote is truly remarkable when viewed in the context of the times. This was the 1950s, a pre–Civil Rights era, and Bart Starr—the son of man who was scarcely a crusader for civil rights— was from Alabama, where the "N" word was tossed around as loosely as names of towns. Yet, Starr resisted the temptation to choose the option that would best ingratiate him with his teammates—that being to do nothing—but rather decided to do the right thing. For Starr it was about personal integrity, one of Russell's eleven principles of leadership. He was, as Russell advised, taking responsibility for what he was doing in his life, standing clearly behind the choices he made, and giving himself to the mission at hand.

In any case, principle would not win him a spot on the '57 Green Bay roster, and so with the military hitch behind him, Starr set about to convince the Packer brain trust that he had a future in the land of beer and cheese. Things did not look good. The Pack spent their #1 draft choice on a quarterback, Heisman Trophy winner Paul Hornung from Notre Dame. There was no way the team would pass over the Golden Boy for the #17 pick of 1956. Moreover, with sturdy but aging

Tobin Rote still at the throttle, Bart Starr figured to be looking for a place to sit in the game of musical chairs. Once again, Starr would not be deterred. His now iron will kicked in and drove him to the limits of his capacities. The words of Tobin Rote, when the veteran observed him as a rookie had not decayed in his brain. "Kid," Rote had said to him early on, "you have to learn to zip the ball a little more. You won't make it in this league throwing cream puffs." So Starr focused on speed and accuracy with his throws as he practiced. And once again, he relied on preparation, believing that if an opportunity was in the divine plan, he would be ready.

In pre-season drills, it appeared Starr was hopelessly slotted as the No. 3 quarterback on a two-man chart. Rote was set. Hornung, however, was found wanting. He could run, block, and kick, but when he passed the ball, bad things happened. He threw what Rote derisively called "cream puffs," tosses that too often were picked off by opponents. Not many gridiron battles are won on the golf course, but it was on the links that opportunity met preparation for Starr. In July of 1957, a day before the beginning of training camp, Rote, Fred Cone, and Starr were on first hole of the Town and Country Golf Club. As Rote was readying himself to swing his 2 iron, Jack Vainisi ran up to the tee and told Tobin, "You've just been traded to the Detroit Lions."

Rote was incensed. Settled in Green Bay, he was now being dispatched to play for a team that already had a Hall of Fame quarterback, Bobby Layne. Starr wondered if Rote was going to bash Vainisi over the head with his golf club. Despite his teammates' willingness to forget about playing the round, Rote insisted they continue. He was, however, very upset as evidenced by his dropping the 2 iron back in his bag and giving the ball a mighty smack with a driver. Rote hit the little white ball with such all-consuming force that it bounced off a house well beyond the green. For Tobin Rote, the trade had a happy ending. He took over the controls when Layne broke his ankle that season and led the men from the Motor City to the NFL championship in a 59-14 drubbing of Paul Brown's Cleveland squad.

What has been left out of the narrative is that the Packers added another signal caller to the mix. He was none other than Vito "Babe" Parilli, Starr's hero from Kentucky. As such, Starr did not enjoy his final golf game with Rote. His thoughts turned to his upcoming joust with Parilli. "I kept thinking back to the summer of 1951," Starr noted, "when Babe worked as hard as I did to improve my quarterback skills. I knew then that I could never repay him, and now I had to compete against him." Starr wondered how Parilli would react when he saw him in camp for the first time in six years.

Babe Parilli was pure class. When he saw Bart, he made the first move, and according to Starr, said, "Bart, I know you probably feel as uncomfortable about this situation as I do. When we worked together in Lexington, I said you could be a great quarterback. Prove it to me. Let's push each other and have some fun." Understandably, Starr had nothing but good things to say about the hero of his youth, a man who tutored him even while competing with him. "There is no end to what Parilli taught me, when he came to Green Bay," he states, "As a matter of fact, he taught me more about basic techniques in playing quarterback than any coach up to that year."

Starr and Parilli maintained an amicable relationship despite their intense competition. The student finished ahead of the teacher. Bart Starr, the self-effacing son of burly Ben Starr, the youngster who had been all but overlooked until his next-to-last season in high school, the young man who spent his senior year on the bench watching his college team go 0-10—that Bart Starr was a starting quarterback in the National Football League.

But that was as far as it went. It proved an illusion. After defeating the hated Chicago Bears in a stirring season-opening triumph, 21-17, the team eagerly awaited the visiting Detroit Lions. The day before the game, Cherry seemed ready to give birth to the family's first child. The dutiful quarterback stayed with his wife throughout the night, but at 8:00 on Sunday morning the moment of nativity had not yet arrived. "We'll do our best," their obstetrician told the anxious Starr as he left reluctantly for the pre-game meal. "Your wife and baby will pull through."

They did, but Starr didn't, at least football-wise. Bryan Bartlett Starr, Jr., was born that evening, after his nervous father played what Starr called "one of the worst games of my life," one in which he made a healthy contribution to a Packer defeat. The Green Bay Packers turned in a dismal 3-9 season, with Starr sharing time with Parilli ("Babe actually played more than I did," he said.) Starr did improve on his 1956 statistics. Completing 57 of his 215 passes, he threw for 1489 yards and eight TDs, yielding ten interceptions. It was good enough for a .544 completion percentage and a 69.3 rating.

Liz Blackbourn was gone—back to Marquette—but not forgotten. Curiously, he approached Starr with an alluring angle, as Schoor relates it. Blackbourn reportedly told Starr he would never be more than a backup quarterback. "Is that what you want?" he queried rhetorically.

"No, sir."

"Of course that's not what you want. You play backup a couple of years, and then you're out," predicted the deposed mentor.

"That's not my way of looking at it, sir."

Then Blackbourn made his move. "You understand the game all right. You've learned a lot these last couple of years. You learn fast. You've got a fine head on your shoulders, but I don't know about being No. 1. I think you could be a great help teaching. You're a natural."

"School?" said the taken-aback Starr.

"I mean coaching. I think you'd be a great help coaching quarterbacks." After a few more exchanges, Blackbourn delivered the punchline. "How about coming with me to Marquette University?"

Blackbourn was making a truly amazing offer. He was proposing to place a 23-year-old football player and father on a career path in coaching, one that would begin at the college level. Given the paltry salaries of the not-yet-big-league NFL, and Marquette's status as having run a reputable college football program, one might have expected the conservative Starr to grab this career life raft and climb aboard with the generally respected Blackbourn. But he didn't.

After thanking his former mentor, Starr explained himself. "I'm not moving. Not just yet. I'm going to stay in Green Bay as long as I can, as long as they'll have me. I've got to try to make it as a pro quarterback before I try anything else." Will won out. So did personal integrity. "Many people," noted Russell in defining leadership, "ponder career choices when they are young and believe that unless they find exactly the right job or career path for themselves they will be eternally miserable. That is a mistake. What is essential is the inner commitment we make—the commitment to our integrity—to do whatever it is we decide to do." In that sense, Starr again was clearly a leader. He had the integrity to lead his own life. What remained was for him to become a leader on the field.

Nonetheless, the 1957 season had ended badly. Little did Starr know that the dim nature of 1957 would give rise to a full-scale football brownout in 1958.

CHAPTER 10

Brownout

THERE WAS every reason to be hopeful as the Packers readied themselves for the 1958 season. Liz Blackbourn had resigned and headed back to Marquette and was replaced by popular, affable, assistant, Ray "Scooter" McLean. Furthermore, the Packers were assembling a cache of solid talent. They already had Starr, tackles Forrest Gregg and Bob Skoronski, tight end Ron Kramer, and center Dan Currie, along with Jim Taylor and Paul Hornung on offense. Ray Nitschke had also arrived from Illinois, along with guard Jerry Kramer out of Idaho, to begin their sterling careers as bellwethers of future Green Bay success.

This was an estimable bunch. Five of them lasted through the championship years, and five—Starr, Gregg, Hornung, Taylor, and Nitschke—are in the Hall of Fame. That Jerry Kramer is not remains one of the greatest mysteries in all of sport. Currie and Skoronski were extremely solid players, with the latter serving as the team co-captain, while the mercurial Ron Kramer became the best tight end in the league outside of Mike Ditka.

After losing the opener to the hated Bears, 34-20, the Pack knotted the Lions at home 13-13. On the local WBAY Quarterback Club show there was optimism in the air. The team was young and but a point short of being 1-1. One of the show's regulars, though disappointed with the tie, reminded the fans, "We'll get another crack at the Lions come Turkey Day." After dropping the next two to the powerful Baltimore Colts and the far less capable Washington Redskins, the 0-3-1 Packers played host to the Philadelphia Eagles. The bad news is that the Eagles closed the game scoring 28 consecutive points. The good news is that Green Bay was ahead 38-7 when the deluge happened. The 38-35 triumph spurred some hope among the faithful. It lasted exactly one week. In their next game, Green Bay took a 56-0 pounding from the Colts, and then went on to lose their last six outings, finishing the campaign in a near-fatal, J.D. Whitworth–like 1-10-1. It is easy to write off the '58 season as an aberration, but it was so ghastly that it merits at least a brief recap. Here in capsule form is how the Packers accomplished the amazing feat of winning one game in an entire season.

- Chicago 34, Green Bay 20. Not as close as it looks, the team scored only 7 points in the second half of this home opener. Starr's fumble on the 12 set up a Bears' score.
- Detroit 13, Green Bay 13. Another home game, one in which the Pack outgained the Lions. Starr hit on 19 of 31, but went out with an ankle injury.
- Baltimore 24, Green Bay 17. This game, played in Milwaukee, was perhaps the highlight of the season, given the team's coming within a touchdown of the eventual NFL champions. At one point, the Packers led 17-0. Starr threw for 320 yards, but saw four of his throws intercepted.
- Washington 37, Green Bay 21. It was 34-0 after three quarters. Starr left with an injury.
- Green Bay 38, Philadelphia 35. Babe Parilli was the hero of the team's lone win on a cold, rainy day in Green Bay.
- Baltimore 56 Green Bay 0. The three quarterbacks were a combined 5-for-26 in the worst defeat in Packer history. There were public references to "defeatism" by a frustrated McLean.
- Chicago 24, Green Bay 10. "I figure we had 35 boys out there trying today," was McLean's benediction after this loss in Chicago.
- Los Angeles 20, Green Bay 7. The team never scored after the first quarter, but "The boys were trying . . . sure they were," said McLean.
- San Francisco 33, Green Bay 12. Tied after three quarters, the 49ers

scored 21 unanswered points in the final period. The Pack was outgained 539-230.

- Detroit 24, Green Bay 14. "It's disgusting," said McLean of this mistake-ridden game, "when you have the momentum we had, the opportunities we had, then throw the game away." Quarterback Tobin Rote and Coach George Wilson were gracious winners, with the latter saying, "They went all out to win for Scooter." The Pack have been nearly doubled up in scoring (300-152) after ten games.
- San Francisco 48, Green Bay 21. Three interceptions and a fumble and the team was behind 27-0. Starr started but was benched, as the team threatened to exceed the record 2-10 futility of the 1949 squad.
- Los Angeles 34, Green Bay 20. "Packers Make Gallant Try But Lose Last One 34-20," was the headline of a game in which the team gained 84 yards passing.

Not much has been written about that season and it is likely not much ever will be. A few comments do need to be made. When a team is assessed in terms of "trying," rather than succeeding, you know the bar has been lowered to accommodate a losing season. How bad were the '58 Packers? They scored just 193 points. Only one other team scored less than 246. The Pack yielded 382 points—199 more than the New York Giants, and 36 more than the second-worst (2-9-1) Chicago Cardinals. Their 189 net points performance was over 100 points worse than the Cardinals, and 148 worse than the 2-9-1 Eagle team they defeated.

The '58 season was a testament to the importance of the mental aspect of the game. Not very many teams go 1-10-1; even fewer do it with five future Hall-of-Famers on it, even if they are in their early years. This one did, and did it in large part because it really was not a team. It was a collection of factions, battling one another rather than the fellows on the other side of the line of scrimmage.

Disillusionment and dubious coaching decisions were everywhere. Among the most disheartened was rookie Ray Nitschke. After starting the first four games, the defensive tornado, who was later referred to by one writer as playing "middle maniac" for the Packers, was benched after Washington's Johnny Olszewski racked up 156 yards rushing in a

37-21 Packer loss. Author Edward Gruver notes that Nitschke was not buying the coaching decision. "Nitschke wasn't so sure," he writes, "he found himself wrapping up Olszewski well beyond the line of scrimmage, indicating to him that the Packer front wasn't doing its job. Nitschke took the benching grudgingly and took out his frustrations the rest of the season as a kamikaze member of the suicide squad."

The consensus was that McLean—who went on to Detroit at season's end—just did not have the stomach to take the whip in hand and move the team forward. Due to his tenure as an assistant, he had friendly alliances with a number of veterans, players that now needed discipline that he did not mete out. Perhaps his partiality to the veterans is what was the most costly. Again, to have the type of young talent this coaching staff had and win but one game is inexplicable. But that is what happened. McLean entered the head coaching post a nice guy and solid football man. He left at the end of the season a nice guy.

The story of the '58 debacle might have been fit subject for such hilarities as "NFL Follies," had the campaign been less depressing. The Packers resembled an amateur beer league squad more than an NFL contingent, given their antics. McLean himself was the ultimate enabler. A hale fellow very well met, McLean had established few and very loose boundaries with players. He played poker with the veterans, usually losing as much respect as money in the process. He thought players like Max McGee and Billy Howton cut the cards with him because of their affinity for the coach. Instead, they enjoyed gutting the mentor in an era in which times were tough and dollars scarce.

Maraniss tells of an evening in Washington in which Knafelc, Bettis, and John Symank walked by McLean's hotel room on the way to eat on the night before a game. They did not see a coach hunched over a yellow legal pad, or one looking at film, or even one addressing his assistants or key players in preparation for the next day's confrontation. What they saw was a room decorated by blue smoke and occupied with focused poker players, chief of whom was Head Coach McLean. Noticing the players, the untroubled Scooter simply reminded them to return in time for bed check. Knafelc put this cap on McLean's tenure: "He was a great guy but he had no leadership qualities. He was not demanding. If you've been around ballplayers, you know they'll take you to the hilt every time. They'll drive you. They'll get everything they can out of you. And we took Scooter in every way."

And so they did. After a losing effort against the Bears in Chicago, Paul Hornung and Max McGee tried to persuade McLean to allow them to spend the night in Windy City rather than ride the train back to Green Bay with the rest of the squad. McLean, concerned about the two generating negative publicity by partying after the game, reluctantly relented. The two headed for the Playboy Club where entertainer Don Rickles fired a few of his sarcastic salvos at them, and then topped off the evening by keeping company with several of the dancing girls at the Chez Paree night club. To the coach's dismay, the nocturnal antics of Hornung and McGee made it into Irv Kupcinet's popular newspaper columns. The two were fined, but McGee noted that implementing this very common disciplinary procedure seemed to hurt McLean more than the culprits.

As for rules, there were essentially none. Curfews were ignored and dress codes were non-existent. Even team meetings were cut by players—amazingly often without McLean's awareness, given his tendency to daydream while the film projector was running. One likely fictional tale had it that McLean once lapsed into a deep sleep and awakened to an empty room.

The team seemed asleep on the field. "Excellence meant absolutely nothing," wrote Jerry Kramer. "I remember in our exhibition game against the Giants, somebody threw a long pass to Max McGee and he just stuck a hand up and didn't make any more effort than the man in the moon to catch the ball. He slapped it with his hand and knocked it up in the air and then caught it when it came down. Max made a big gain on the play, but he couldn't have cared less. That was typical of the season. If you did something, you did it, and if you didn't, don't worry about it; there were much more important things to do after the game."

As for practices, they were like picnics to Kramer. In fact, whereas players almost universally lose weight over the year due to the rigors of the NFL season, Kramer put on 17 pounds. As for the head coach, "Scooter McLean was a great guy, a really nice guy who seldom got angry and seldom raised his voice. He was just one of the guys." The guys cared about McLean but were as impotent as competitors as was

McLean as a leader. "We went out to the West Coast for our last two games of the year, against San Francisco and Los Angeles," related Kramer, "knowing that if we didn't win one or both of those games, Scooter would lose his job. No Packer team in history had ever won fewer than two games. We really liked Scooter, and we really wanted to win for him, but we didn't know how to win. Instead, we made Packer history. We lost both games, and Scooter didn't wait to be fired. He quit and ran to Detroit as an assistant coach."

McLean was a pathetic, almost tragicomic figure. As the losses swelled, he showed all the symptoms of man in touch with his own professional impotence. According to Maraniss, McLean would stop by Paul's Standard Service gas station on the way to work each morning. He would commiserate with owner, asking what was wrong and what he could do. "He'd get very emotional," recalled Paul Mazzoleni, "and he started to cry. He could see his job was on the line." There was pressure all around the beleaguered coach. The Packer brass needed to fill its new 32,150 seat City Stadium, which opened in 1957.

Members of the executive board would grill McLean weekly after defeats. It was a humiliating, depressing experience, albeit understandable given the need for some modicum of accountability amid defeat after defeat. Board members were ambivalent. "I knew Scooter and played against him and liked him," said Packer great Tony Canadeo. "But Scooter had no control of the team. Deep down in his heart he knew things had to change." Legendary play-by-play announcer Ray Scott watched as players back-doored the helpless coach. "If you were a Packer who knew someone on the committee and you thought you should be getting more playing time," said Scott who witnessed the sad charade, "you'd go to a committee member, who'd go to the coach. Oh, it was awful."

His leaving was not altogether popular, however. On Christmas Eve, the office staff held a party for the lovable but doomed coach. Liberal allotments of gin, bourbon, and beer were guzzled and the rug rolled back with the furniture moved to the perimeter to enable the participants to dance to the big-band and polka music that filled the room. Scooter's wake stood in contrast to the low regard in which the staff held Packer president Dominic Olejniczak as evidenced by the president's effigy swinging from an outdoor lamppost a few nights before McLean's leaving. Green Bay is a small town and it reacted to the two accordingly. Clearly, McLean had to go and it was up to Olejniczak to make that happen. The problem, however, was that it galled them that the powerful former city mayor—president for just one year—would be executing such a wonderful guy. Besides, calamitous as Scooter's reign turned out to be, he was hardly the successor to highly successful Green Bay coaching giants. Just a year previous, a bitter, cursing Blackbourn left before the axe fell on his four losing seasons. Gene Ronzani preceded Blackbourn with another four-year tenure marked by consistent losing. The team was winning less than one in three games. Scooter was just one more failure among a series of losing coaches.

At least the local press carried the popular coach. After all, he played poker with them too. On New Year's Eve, McLean's final night in Green Bay, the coach wound up at Green Bay *Press-Gazette* sportswriter Art Daley's home at two in the morning. "He took it all right," said Daley in reference to the helpless McLean's being pushed out. They ate some eggs, lifted a few libations to toast auld lang syne, and with that the Scooter was off to Detroit.

As for the players, any sense of team had been shattered by the end of the season. Divisions were even deeper and players wanted out. Other coaches around the league reportedly used the threat of sending their under-achieving players to Green Bay as a motivational device. Green Bay was the lowest rung on the football food chain. The town was small, the weather was cold, and defeat was everywhere. Paul Hornung put it succinctly, "Green Bay was the Siberia of pro football."

For the disciplined, incisive, and fully prepared Bart Starr, 1958 may as well not have existed.

The competitive Ben Starr had not raised his son with a casual tolerance for losing. "Miserable, sickening, disappointing, testing," was Starr's way of describing the '58 experience to Maraniss. "Babe Parilli was in there most of the time, and when Joe Francis wasn't calling the signals, McLean would send me in." And, of course, how much a quarterback played depended totally on what he had done for the team on the last play. "If you made an error you went out and if the other guy made an error you went back in. Not only does it test your resolve, it tests your reasoning, where you're going wrong. You're not accomplishing what you want to. It was a tough terrible year."

"It was like musical chairs," said Starr in describing his Nitschke-like experience of trading off with fellow quarterbacks Parilli and young Joe Francis. Starr was essentially the No. 3 man much of the time in the derby, although no roles were firmly established. In fact, nothing about that team was firmly established other than losing. What little confidence Starr had mustered after two years had eroded badly. "I lost confidence," he said, "I wasn't sure about the plays I called. I lost confidence in my passing."

A dozen of his 157 passes were picked off and it just ate him up. "Every time I was intercepted, it would kill me. It would have me worried the rest of the game," he explained to Schoor. "You can't play a good game when you're worried that way. In 1958, I was worried all the time." Failure affected his otherwise stable and optimistic mood. On one hand, he became excessively sensitive to criticism; on the other he never called out a teammate who messed up a play. Once he hollered, "Let's go, Jerry," to rookie Jerry Kramer. Later he apologized for "hollering" at him.

At season's end, despair was Starr's companion. The ugly memory of his senior year at Alabama hung over him. Coach Whitworth's no-confidence vote had had a lingering effect on Starr. So much of professional sports is a mind game. All the players have talent. Some release it, while others bottle it up in nerves. The cycle is vicious. A lack of confidence erodes performance, and poor performance destroys confidence. It leaves one with a variation of Parcells' question: Will I ever succeed again?

"Confidence is the result of success," Starr said. "There aren't any confident losers. Success comes first. Then confidence follows. For three or four years, I haven't succeeded in anything in football. When I went into a game I acted confident, but that was only on the surface. Inside I was expecting to fail and so I did." Starr lacked confidence long before he became a member of the Crimson Tide. He lacked it growing up with Hilton, hearing the stinging critiques of his father, and riding the bench in high school. Bart Starr earned everything he ever got, and he would have to earn self-confidence as well.

In retrospect, Starr's leadership traits emerged as he took responsibility for his ineptitude. "I wasn't mature enough," he says. "I wasn't emotionally mature enough to give Green Bay the kind of leadership a quarterback is expected to give his club." Indeed, he did not lead. "The quarterbacks were Babe Parilli and Bart Starr," wrote Kramer recalling the 1958 debacle in his memoir, *Farewell to Football,* "and I swear I have absolutely no recollection of Bart at all. He threw more than 150 passes that year, so I must've seen a lot of him, but he made no impression. He was a complete blank." And he most certainly performed poorly, completing 78 of 157 passes for just 875 yards, while registering only three touchdowns against the twelve interceptions. His quarterback rating was a puny 41.2. Though basically an optimist, Starr was close to hitting bottom. "I was discouraged," said Starr. "I knew perhaps better than anyone else how poorly I had performed for the Packers."

Starr was too bright to fool himself into thinking he was a quality "field general." "I really didn't have faith in myself, and that's the one thing you can't hide in a family as close as a pro football club," said Starr in summary. "I couldn't inspire confidence in the players. I couldn't be a leader, and leadership is probably the one most important quality a quarterback has to have."

And he wasn't fooling anyone else, either. His teammates knew. "No one, absolutely no one, expected Bart to become a great quarterback," noted Kramer. "His physical equipment was not impressive; he wasn't particularly big or particularly strong, and he didn't have an exceptional arm." But beyond his not measuring up physically to his teammates, he had zero impact from the neck up, according to Kramer. "He was not loud, he was not funny, he was not full of enthusiasm. Bart was like methane gas—colorless, odorless, tasteless—virtually invisible."

Season's end brought on a time of soul-searching for Starr. Perhaps Blackbourn had been correct; Starr would never emerge from the shadow of being a backup into the sunshine of stardom. And worse, as his former coached had prophesied, perhaps he would be a backup for only a few years. Perhaps also, the opportunity to join Blackbourn at Marquette had been not only a good one, but one he had been foolish to reject.

Anyway, it was too late now. The curtain had come down on the 1958 season and very likely on the career of Bart Starr.

CHAPTER 11

Turnaround Incarnate

VINCE LOMBARDI waited a long time to become a head coach. He was 45 when he got the Packer post.

From the outset, Lombardi never left any doubt as to who was boss. When early in his tenure he was asked whether he was concerned about how receptive the players would be to him—a reasonable question given the tenure of his predecessor, McLean—Lombardi had the perfect response. "I don't care what they think of me," he roared, "they need to be concerned about what I think of them."

As for Bart Starr, it was reasonable to believe that his football career was probably over by the time they put away the pads after the '58 debacle. Consider the facts. Starr had come to Green Bay about as unheralded as a quarterback could be. Though a short-term high school phenom, he had ridden the bench as a college senior on a winless Alabama team. Fully 198 players had been selected ahead of him in the 1956 draft. And as if that were not enough, the first three Packer teams for which he played had a cumulative record of 8-27-1 and he was not good enough to play regularly for any of them. Only God knows how close NFL history came to being written without Bart Starr—simply because he was out of the league.

"I'm not sure he (Lombardi) really felt Bart was really tough enough," says Boyd Dowler. "Not so much physically, but mentally tough."

Not surprisingly, Vince Lombardi had his own doubts about Bart Starr. "When I joined this team, the opinion around here and in the league was that Starr would never make it," Lombardi wrote. "They said he couldn't throw well enough and wasn't tough enough, that he had no confidence in himself and that no one had confidence in him." Lombardi, however, did his own research. While studying films, he saw some redeeming qualities in Starr. "He was a top student at Alabama so they said he was smart enough, and after looking at the movies that first pre-season I came to the conclusion that he did have the ability—the arm, the ball-handling techniques and the intelligence— but what he needed was confidence." At least Starr deserved a chance.

There are few areas in which Lombardi's scintillating insight was more in evidence than in his understanding of Starr. He had identified the confidence issue when he arrived. Moreover, he saw the confidence issue less as a matter of personal weakness than as a function of Starr's overall psychological makeup and perhaps the context in which Starr had developed. In 1962, after Starr had emerged as a key figure in the Packer football machine, Lombardi still felt confidence may continue to be an issue. "It's just that when you combine sincerity with sensitivity and intelligence, the individual tends to be tense, and I'll have to find the right time this week to try somehow to relax him," he said before a game with Detroit.

The two had a long, difficult road to travel. Starr was the antithesis of Lombardi. Lombardi was a Roman Catholic lineman from the urban east. Starr was a Protestant quarterback from the bible belt. Whereas Lombardi was loud, Starr was quiet. Whereas Lombardi was emotional, Starr was intellectual. Whereas Lombardi was overbearing, Starr was deferent. Worst of all, Starr appeared to be a loser. There were simply no points of intersection for them. That they found a way to build a bond, one that eventuated into mutual love and respect is among the greatest tributes one can make to each of them.

Lombardi wanted an offensive leader. Leadership for him, however, meant force, dominance. By that definition Bart Starr may have been many things, but he was not a leader. He was too soft. This, after all, was football, a paramilitary battle of bodies and wills. Quarterbacks were called "field generals." "Yes sir," "no sir" guys with impeccable manners could hardly have fit the description of a field general, at least in Lombardi's view.

Upon a closer look, there are discernible reasons why Starr and

Lombardi meshed despite their superficial differences. Both were military men and Starr, because of that, did have, under the surface, an authoritarian streak. He could give orders as he had as a quarterback in high school and at Alabama and he could take them. He also had two other characteristics an autocrat like Lombardi valued highly. If he was told how to do something, he was smart enough to grasp it quickly. He was also reliable enough to get it done. In addition, Starr was 100 percent accessible. He was always either present or available, due to his dutiful and predictable life. He was also extraordinarily even-tempered. So much so that he would eventually be a moderating force in the coach's life.

Right from the start, the quarterback was attracted to the tightly organized, linear mind of Lombardi. "We're going to take a step backward, gentlemen," stated the new mentor during the first morning as he handed out the playbooks to his quarterbacks. Lombardi's playbook was substantially less than half the size of McLean's, or the one to which quarterback newcomer Lamar McHan had been exposed in his time with the woeful Chicago Cardinals. According to Maraniss, Lombardi wanted his quarterbacks—Lamar McHan, Joe Francis, and Starr—to empty their brains of all the mush of the past system and play-calling options in order to comprehend a new, simpler, yet far more effective system. The former high school physics teacher would teach his approach to them, and do it simply, clearly, and with endless repetition. This was all a part of Lombardi's thinking. He believed a coach was to be a teacher. "He has to pound the lessons into the players by rote, the same way you teach pupils in the classroom," he explained.

Lombardi's system was in a word, brilliant. The plays were relatively few in number, but there were options within each one of them. Moreover, he taught his quarterbacks how to read defenses swiftly and so determine which option would be most effective. The former New York Giant offensive coordinator's approach was logical rather than intellectually unmanageable. And he had a reason for everything. Lombardi wanted his players to understand. "They call it coaching, but it is teaching," he once said of his pedagogical approach. "You do not just tell them it is so, but you show them the reasons why it is so and you repeat and repeat until they are convinced, until they know."

And Starr loved it. The fog and the foolishness, the needless complexity and confusion evaporated. Everything was suddenly simple, sound, and sensible. Plays were orderly, rational, and labeled clearly. Beyond the intellectual tidiness of Lombardi's system there was his absolute conviction that his approach worked. Vince Lombardi was a professor, salesman, and above all, a leader. It was an exciting new world that the Packers were entering, and Starr knew it. Right from his initial meeting with the players involved in the passing game, the new coach was crackling with charisma. "He had an early camp for the quarterbacks and the receivers in June 1959," recounted Starr in Kramer's *Lombardi*, "and his whole approach—the forcefulness of his voice, his carriage, his very presence—oozed confidence. I knew right away that here was a man who was going to take complete charge, who had absolute confidence in his system, and I couldn't wait to see what the system was going to be like." After the likes of J. D. Whitcomb, Lisle Blackbourn, and Scooter McLean, Lombardi was, for want of a better description, exciting. At the first break, Starr hurried to a pay phone to call his wife and soulmate, Cherry, in Birmingham. The key words in their brief exchange came from Bart. "I think we're going to begin to win," he said joy.

This is testimony to Lombardi's incredible presence. This short, squat man filled every room he entered. After a single meeting with a group of players totally unfamiliar with him, players that had not enjoyed a single winning season in the professional ranks, and were playing for an organization that was backward in every respect from organizational structure to facilities, this small but powerful man put his stamp of victory on their minds. He demanded that the Packer offices be redecorated, pronouncing the dilapidated condition in which he saw them initially, "a disgrace." The Packers were going to win and the offices would look like it.

Lombardi never stopped talking about winning. It was the Darwinian law of the NFL jungle. Once he dramatically pointed to and called each of his assistants by name and said each of them was there for only one reason: to win. The team's goal was to win. In fact, it must win. "If we don't win," Lombardi said, referring to players and coaches alike, "we're gone." In Lombardi's logic, winning was not something you tried to do. Winning was something you chose to do. It was something you willed yourself to do. It was that simple. "The will to excel and the will to win," he stated, "they endure. They are more important than events that occasion them."

And he would exact that will from his players. He made no secret of his expectation that his players be committed to winning. "I will demand a commitment," he told them early on, "to excellence and to victory, and that is what life is all about." He would not try to coax them to commitment. "There are planes and trains leaving here every day," he warned them, "and if you don't produce for me you're going to find yourself on one of them."

If there is a single genius to Lombardi's success it lay in his riveted attention, his unbreakable focus, and single-minded obsession with winning. And he was convincing. "Basically, I feel, Coach Lombardi is a supersalesman," said Starr later to teammate Jerry Kramer, "one of the finest salesmen there's ever been. He has a knack for selling himself and his system and his ideas to football players. He's able to do this because, first, he believes passionately in what he's selling—in himself and his system. And second, he's a great teacher, both on the field and at the blackboard. For nine seasons, I watched him get up in training camp and diagram his favorite play, the sweep, and talk about it, and I never once got tired of his performance. Every single time, I was captivated."

He was not a man without values. Deeply committed to his Catholic faith, the coach was a daily communicant at Mass. He regularly espoused the importance of religion and family. But the work of football to Lombardi was not merely a job. It was a near sacred calling. "When you play here," he said, "only three things are important: your religion, your family, and the Green Bay Packers."

For Starr, the ordered nature of Lombardi's values made perfect sense. "I was the beneficiary of seeing a proper, prioritization of a life because that is the way my parents lived," he explained to the *Birmingham Christian Family* in 2001. "God came first, then family and others. It is something I have tried to emulate all of my life. I believe that one of the most severe problems we have in our society today is our lives are not properly prioritized. I think there are too many I's and We's at the top, and when that is the priority we are in trouble." As for Lombardi's walking the walk, "That was his prioritization and he never wavered. What a joy to be working with someone for nine years who every day, standing in front of you and working with you, was seeking to be the very best he could be. I have never been around anyone more committed to excelling."

As for the Green Bay Packers, the commitment was about winning. "Winning is not everything. It's the only thing," was one of the most famous of the many Lombardi utterances. He expunged all excuses for poor play, all reasons for mediocrity. For Lombardi, there was nothing about his dedication to winning that was inconsistent with the rest of his largely spiritual values. For those in Lombardi's NFL, winning was simply doing one's job. This was professional football. It was not about education, character, or dear old alma mater. It was about pragmatism. You were paid to do one thing—to win. And according to Lombardi's values, you were to earn your paycheck.

Lombardi would earn his by being the leader. "The strength of the group is the strength of the leader," he once declared. "Many mornings when I am worried or depressed, I have to give myself what is almost a pep talk, because I am not going before that ballclub without being able to exude assurance. I must be the first believer, because there is no way you can hoodwink the players." Indeed, he was the first believer, according to Jerry Kramer. "Gentlemen," he said at the outset of his tenure, "I have never been associated with a losing team, and I do not intend to start now."

"Until he came to Green Bay," wrote Kramer, "we had been expected to lose. He was the first person to tell us, without a smile, that we were not going to be losers." He was not the first believer for long. "We knew immediately he could make us into a winning team," said Kramer. "He made us believers, too."

The players would earn their paychecks by their willingness to pay the price of preparation necessary to bring about winning. And he would push them. "With every fiber of my body, I've got to make you the very best football player that I can make you," he promised. "And if I don't succeed the first day, I'll try again. And I'll try again. And you've got to give everything that is in you. You've got to keep yourself in prime physical condition, because fatigue makes cowards of us all." Indeed his team would be physically fit. He insisted on it. On the first day of camp, he told linebacker Tom Bettis and Dave "Hawg" Hanner, the veteran defensive tackle from Arkansas, to drop twenty pounds in two weeks or "get out of camp!" Lombardi made his contribution to the team's conditioning in the form of a brutal dose of conditioning in training camp. He began with three laps around the goalposts in the summer heat, followed by twenty minutes of intense West Point style calisthenics, culminating in the dreaded grass drills. Players would have to run in place, lifting their knees as high as possible for anywhere from ten to thirty seconds. Then, on the command "Down!" they dove on their stomachs, only to leap to their feet and resume the knees-high running in place at the sound of "Up!" Hanner lost eighteen pounds in two days, and by the end of the second day of practice, he collapsed from sunstroke. He was taken to the aptly named St. Vincent Hospital for intravenous liquids. After the first few practices, the team lost an average of twelve pounds per man.

At the conclusion of practice, the players ran another lap around the field. To keep everyone hustling, the last three finishers did an additional lap. For any practice in which Lombardi deemed a player was giving less than his best, extra laps were ordered. Soon the players realized it was in their best interest to exert maximum effort during practice rather than after it. Difficult as it was, it worked. Years later, Kramer met a successful businessman who characterized a successful person as one who can and will do the things that an unsuccessful person cannot and will not do. "Lombardi showed us what we could do," he noted, "and he made certain that we would do it. He pounded success into us."

Conditioning was mental, physical, and behavioral. "Wherever you go," he directed them, "you represent the team. You will talk like, you will look like, and you will act like the most dignified professional in your hometown."

Lombardi would not brook even the slightest deviation from his rules. And in that first year, the rules went into effect the moment a player entered camp, even if he was an early arrival. Max McGee and fullback Howie Ferguson found that out quickly. The two got to camp several days early. On the first night, they ate dinner in the team dining room and then took off for an evening of libations. The following morning at breakfast, the new coach made his presence known. "You start working out today, and you start keeping curfew today," he announced loudly. "As far as I'm concerned, when you ate a meal here yesterday, you became part of this camp. Therefore, you abide by all my rules."

Ferguson was hot. Who was this first-year head coach to get in the face of veterans like he and McGee? "What are you talking about?" challenged Ferguson. "We don't have to report for two more days."

Lombardi erupted. "Listen, mister," hollered the coach using one his favorite words to address people with whom he was displeased, "you get your butt out there on the field, or you get your butt out of here!" The argument did not end as Ferguson and Lombardi shouted at one another. The coach, however, did not relent.

The rules were specific—to the letter. During the initial training camp, lights out curfew was 11:00 P.M. Lombardi entered Jim Taylor and Jerry Kramer's room at exactly eleven only to find Taylor, dressed in just his socks and shorts, sitting on the edge of the bed.

"Jimmy, what time you got?" queried Lombardi.

Taylor took out his watch. "I've got eleven o'clock, sir."

"Jimmy, you're supposed to be in bed at eleven, aren't you?" Lombardi asked.

"Yes, sir," Taylor responded.

Lombardi fined him.

The next night Ray Nitschke was in the phone booth two or three minutes after eleven. Lombardi fined him as well. Forgetting that the McLean regime was history, Jerry Kramer, Dan Currie, Jesse Whitten-ton, and Fuzzy Thurston tried to sneak out of the dormitory at St. Norbert College in West De Pere, Wisconsin, site of the training camp. Assistant Coach Red Cochran saw them in a bar. The players believed their old pal Red would cover for them. They were wrong.

Lombardi fined them. "The fines weren't nearly as bad as the tongue-lashing Vince gave us," wrote Kramer. But there was more after the next practice. "You four guys, come over here," he hollered. "You four guys who broke curfew, come here." The compliant players hurried over, hoping the coach would be merciful. He was not. "Start right here on the goal line," he said, "and go down the sideline to the other goal line, then go across the end zone, up the other side of the field and back here." Then came the clincher. "And I want you to play leapfrog all the way."

None of the exacting behavior was at all difficult for Starr. First, he was a rule-follower, not at all given to pranks or testing limits. Further, he was the son of an autocratic military man. As far as the quarterback was concerned, the man in charge had the right to make the rules, and provided that he was even-handed about enforcing them, a player was expected to comply.

Throughout his tenure, the coach would infuriate his players with Olympian chewings-out. In 1962, long after Kramer had established himself as one of the NFL's elite interior linemen, he unknowingly practiced with two broken ribs. What he did know was that his ribs were incredibly sore and it affected the way he practiced. On one play backup guard Ed Blaine fell over. Kramer, unable to jump over or run around Blaine, simply stopped. The next thing he heard was Lombardi's voice. "Good guards, my tail!" the coach bellowed, "We got the worst guards in the league!" Kramer was enraged and glared at Lombardi who would not meet his gaze. When practice ended, the coach, ever astute at picking his spots, came up to Kramer, patted him on the back and mussed up his hair. "I'm sorry," he said, "I didn't mean that. I wasn't talking about you, you know that."

On another occasion in Lombardi's inaugural season, he scorched Kramer with criticism throughout a grueling practice session. "Son," he said, exhibiting expert timing in addressing his dispirited young lineman after the practice, "one of these days you're going to be the greatest guard in football."

He worked the same psychological game on others. Max McGee, an essentially shy man beneath a maverick exterior, could not bear to be humiliated in front of his teammates. That, of course, did not stop Lombardi. Early in a practice week, the coach would severely work over his wide receiver. By the end of the week, however, he would ingratiate himself with McGee. "Hey, Maxie, how're you doing there?" he would say with a husky laugh.

"I hadn't talked to him for three days because he'd embarrassed me," McGee said, "but he was afraid it was getting close to game time and I was a big play kind of guy and he didn't want me going into the game mad at him, so the next two days he'd be making up to me for chewing me out in front of my buddies. It worked every time."

Lombardi was confident and comfortable working the psyche of his players. "There are other coaches who know more about X's and O's," Lombardi confessed to his friend Jack Koeppler, according to Maraniss, "but I've got an edge. I know more about football players than they do."

From the beginning in 1959, this turnaround incarnate seared a whole new mindset into his charges. "He destroyed the defeatist attitude that had afflicted the Packers for so many years," wrote Kramer. He did it by remolding the players he kept and ridding the team of others. In that era, five to six players constituted a normal roster turnover from year to year. Between '58 and '59 it was fifteen. Some retired, others were cut, and still others traded. In every instance, the new player was someone who was used to winning.

Little wonder that the man from New Jersey had such an incredible impact. "All men are not created equal," he once said. "The difference between success and failure is in energy." And Lombardi had plenty of energy. Everything about Lombardi was larger than life. He talked loudly. He laughed loudly. He criticized loudly. Incredibly emotional and mercurial, the coach was what would be called bipolar today. He could go from reflection to rage to laughter in seconds. His temperament brought zest to repetition, and intensity to otherwise dull, midseason practices. What never changed, however, was his dominance. Vince Lombardi was never not in charge. One writer spoke of a dinner party held at the coach's home for media and friends. Although the occasion was convivial and joyous, it was not loose. Everything was done in order. When Lombardi announced over the cocktail-clinking din that dinner was served, glasses were set down as one and conformity triumphed.

Lombardi was driven by yet another force, one similar to his shaky young quarterback. He had something to prove. Stop after stop, year after year, he had executed his tasks with excellence. Yet, he watched helplessly as other, less competent coaches were elevated for political and ethnic reasons. He once applied for the head coaching position at Wake Forest, confident that he was the most qualified for the job. When the school did not call, Lombardi called an insider friend who told him, "Wake will never hire a coach whose last name ends in a vowel," something Lombardi himself said, when he was removed from consideration for the Army head coaching position when the renowned

Earl "Red" Blaik—on whose staff he served—resigned, also after the '58 season. Lombardi was an Italian Catholic in an era of Waspish (and, in some parts of the gridiron world, Irish and Polish Catholic) dominance.

No one questioned his competence, and his resume was sparkling. He had coached under Blaik at Army, and had been the architect of the powerful New York Giants' offense under Jim Lee Howell, while Tom Landry expressed his football genius running the defense. A perhaps apocryphal story made the rounds that one day a visitor made his way to the Giants' facility. He entered the complex and looked into one room. There was Tom Landry with the defense, peering at the screen as the projector whirred. He walked further and looked in another. There he saw Lombardi, lecturing the offensive players, chalk in hand. The visitor then went down to the end of the hall to the head coach's office. There was Howell, shoes up on his desk, comfortably reading the paper.

Lombardi was not really the Packers' clearcut first choice. Forrest Evashevski, the highly successful Iowa coach, had been interviewed and seriously considered. A gritty, proven winner from the Midwest's Big Ten, the man with the Polish surname would certainly be received warmly in Packerland. There was also intense sentiment to bring back Earl "Curly" Lambeau, the man who had founded the team and made it a winner, claiming six championships between 1929 and 1944. And Curly wanted back in. Fortunately for Lombardi, he had the recommendations of the Giants' Wellington Mara (who, truth be told, did not want the Pack to take his prized assistant), George Halas, Paul Brown, Red Blaik, and even Commissioner Bert Bell. Nonetheless, it was the inimitable Jack Vainisi, who behind the scenes, did the due diligence on Lombardi and then sold his ideas to Olejniczak.

The executive committee knew the choice of head coach was a critical one. There was intense community pressure to make the right pick. The Packers were Green Bay. The team and the town's identity were one. More important, however, the NFL no longer consisted of a collection of small town contingents from Decatur, Illinois; Hammond, Indiana; and Canton, Ohio. The Packers had turned to its Green Bay citizens in 1949, offering stock in a non-profit corporation, in an effort to salvage the local franchise. Now the Packers were in jeopardy once again. The time had come for the team to win, to fill its stadium, and to return to NFL respectability, quelling the sentiment throughout the league that no franchise should be located in a hamlet like that of this small Wisconsin city.

When Lombardi met with Jerry Atkinson, one of the directors, Atkinson offered him good money and substantial autonomy in the form of the dual title of Coach and General Manager. According to Maraniss, Lombardi had listened well to Vainisi's directive to take command. Rather than agreeing to the contract with grateful humility, he opened by asking for more money. He got it. The deal had to go to what Oliver Kuechle, long time sportswriter for the *Milwaukee Journal* called the "Soviet Supreme," the full board of directors. The board was not without reservations regarding this unknown former assistant from the East. Why couldn't they get Evashevski? Why not bring Curly Lambeau back? After all he had built the Pack and brought it to greatness and now wanted back in. In the end, however, it was Lombardi.

Vince Lombardi did not come in like a lamb and go out like a lion. He came in like a lion and never stopped roaring. The night before Lombardi signed the five-year pact, he spent extended time in his office with his secretary, Ruth McKloskey, deleting clauses from his contract that he felt might in some way limit his power. Moreover, he was done with any and all meddling from members of the Soviet Supreme, telling them at his meeting with them that were he to need any help, he would request it. "I want it understood that I am in complete control," he announced to what must have been bewildered members of the committee. Furthermore, as a symbol of his omnipotence, Lombardi took over Olejniczak's parking space.

For most of the Packers, Lombardi's hiring was greeted by a "Vince who?" response. After a parade of less than successful mentors, Lombardi figured to be just another low-profile mediocrity that Packer brass could hire at a bargain price. Surely, no difference in the team's gridiron success should be expected. Starr, however, with his elephantine memory, remembered the bellicose coach the instant he saw Lombardi's picture in the papers. In a preseason exhibition against the Giants, played in Boston's Fenway Park, Green Bay won in the closing seconds. Starr, when he left the field after holding for the PAT, saw one of the Giant coaches excoriating the defense for allowing the touch-down. The face he saw in the papers as the new Green Bay coach belonged to the same man on the sidelines in Boston: Vincent Thomas Lombardi. That Lombardi, an offensive coach who had the temerity to tear into the defense, told Starr that the Scooter McLean days were over.

Vince Lombardi was the original control freak.

Lombardi understood leadership, something he would model for Starr. "I hold it more important to have the players' confidence," he said, "than their affection." Starr, lacking in confidence, had inspired none from his teammates. A new day was dawning, but for Bart Starr, the future was still uncertain.

CHAPTER 12

Sudden Impact

OOTBALL IS a 'now' game," said Buddy Ryan when he took over the moribund Philadelphia Eagles in 1986. "You have to win now, or at least soon." Lombardi understood this Ryan doctrine. The Packers would win now—and they did, taking four of their six exhibition games.

To Lombardi, football was controlled violence and he drove the team with that in mind. One of his favorite line drills was the nutcracker. Two blocking dummies were set up five feet apart as boundaries for the mayhem. A running play was then executed in that five-foot space. The key to the drill was the battle for hegemony between the offensive and defensive linemen. Depending on the outcome of that confrontation, either the run would succeed or the defender would fight off the block and tackle the ball carrier. The blocker knew the snap count and could initiate the contact. The defender, however, knew the play, creating a checks and balances situation.

Violence is about pain, something Lombardi understood. "A small injury," he once said, "is one that is painful but not disabling." Pain was fought with mental toughness. "I think it is singleness of purpose and, once you have agreed upon the price that you and your family must pay for success, it enables you to forget that price," he wrote. "The harder you work," Lombardi would say, "the harder it is to give up." Moreover, he believed that singleness of purpose enabled an athlete to ignore the minor hurts.

"I remember my first year here. I remember that first day of practice in training camp, and when I walked back to the dressing room I wanted to cry. The lackadaisical ineptitude, almost passive resistance, was like an insidious disease that had infected almost a whole squad. The next morning, when I walked into the training room, there must have been fifteen or twenty of them waiting for the whirlpool bath or the diathermy or for rubdowns." Lombardi erupted. "What is this?" he hollered. "An emergency casualty ward? Now get this straight. When you're hurt, you have every right to be in here. When you're hurt, you'll get the best medical attention we can provide. We've got too much money invested in you to think otherwise, but this has got to stop. This is disgraceful. I have no patience with small hurts that are bothering most of you. You're going to have to learn to live with small hurts and play with small hurts if you're going to play for me. Now I don't want to see anything like this again."

"Coach Lombardi never takes second place when it comes to Oral Roberts or any of the rest of the faith healers," said Jerry Kramer later in *Instant Replay*. "He can just walk into a training room filled with injured players, and he'll say, 'What's wrong with you guys? There's nobody here hurt.' And the dressing room will clear immediately. And all the wounded will be healed."

That was the case on the day following Lombardi's training camp eruption. Only two players were in the training room. Lombardi's impact was immediate.

As the season approached, the challenge was daunting. The pro football observers saw the Packers as Western Conference cellar-dwellers. "Last and probably least—that's the sad forecast for the once-proud Packers," were the words of *Sport* magazine. "They've got a new coach in Vince Lombardi, but he might as well kiss this one off as a rebuilding year."

The opener would be in Green Bay against the hated Chicago Bears. Lombardi opted to prepare for it with a week of practice just outside of Milwaukee at a private boarding school in Pewaukee. Final cuts having been made, family members were encouraged to be part of the week. Offensively, the primary focus was Lombardi's signature play in New York and now in Wisconsin, the mighty power sweep. The joke on the team was that Lombardi would run that play in practice until finally even he was tired. The coach absolutely loved that play. It was in one sense, incredibly simple; in another endlessly complex. It was simple enough to draw with ease on a blackboard—"What we want is to get a seal here, and seal here," Lombardi would say as he drew two white vertical lines across the left end of the horizontally arranged X's and O's, "and run this play in the alley"—yet there were seemingly endless variations that flowed out of the sweep, and its success depended on the synchronized movement of all eleven offensive players.

Lombardi ground his ideas into the team's head, using fear and logic. "You're watching this day after day," said Bob Skoronski in Maraniss' book, "and it starts sinking in, becoming second nature. And after awhile you say, 'I don't care what happens, we can make this go.'" That was the coach's intention. He was going to make the execution of the plays a matter of sheer determination and practice. There would be no "if" this, and "we hope" that. The Packers would exert their will on the gridiron with such determination that concern about the opposition evaporated.

The practices in Pewaukee leading up to the bigger-than-life opener were brutal. On offense, everything was set except at tight end, where Gary Knafelc had to step in for an injured Ron Kramer. During the final half-hour drill, Lombardi ran sweep after sweep against a defense knowing it was coming. "Again!" he would shout after each run of the same play. "It was the modern equivalent," Maraniss wrote in describing the practice, "of Bloody Wednesday for the Seven Blocks back on the practice field on Rose Hill, the smell of wet autumn leaves, smack and thud and up for more."

For Knafelc, it was torturous. He was taking pounding after pounding from linebackers Dan Currie and the violent Ray Nitschke. "Move! Knafelc! Seal it! Seal it! Again!" Lombardi would shout, his voice piercing the psyche of the exhausted player. Lombardi the perfectionist was not satisfied. "It's sticky, it doesn't look good!" he would scream in displeasure. Finally, Knafelc had reached the limit of his endurance and he turned on the raging Lombardi. "Coach," he said sarcastically, "by this time I think even Ray knows it's a sweep."

With that, Lombardi was satisfied. "Everybody in," he shouted.

It had been a painful, embarrassing, and humiliating experience for Knafelc, so much so that one of his youngsters ran up to him and shouted, "Daddy, I still love you!" The coach had done everything to help him feel afraid, inadequate, and anxious. And he had succeeded. But Lombardi was one step ahead. A master of timing as well as psychological manipulation, he waited until the next morning at breakfast to make his move. He walked up to Knafelc's table and said just loud enough for his family to hear, "You're starting Sunday." With those simple words, the coach had made it all worthwhile.

Knafelc, like virtually every other Packer, never forgot Lombardi. "Not a day goes by," he said in a choking voice on an ESPN *Sports Century* feature on Lombardi, three decades after the coach's death, "that you don't think of him. One way or the other, you think about him."

For Bart Starr, like his roommate Knafelc, nothing came easily. Despite his enthusiasm about Lombardi and his system, Bart was not the coach's choice to start the 1959 season at quarterback. The job went to journeyman signal-caller Lamar McHan, who Lombardi had picked up from the hapless Chicago Cardinals. "That was a real shock, I wasn't happy at all when Mr. Lombardi traded for another quarterback," said Starr with typical understatement. "I had been in the league for three years and it looked like I might be the No. 2 quarterback for the rest of my life." Lombardi was familiar with McHan, because the Chicago Cardinals were in the Eastern Conference and therefore twice-annual opponents of the Giants. McHan was large and had the big arm to go with a fiercely competitive spirit, all attributes Lombardi prized. Though saddled with playing for the losing Chicago entry that played its games on the Windy City's south side—in Comiskey Park—McHan had been a single-wing tailback at Arkansas, evidence of his run-pass athleticism.

McHan was not the only player the aggressive coach brought in. He acquired Fred "Fuzzy" Thurston from Baltimore, and Henry Jordan, Lew Carpenter, Bobby Freeman, and cantankerous Bill Quinlan from Cleveland. In addition, he pulled in Emlen Tunnell from the Giants, and guard John Dittrich. One of the rookies who stuck was Boyd Dowler, a wonderful pick out of Colorado.

As for the quarterback position, Lombardi made no secret of his preference for McHan, naming him the starter during training camp ("You're going to lead the league in passing," he told McHan), and leaving Starr to vie with Parilli for the backup spot. In his first scrimmage, the nervous Starr threw an interception. "One more like that and you're through!" exclaimed the displeased Lombardi in his typically intimidating style. Although the dire prediction of Lisle Blackbourn was beginning to look prescient, Starr's spirit—driven by faith and will—would not be broken. "I never even considered quitting," he said. "It was another challenge."

And he was developing. By the time training camp opened, he had memorized the playbook cold. "I could see in my own mind, day by day, week by week, that this was going to be a lengthy process," he said, revealing the army mentality he had gotten from Ben, "because trust and respect should never just be handed out to somebody. You have to earn it." That was all right with Starr. He was used to having to prove himself. He had earned everything he had ever received on a football field, so why should he stop now?

Starr won out over his hero, Parilli, with young Joe Francis being the other reserve signal caller. "I had mixed feelings when Lombardi released Babe," he wrote, uncomfortable about displacing his boyhood hero and mentor. "Babe was four years older and I was retained primarily because of the difference in our ages. It was obviously not a vote of confidence from Lombardi."

On September 27th the dress rehearsals were over. For better or for worse, the Lombardi era would begin. "There are no notebooks now," Lombardi would later say about game day for his quarterbacks, "because what they have in those notebooks and playbooks isn't going to help them, or us, if it isn't in their heads." The locker room was alive with mental, physical, and emotional energy. Yet the players felt a sense of calm resolution and confident certitude as they prepared to meet the Bears. They were ready. Lombardi's system was simple yet brilliant. "By this time I have cut the number of our running plays down to a dozen and our passes to half a dozen, and I recite them," he later said, explaining how he worked with his quarterbacks. On this particular, very special day, the coach tried to keep the atmosphere controlled, greeting and shaking hands with the players calmly. When it came time for his pre-game speech, however, the intensity spilled out of the passionate Lombardi. His body shook with emotion as he addressed the team, advocating victory. He said later that he had told the team about the great football tradition of the Green Bay Packers, and that "we have a chance to do something about it." The emotional advocate of single-mindedness then worked up to his final charge. "Now go through that door and bring back a victory!" he cried in conclusion. Linebacker Bill Forester was so psyched he accidentally banged his head on a metal locker as he leaped up in anticipation of leading the 1959 edition of the Green Bay Packers out on the field before the throng of 32,150 Packer faithful.

"Packers Carry Lombardi Off Field After Victory," the next day's headline screamed. In a simply amazing game, the Packers defeated Chicago in the opener, 9-6. A year ago, the 8-4 Bears had beaten the Pack twice, each time by 14 points. Now a year later, this team that had yielded an average of nearly 32 points a game a season previous, slammed the door on their arch-rivals, limiting them to two 46-yard field goals.

The game was dramatic, with the Packers trailing much of the way. When fullback Jimmy Taylor circled the end for five yards and a touchdown late in the final period, City Stadium exploded. Was it possible? Were these pathetic Packers going to win? Was this blustery coach for real? Many were afraid to believe, but not too afraid to hope. When the final gun went off, it was bedlam in Green Bay. The Packers had struck a mighty blow for NFL respectability. You could feel that things were different with this team under this incredibly forceful coach.

Lombardi was jubilant and the tiny Wisconsin town was delirious. Ironically, it was the defense, steered by Phil Bengtson, that won for the offensively geared Lombardi. "We worked ten weeks on this defense," said the animated coach. "We planned the game the way the defense played it." Despite the closeness of the score, the Pack dominated. They outgained the Bears by more than a hundred yards. And it was not as if the team's offense was inept, as Green Bay churned out 176 yards on the ground against the usually stubborn bruin defense. Lombardi was confident. "It was first game tenseness," he said, referring to the lack of scoring. "Now that the defense is working, we'll have to sharpen the offense."

"We were outplayed," said Chicago quarterback Ed Brown. "We couldn't get anything."

The next week, with the wind at their back psychologically, the team rolled over the Lions, 28-10 at home. It was all Lamar McHan, with his four touchdown strikes, while Starr was rapidly becoming the invisible man. "If the Green Bay Packers become the Cinderella team of the National Football League this season," wrote Ray Doherty of the Associated Press, "and they seem to be on their way—quarterback Lamar McHan will fill the role of Prince Charming very nicely." Lombardi lauded his quarterback. "Lamar was simply great," he enthused. "Lamar gives us the long bomb we needed." All that was missing was the clause, "that Starr cannot give us." Still another win followed, this one over San Francisco, 21-20. The once defeatist, impotent Pack now stood alone atop the Western Conference, leading the 49ers and Colts by a game.

That same day, Commissioner Bert Bell died of a heart attack at Franklin Field in Philadelphia while watching the Eagles defeat the Pittsburgh Steelers. Three major candidates emerged as his successor. They included then 64-year-old George Halas, a league founder and patriarch; Edwin J. Anderson, who was president of the Detroit Lions; and former baseball commissioner and color line breaker, A. B. "Happy" Chandler. Alvin "Pete" Rozelle, perhaps the greatest commissioner in the history of sport, seemed no more likely to be the NFL czar than Bart Starr would be the starting quarterback for the Green Bay Packers.

By now, according to Jerry Kramer in *Farewell to Football*, the whole town of Green Bay had gone crazy with glee. Kramer told of losing his shaving kit and going to the local Holzer's drugstore to purchase a replacement.

"Here's just what you need," said owner John Holzer, as he presented the kit to Kramer.

"How much is that?" Kramer asked.

"No, no, no . . . it's yours, keep it."

And not just the kit, but the shaving cream, a razor, and even a pie Kramer had been gazing at. Although he needed several other things, Kramer left the store, not wanting to take advantage of his celebrity.

The magic carpet ride ended for the Packers the following week in Milwaukee County Stadium where the Rams trounced them, 45-6. "No excuses today," said the no-longer undefeated head mentor, "but we better bounce back next week." The team had been inexplicably tight, according to Lombardi. "Our boys were tense today," he said in his post-game remarks, "and I don't know why. We didn't see anything we didn't expect." Johnny Unitas and the Colts put the Pack away the following week, 38-21. And it didn't end there. Three more losses followed, such that at the season's two-thirds pole, the team was 3-5, riding a five-game losing streak and having been outscored on the year by 66 points. Especially galling to the proud Lombardi was that the defeats included a loss at the hands of his former team from New York and another in Chicago in a rematch with the Bears.

More than the losses were painful to Starr. In game five—a loss at Baltimore—McHan hurt his shoulder. He tried to fight through the pain the following week in New York but couldn't do it. "It was so stiff out there," said an empathetic Lombardi, "he could hardly raise it to throw. I made a mistake in starting him, but he told me he was all right." The always-prepared Starr's chance had come. At least, so it seemed.

"Francis," shouted Lombardi, summoning the former Oregon State tailback from the bench. Starr felt terrible. "While the Packers absorbed a 20-3 thrashing," he noted, "I stood on the sidelines feeling unwanted and betrayed. I hadn't experienced so much frustration and helplessness since my senior year at Alabama." Repeated thoughts of failure, about the worst thoughts a would-be leader can have, were now taking up residence in his mind. Starr was not underplaying the level of his despair. After the game, he joined tight end Ron Kramer, who was also held out of the game, in a wholly uncharacteristic (for Starr) venture into the Manhattan night. "I don't remember where we went that night or how many bars we went to," Starr noted. "I don't know how much I drank ("Bart had four beers," reported Kramer with amazement. "Miller High Lifes. It was the last time anyone saw him like that."), and I don't recall returning to the hotel. Fortunately, Ron was big and strong enough to carry me back. The only thing I do remember about that night is that it was the first and only time in my life that I have been drunk. With each succeeding drink, I became more convinced that Lombardi was responsible for my stupor."

The following week in Chicago, McHan got hurt again, injuring his leg. This time it was not Joe Francis who received the call. It was Bart Starr. But he did not perform as he did against Tuscaloosa nearly a decade earlier. He completed but three of ten passes for a measly 20 yards in a 28-17 defeat. Nevertheless, Lombardi stuck with Starr the following week in Baltimore, against the reigning NFL champions. Bart threw 40 times, hitting just 14 for 242 yards, and having a couple picked off by the opportunistic Colts. He showed some toughness, however, shaking off several injuries and calling his own passing number 40 times.

Despite the losing streak, Lombardi had taught his charges well. There was no evidence of the defeatism that suffused the '58 squad during the five-game skid. Besides, four of the five losses came against winning teams, three against eventual conference champions. The next game—at home against Washington—would be a genuine test because it would pit the Packers against a team with an identical 3-5 mark.

Starr got the start. Faith, will, and preparation paid off as he made the most of it, completing 11 of 19 for two TDs in a 21-0 rout. Lombardi was pleased and made no secret of it. "This was the best combined effort of our offense and defense," he crowed. "If we did anything wrong it certainly wasn't much." As for his quarterback, "Bart Starr played an especially fine game," the coach said. "He threw well and called an intelligent game."

It could be said that the Washington game was symbolic of what Bart Starr would become—a quarterback who threw well and called an intelligent game. And for the Packers, that is what a quarterback needed to do. The running game was taking shape with Jim Taylor and Paul Hornung supplying the one-two punch behind a tough line. What was needed was an accurate air game with a cool, intellectual wizard at the controls.

"Starr Pilots Packers . . ." was the headline the following week, as the Pack enjoyed Thanksgiving, feasting on the Lions, 24-17 on national television. Rookie Boyd Dowler grabbed four Starr aerials for 107 yards, in an accurate, interception-free game for Bart. Lombardi was now seeing the Packer offense become a machine. "The most important thing is consistent execution," he explained. "Consistent execution wins ball games." The now .500 Packers went on to avenge their earlier 45-6 blowout at the hands of the Rams, by pounding Los

Angeles, 38-20, and closed the season with rousing 36-14 conquest of the 49ers on the West Coast.

Lombardi was ecstatic, describing Starr's performance as "brilliant" and "great," after his quarterback threw for two TDs without an interception in San Francisco. The coach was especially pleased with Starr's accuracy and execution. "He was just automatic about 90 percent of the time," he said. The '59 season could not have ended on a brighter note for Starr. "I had studied Lombardi's offense and his ideas about attacking the different defenses," he said to Tex Maule, getting into the complexities of the game. "A lot of the success depends on the ability of the quarterback to read keys, the things a defensive player does to indicate what kind of defense they are playing. Defenses are complicated, and they change from play to play, from man-to-man to zone to combination zone and man-to-man, and if you don't recognize them immediately, you get in trouble. I knew all the theory; I mean, I knew what keys to look for and I had spent a lot of time watching movies of the other teams' defenses, but in the middle of a game, when you're dropping back to set up to throw the ball, it looks different, not as clear."

San Francisco, however, had been the breakout game. "But on that afternoon in San Francisco, all at once, everything fell into place. It was like someone had taken a veil from in front of my face. I knew the keys." Now he could look over the line of scrimmage and change the play in a midnight second. Everything crystallized for Starr. The confusing fog lifted and clarity and leadership broke through. He even told the always loose Max McGee to "hush up" in the huddle. It so startled his teammates that Ringo called a timeout so that the linemen could stop laughing.

The skies looked very bright for Packer fans as the team closed the season with four straight wins, outscoring their foes 119-51. The effect of Lombardi was one of sudden impact. "The game was the climax of one of the finest comebacks in NFL history," wrote Hal Wood of UPI. "A year ago the Packers had finished last in the Western Division, at 1-10-1.

"This was the first Packer team to finish above the .500 mark since 1947, when the Bays had a 6-5-1 season. And to find a better record than 7-5, one has to go back to the 1944 world champions Packers, who won nine games, including the playoff, and lost two."

Forget about Lisle Blackbourn, J. D. Whitworth, and for that matter, even Ben Starr. Bart Starr was now a starting quarterback on a winning team. Although his overall statistics were rather ordinary—70 completions of 134 passes, 972 yards, 6 TDs and 7 interceptions—he had delivered down the stretch, connecting on 52 of 79 passes for 699 yards and 6 touchdowns. More important, he had begun to establish himself as a leader in his own mind and in the minds of his teammates. "I gained more confidence in my ability to lead our team," he wrote. "In addition, I could detect that my teammates were beginning to believe in their quarterback for the first time since Tobin Rote was traded." Even more than that, Starr now had the unqualified support of his coach. After the season, the ever-demanding Lombardi gave Starr his blessing on Frank Gifford's "It's Sports Time" radio show in New York. "We have great determination," he stated. "And in Bart Starr we're going to have one of the great quarterbacks in football."

CHAPTER 13

Never Again

Packer fans all but ripped the days off the calendar in anticipation of the 1960 season. Had the '59 team beaten the NFL champion Colts in either of the two games in which they played
Baltimore, the Packers would have finished in a three-way tie with the
Colts and the Bears for the Western Conference title. It had been that
close. None of this was lost on either Starr or Lombardi. In the off-
season, the coach had his quarterback study composite films of the
great Johnny Unitas, for a very good reason. "Unitas was a proven
championship quarterback," Starr noted, never too proud to improve,
"and I was not." Moreover, Lombardi believed such study would improve Starr's passing, given that he and Unitas had similar deliveries.
"I studied the films diligently," Starr stated. "They provided a frame of
reference from which I could improve the mechanics of my throwing
technique, especially my follow-through. When I reported to training
camp in July 1960, I felt that I was a more able and disciplined passer."

It is easy to get caught up in the substance of Starr's remarks, and
fail to notice another of his leadership traits—the continued commitment to work at his craft. Rather than celebrate his sudden emergence
with swagger, he was never fully satisfied with his performance, and he
had the humility to study a rival to build his game. In any case, there
was no question as to the identity of the starting quarterback for the
Green Bay Packers at the beginning of the much-awaited 1960 season.
Nonetheless, Starr's new, lofty status lasted but a single game, as the
team dropped the opener at home to the Chicago Bears, 17-14.

It was an ugly contest, one in which the Pack gained a pitiful 77 yards in the air, and were outgained as a team, 333-230. Even worse for Starr, an interception off a deflected pass set up the Bears' winning field goal, delivered by John Aveni with 35 seconds remaining. Meanwhile, McHan, a feisty individual was unhappy with his backup role. "You should have been playing me," the unabashed McHan said to the head coach. Evidently, the Packer mentor, understandably unhappy with Starr's performance, agreed. Lamar McHan would quarterback the Green Bay Packers against the Lions in game two. Three games later, the team was 3-1, with Starr standing unhappily on the sidelines as he watched the brash McHan lead the team.

Despite the close in 1959, Lombardi obviously was not sold on Starr as his field general. "That was a real wake-up call for me," Starr told Maraniss. "A real punch in the side." Typically, he blamed himself. "I had let him down! Here's the man who had brought me along and given me the opportunity and I failed when I got the chance. So I was even more determined to get back." Two things jump out here. First, rather than deflect the blame about being yanked after a single game on the heels of a remarkable down-the-stretch performance of the previous year, Starr accepted responsibility for his benching. He would not hang his head. Victims make poor leaders and he would no longer be a victim. More important, Starr was becoming the never-say-die army guy of character, down but not out. Instead of sulking, too often the norm for replaced quarterbacks with bruised egos, he studied ways of cracking opposing defenses even harder. And when he got another chance, he was ready.

It came in game five. Green Bay was floundering on offense, and Lombardi decided to let Starr open the second half under center. "Packers Take Over First Place," the next day's headline screamed, with "Starr Leaves Bench, Leads Pack in Rally," as the subhead. With Green Bay down by a point late in the final quarter, Starr sprung the trap on the Steeler secondary, by suckering the defenders in on short throws to Knafelc. "Later, with the Steeler secondary expecting another short pass to him," recalled Starr, "I sent Dowler down the middle on a deep post pattern. Dowler split the seam in the Steeler zone and was five yards from the nearest defender when he caught my pass to set up our only touchdown, a one-yard plunge by Jimmy Taylor (with 63 seconds left)." The 19-13 triumph gave the team four straight wins and first place in the West.

Not everyone was in a celebrative mood after the stirring win. Lamar McHan was very upset about being pulled after two quarters. On the plane back to Green Bay, the frustrated signal-caller confronted Knafelc. "You never catch my passes the way you did today for Bart," he said with typical bluntness.

"That's because you never throw me the ball," the end snapped back.

McHan then turned on his roommate Boyd Dowler. "You didn't catch my passes."

There was little Boyd could say. But McHan was not through registering his complaints. Later in a restaurant at which a group of players stopped to eat, he headed for the separate room in which Lombardi was dining with members of the executive board. The angry quarterback managed to insert the word *dago* into his address to the coach. You don't have to possess great insight to conclude that with that incident, McHan had all but written his professional obituary with the Green Bay Packers.

Lombardi wasted no time. Before the team meeting the following morning, he summoned Starr to his office. "Your performance in the Chicago game led me to believe we had to make a change," he explained, leading with the negative. "That's why I went with McHan. I haven't been all that happy with his performances either, but stayed with him because we were winning. After the way you brought us back yesterday, however, you're my quarterback and I'm not changing again."

Despite the good news, Starr was not feeling altogether affirmed as the team leader. "Although I had secured the starting position," he wrote, "I don't think Lombardi was totally convinced that I was the quarterback he was looking for. Norb Hecker, a Packer assistant coach, said that Lombardi saw leadership potential that could be developed, but questioned the strength of my arm. As a result, he had an interest in obtaining a more established quarterback for at least another year."

Part of a leader's strength, and one rarely mentioned, is his ability to tolerate ambiguity. This is an attribute Starr had developed long ago. Not only did he repeatedly have to prove himself, he almost never knew when he would get the opportunity to do so. Yet, as a youngster with favored Hilton, in high school behind Don Shannon, on the bench at Alabama, and again and again in the NFL, Starr endured— always ready, always believing, or at least hoping in faith, that his moment would come.

As for 1960, the race was on for the Western Conference crown, and the ride proved bumpy. The following week, in spite of scoring 24 points against the mighty Colts, the team fell 38-24 in Baltimore. More than 2,500 fans awaited the Pack's arrival in Green Bay. "I'm very proud of a very great performance, both offensively and defensively," said Lombardi, undoubtedly spinning a bit for the press and fans. "We got beat on four plays because of inexperienced personnel, but I don't want this to be taken as an excuse." Though he praised Starr's 23 for 59, 259-yard effort, he couldn't have been happy with the four interceptions his quarterback threw.

It was after this game that Lombardi passed the test of greatness in the eyes of then inexperienced rookie and future Hall-of-Famer, Willie Wood. Wood had been burned by the great Unitas–Raymond Berry aerial combination. At the airport, after the game, Willie Davis and Jim Ringo needled the young defensive back, telling him to prepare for a return to his hometown, Washington, D.C., in anticipation of Lombardi's likely reaction in the wake of his scorching in nearby Baltimore. "Don't you believe anything those fellows say," were the coach's words to the insecure rookie, one whose talents and concerns Lombardi could recognize incisively. "You're not going anywhere. You're staying right with me. Every one of those guys making fun of you has had the same thing happen to them. You're going to be here as long as I'm here." And he was.

This ability to assess talent and see into a player's psyche was a large part of Lombardi's genius. He knew who could play and who could not. He was not, however, always as sensitive as he was to Wood. After the 1967 season, Lombardi's final campaign as head coach, he saw Fuzzy Thurston at the annual 1,000-Yard Club banquet. Thurston, who had hoped to continue his career along with his counterpart at guard, Jerry Kramer, under Phil Bengtson, was hardly ready for Lombardi's comment. "By the way, Fuzzy," Vince said, "when are you going to announce your retirement?"

"He was telling me to retire, and he really hurt me," Thurston told Kramer. "I hated him then, too, hated him for telling me I was through." Thurston, however, did not dismiss Lombardi's remark. "But, you know," he said, "I thought a lot about it afterward, and he was right. It was time to retire. I just didn't like the way he did it."

A 41-7 drubbing of the expansion Cowboys was followed by a desultory 33-31 defeat at the hands of the Rams in Milwaukee. Lombardi was angry. "We didn't come here to play football," he told the media. "It was evident all week long in practice." Green Bay now trailed the Colts by a game with only four left—this in a pre–wild card era.

Another loss followed; this one to Detroit on Thanksgiving Day, 23-10. The air game had been weak in the two defeats. Despite having halfback Paul Hornung available to throw out of the option at any time, the team had completed 19 of 60 tosses for 244 yards in the two setbacks. "I guess you'd have to say we're out of it," said the dejected head coach in Detroit on the national day of gratitude.

There was much to be concerned about. A season of promise was turning into one of mediocrity, as the Packers' 5-4 record attested. Moreover, given the thunder and lightning effectiveness of the Taylor-Hornung ground game, the problem on offense appeared to be at the quarterback position, where Starr was throwing too many interceptions.

Although publicly resigned to a disappointing year, Lombardi, of course, was not quitting. He decided to reverse the psychological field on his team. Instead of reaming them out for another futile defeat, he allowed them to drink on the flight home, spoke encouragingly about how they would turn the rest of the season in a positive direction, and later took them all downtown with their families for a turkey feast at the Elks Club. Lombardi's kindness and, to a much greater degree, the death of Jack Vainisi three days later, put the loss in perspective.

By the end of the following week's games, with Baltimore having inexplicably lost two straight while the Packers disposed of the Bears, 41-13, Green Bay was tied for first place with the Colts and 49ers at 6-4. Starr hit on 17 of 23 passes for 218 yards and two TDs against the arch-rivals from the Windy City. Despite throwing a pair of interceptions, his performance elicited praise. "Bart Starr called a fabulous game," said Hornung, who tallied 23 points on route to a record 176 for the season. "In fact, it was a perfect game." Much of Starr's leadership was rooted in his ability to maneuver a team down the field by outsmarting the defenses, much like a baseball catcher's capacity to call the right pitches.

Hornung wasn't the only one impressed with Starr's take-charge quality in that game. "We went to Chicago to play the Bears," wrote Kramer recalling the game, "and this turned out be one of the most significant games in my whole Packer career, partly because of what it meant in the Western Conference race and partly because, for the first time, Bart Starr showed me and the whole team that there was a lot of steel in him." Up until that contest, his teammates had their doubts. "He'd played pretty well for us," Kramer noted, "but there was still some suspicion that he might be a bit of a pussycat, a little delicate, a little fragile, maybe even a little short of guts. In the Bear game, Bart destroyed all the suspicions."

Early in the game, rugged middle linebacker Bill George blitzed and crashed into Starr, flattening him and delivering a cheap but severe shot to the mouth, splitting his lip up to his nose. George looked at the quarterback, with blood oozing from his cut lip, and challenged his manhood in the way athletes love to do.

It was showdown time for Starr; he could roll over or fight back. Either way, his teammates would notice. Spitting blood, Starr delivered a stream of invectives in the direction of George, using words unlikely to be heard in his Methodist church. "I think that was the first, and probably the last, time I ever heard Bart Starr swear, and he came back strong, tough, and unafraid. He established a controlled, intelligent attack.

"We led the Bears at half time by only 13-7, but in the second half, Bart completed nine out of ten passes—including his first two touchdown passes of the season—and we beat Chicago, 41-13. I began to believe in Bart Starr that day, and I've believed in him ever since."

Starr also initiated a change in his relationship with Lombardi. During a workout, Starr had thrown an interception and the volatile Lombardi had exploded in front of the team. Tired of the humiliation, Starr picked his spot to take a stand. After the practice, he headed for Lombardi's office and confronted the coach—an incredible move for a young man who still addressed his elders as "sir," obeyed orders almost compulsively, and had—by his own admission—badly lacked confidence. First off, Starr knew the error was not his. The ball had been tipped. Armed with the facts, he stood his ground with Lombardi. He told the coach the interception was not his fault, but that was not what he came in to talk about. There are varying versions of what he said next, but it went something along these lines, "Coach, you're asking me to be the leader of this team, and I'm challenged by that. I want to be the best leader I can be, but I can't be if you're chewing me out in front of the team you want me to lead. You'll see later (on film) that the error (in judgment) was yours. The ball was tipped and intercepted. Now I can take any chewing out you want to deliver, and if you feel I have it coming, have at it. But please do so in the privacy of your office, here where you can make your apologies to me. I will be an even better leader for you if you do that."

Right there Starr demonstrated two things: that it was his mission to lead, and that he understood leadership. More important, he was right. In the military, the officer cannot lead if the troops see him humiliated. Lombardi knew it; he had coached at West Point. Lombardi, for all his virtues, would both rise to confrontation but also was repulsed by weakness. He had felt Starr was too polite, too nice, and not tough enough. It had to aggravate him, even bring out a bit of the bully in him. He was, however, also big enough to realize he was wrong. "I hear you," he said quietly to Starr.

And he had. Lombardi never criticized Starr in front of the team again.

After a 13-0 win in San Francisco, coupled with the Colts' 10-3 loss in Los Angeles, the Green Bay Packers stood alone atop the West by a game over Baltimore and San Francisco. It all came down to a Saturday game on the road against the Rams. With the team's first title since 1944 in the offing, Starr was nervous. He and roommate Knafelc were up at 5:30 A.M. Starr performed his usual game day routine of showering and dressing without shaving. He and Knafelc left to take what they hoped would be a relaxing walk along the Santa Monica beach. Because they left the pre-game meal early, they failed to hear the announcement that the team bus would be leaving at 10:15 rather than 10:30.

Players regularly joked about Lombardi Time—15 minutes early. The coach was so obsessed with punctuality that being on time was to be late, at least by Lombardi Standard Time. Jim Taylor—who Dick Schaap once said spent four years in college emerging unscarred by education—would occasionally irk the intense mentor by dawdling outside the bus until nearly the last minute. Although thinking they were on Lombardi Time, that is what Starr and Knafelc did by making it to the bus about seven minutes before its departure. With a championship on the line, Lombardi was in no mood for humor or testing. "This will cost you a bundle!" snapped the irate coach, standing in the doorway of the loaded bus with his finger pointed at the two (actually on time) players. Starr was embarrassed. "It was the first time I had ever been late for anything in my life," he wrote.

Starr felt loose in the pre-game drills, then headed back into the dressing room to put on his pads and attend the players' meeting. There, Dave Hanner and Em Tunnell held court. "Em says the most intelligent things before the games," Starr noted. "He sizes up the situation perfectly. Only mistakes would beat us, he told the squad." After the players recited the Lord's Prayer, Lombardi entered the room. Starr was eager to hear what he would have to say. "He said three weeks ago they had counted us out and now we were getting a second chance," Starr told Maraniss. "He said he didn't have to tell us what this game meant but warned us about keying ourselves up too much. He told us how big the Rams are and kept reminding us that football is two things—blocking and tackling, plus running the ball. And play the game with abandon, because every time you played with abandon you won, the coach said. He always does an extremely fine job of getting us worked up. You could run through the wall when he lets you go. He doesn't plead. He just stands there telling us what to do in his very authoritative voice. We rushed out of the dressing room door with a shout and I felt well prepared to play the game."

No irreparable harm was done by Starr and Knafelc's tardiness. The Packers blew away the Rams, 35-21. After falling behind 7-0, Green Bay detonated for 28 points in just eleven minutes, with Starr as one of the main-stage performers, owing to his TD passes of 57 and 91 yards to McGee and Dowler, respectively. "These players never quit," exuded the delighted Lombardi to the media. "They had desire all the way. We'll be ready for the title game with the Philadelphia Eagles."

He had not forgotten Starr and Knafelc's "transgression," although he decided to extend some grace. "Forget the fine," he told the two, without offering any compliment of any kind to the "culprits."

Starr had not only been embarrassed by his "tardiness," he had also been sick. "Coach Lombardi was so demanding and so short of praise," he told Jerry Kramer years later, "that I would do anything to gain his acceptance, to get a kind word out of him. I ignored injuries because he shamed me into it. He would walk into the training room and see a bunch of guys sitting around getting treatments, and he'd say, 'Who do you think you are? You're not hurting. You're football players.' I remember I played an exhibition against Cleveland with a shoulder separation and I'll admit it, I played lousy. But my shoulder was killing me. And he came up to me during the game and said, 'You're playing like you're crippled!' And I didn't say a word to him about my shoulder because I had too much respect for him. And in 1960, when we had to beat Los Angeles in the final game of the season to clinch the conference title, I was really ill. I got violently sick to my stomach during the game. But I kept playing—I was mentally tough; I wouldn't give in to my sickness—and we won the game."

Back in Packerland, Green Bay was up for grabs. The team plane was greeted by 15,000 cheering fans in sub-freezing Wisconsin winter weather. But who cared? Signs abounded. "T'was a CINCH with VINCE," said one. "Just One More, World Champs," read another. "Mr. Touchdown U.S.A., Paul Hornung," read yet another. Even Starr was a star, as the "Mr. Quarterback U.S.A.," sign attested. For Starr, however, praise was always provisional, forever balanced off against a lack of belief in his competence. "I think the Packers are a better team than Philly," said New York Giants Head Coach Jim Lee Howell in assessing the game, "but they are a little weak at quarterback."

"I'll be home for Christmas," enthused the happy Philadelphia native, Em Tunnell. "And I'm the only one." Tunnell, however, was unprepared for the 19-degree Green Bay climate. "Man, am I glad to see you," the coatless defensive back said to a friend. "I don't have any warm clothes here. I sent them all home after the Detroit game."

Later at Speed's, a popular watering hole inhabited by fans and players, where the official capacity was 150, over 300 celebrants howled into the night. "We'll win the title. We'll beat the Eagles," said the brash Bill Quinlan along with the team's other defensive end, Willie Davis.

Jimmy Taylor, swilling champagne, agreed. "Look, the team with heart is going to win it," said the man from LSU who had finished right behind the vaunted Jim Brown for the league rushing title. "We've got heart. We're going to be the champions of the National Football League. We never gave up hope and we're not going to quit now."

Taylor was in a talkative mood. "We've got the best team in the league because we wanted to win right from the start. How about that?"

One more game to go. This one was on the day after Christmas in Philly, against the 10-2 Eagles and their great quarterback Norm Van Brocklin. Ironically, this game would match two of the worst teams in the league just two years previous—"dogs of the National Football League," in the words of the great Red Smith of the *New York Herald Tribune*. The Eagles' 2-9-1 mark in '58 meant the two championship squads had been resurrected from a combined 3-19-2 record in just two seasons. It would also pit Lombardi against the team that had offered him their head coaching position the same year Green Bay had. He elected to follow the advice of Giants' owner, Wellington Mara, who felt taking the Philadelphia job would be a mistake. "You'll never get along with them," said Mara, referring to the Eagles' ownership. "They'll never let you run the team the way you want to do it." Mara also told Lombardi that the short-term deal the Eagles had put on the table would not allow him sufficient time to rebuild the team. Mara's counsel was not altogether devoid of self-interest. Knowing Lombardi's worth, he wanted to keep the coach; he had his wife call Marie Lombardi, Vince's wife, an instant later, urging her to help keep Vince in New York. Mara went beyond that, offering Lombardi a raise along with the assurance that he would succeed Howell as the Giants' head coach. In fact, one of the conditions Mara insisted upon in permitting Lombardi to negotiate with Green Bay was that the Packers would agree to release him from his contract, should he be offered, and wish to take, the Giants' head coaching post after Howell left.

As for the upcoming game, there was much to be said for Green Bay's chances. "The Eagles don't have enough ball control to handle them," said Ram coach Bob Waterfield, who once reluctantly split time

According to Lombardi, no one prepared more conscientiously for a game than Bart Starr.

A better athlete than many thought, Starr fights for yardage against the Detroit Lions early in his career.

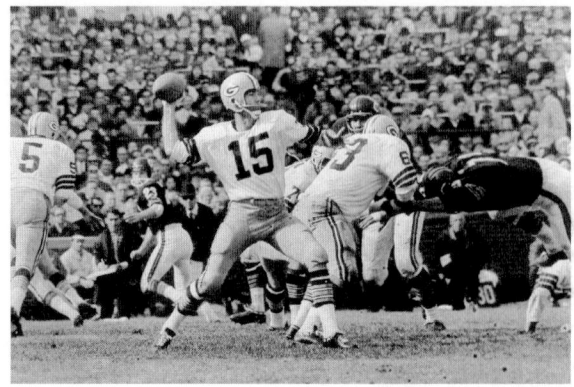

A pinpoint passer, Starr strikes a classic pose against the Bears in nearly perfect 1962.

Starr, warming up for the 1965 title game against the Cleveland Browns, put up impressive championship game numbers in less than ideal conditions.

Starr hurls a strike on the muddy Green Bay turf as the Packers defeat the Browns, 23–12, to win the 1965 NFL championship.

An ultimate leader, Starr called his own plays.

Once intimidated by the bellicose Lombardi, Starr eventually became his confident on-field alter ego.

Starr pitches out to fullback Jim Taylor, the backbone of the Pack's vaunted ground game during much of Starr's tenure.

Packer faithful follow their leaders to Dallas for the 1966 NFL title game—the championship season in which Starr was the league MVP.

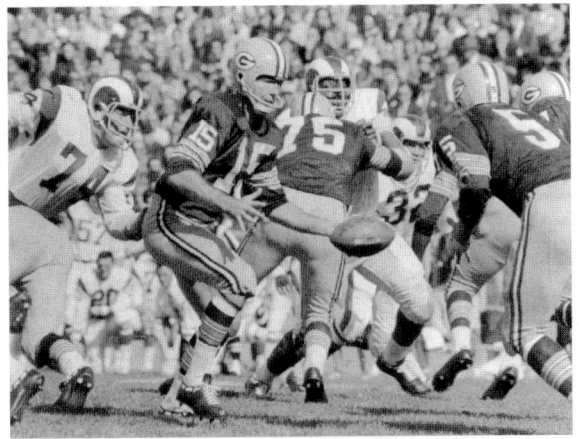

Three Hall of Famers: Starr handing off to Paul Hornung, who follows Forrest Gregg's block in a 1966 game against the Rams.

The most famous quarterback sneak in history: Starr's teammates did not know he would carry the ball in the winning play in the 1967 Ice Bowl.

Game MVP Starr looks on as the Packers score en route to a 35-10 conquest of the Kansas City Chiefs in Super Bowl I.

The Roadrunner, Travis Williams, takes the ball from game MVP Starr and follows All-Pro pulling guard, Gale Gillingham, in Super Bowl II.

An emotional day: Starr's wife, Cherry, and Head Coach Dan Devine are seated next to Bart as he announces his retirement after the 1971 season.

The leader again: Starr fields reporters' questions at the press conference announcing his appointment as head coach and general manager just four years after retiring as a player.

Hail to the Chief: President Nixon came to Green Bay to recognize the Packers' leader on Bart Starr Day. Head Coach Phil Bengtson is seated behind Starr while Bart's parents are to Bart's left.

The crowning moment: Bart and Cherry pose in front of Bart's Hall of Fame induction bust and plaque. Starr was inducted into the Hall of Fame in 1977.

Still smarting from being fired as head coach in 1983, the classy Starr appeared at the Packers' reunion the following season and received a warm welcome from adoring fans.

with Van Brocklin in his playing days with the Rams. Starr saw lots of daylight in the Eagles' defense. "Successful coaches believe that championships are won primarily with a strong defense," he noted. "The Eagles, however, were a team that possessed only a marginal defense." Philadelphia had yielded 246 points in 1960, only 7th best among the league's thirteen teams. They had scored 321. By contrast, Green Bay had outscored its opponents by a 332-209 margin. The oddsmakers installed the Packers as two-point favorites.

With the team in the City of Brotherly Love, Lombardi gave each player a tie on Christmas night as a token of appreciation for winning the Western Conference championship. Perennial All-Pro center and team leader Jim Ringo had something more substantial than a tie in mind as a suitable gift for having posted the organization's first title in 16 years. After the meeting, Ringo collected 30 ties, went to his fifth floor room, and leaned out a window as he cut the ties in pieces with scissors, much to the amusement of several of his teammates who witnessed the surgeries. Ultimately, Lombardi would get even, as he always did. Realizing that the Packer head coach and general manager threw nickels around like manhole covers (as Mike Ditka once described Chicago football potentate, George Halas), Ringo decided to bring an agent with him when he was to meet with Lombardi to discuss his contract. For the man from Fordham, this was an unspeakable misdeed, and he promptly traded the malcontent to the Eagles without ever talking contract numbers.

For Starr, the good news in the championship game was that he completed 21 of 34 passes for 178 yards and a TD, in a game free of Packer interceptions. The bad news was that the Eagle defense—led by both-ways stalwart Chuck Bednarik—was not at all marginal on this afternoon, and the Philadelphians won the NFL title, 17-13. What made the loss particularly galling was how the game ended. The Pack took over the ball on their own 37 with 1:20 left. Starr, who had been struggling all day against an Eagle defense that denied him anything but a short completion, then took over with an air of calm resolution. After completing three straight passes, along with an end sweep by Taylor, the team was down around the Philadelphia 30. After misfiring on a throw, he hit his roommate Knafelc, and the Pack was down at the Eagle 22, where Bednarik sat on the receiver as the precious seconds evaporated. There was time for one more play. With a field goal doing them no good, and Eagles covering deep, Starr delivered the ball to his ace ballcarrier Jimmy Taylor, in the flat. Red Smith, having been born in Green Bay, was all but pulling for Taylor openly, as he wrote, "From the Philadelphia 22 yard line, Bart Starr passed to Jim Taylor. That wonderful runner ducked his head like a charging bull, bolted like an enraged beer truck into the Philadelphia congested secondary, twisted, staggered, bucked, and wrestled one step at a time. . . ."

Packer cameraman Robert Riger was positioned to get a snap a photographer would die for. In the end zone, he readied himself to record the winning touchdown head on, much as the AP wirephoto had caught Alan Ameche's immortal plunge to win the '58 title for the Colts in overtime. And the play looked perfect. "Come to Poppa," he had said to himself, "and I'll give you the whole town of Green Bay." The play started with a pass in the flat to the fullback, premised on the notion that Taylor—who could run over tacklers like no other— would, with a full head of steam, blast his way into the gridiron Promised Land. "He took it and cut back over the center and had one man to beat," Riger recalled for Maraniss, "a rookie in a spanking clean uniform who had just been sent in—Bobby Jackson—and the kid made the stop. Bednarik came over and there was a big pileup, but had Taylor gotten by Jackson, Green Bay would have won and I would have had the picture."

The Eagles had won the NFL championship in the final game of Van Brocklin's and Head Coach Buck Shaw's careers. For Lombardi, the wrenching loss was only the beginning, something he made clear to his team after the press had left the dressing room. "Perhaps you didn't realize that you could have won this game," he told his disappointed troops, "but I think there's no doubt in your minds now. And that's why you will win it all next year." He finished with that prophetic statement—vintage Lombardi. "This will never happen again. You will never lose another championship."

CHAPTER 14

Titletown's Quarterback

DESPITE THE coach's glowing words to Frank Gifford in '59—"And in Bart Starr we're going to have one of the great quarterbacks in football"—and Starr's emergence as the team leader in the banner year of 1960, Vince Lombardi still had his doubts about Bart Starr. As usual, it was never enough.

There was reason for Lombardi's concern. The only imperfection in the otherwise flawless game of football, according to him, was the excessive importance of the quarterback. A pitcher may dominate a baseball game, but a team had a pitching staff, not a pitcher. "Since in the T formation he handles the ball on every play, and because so much of the pro attack has to do with passing, a quarterback must have sure hands and be an excellent passer," Lombardi wrote. Then there was the need for intelligence and knowledge of every player's role on the field, in addition to the tendencies of the opponent.

Statistically, Starr had not had a breakout year in '60. He did complete 57 percent of his passes (98 of 172), but he tallied only 1,358 yards and threw twice as many interceptions—eight—as touchdown passes, for a mediocre 70.8 quarterback rating. The nagging question remained: Did Bart Starr have enough of the right stuff? Was he perhaps too polite, too self-effacing, and too lacking in swagger to lead an NFL team at a championship level? One player who did seem to have what it took was playing for Lombardi's former colleague in Dallas—Don Meredith.

This came out during the league meetings in a conversation over dinner with Jim Kensil, the director of public relations for the NFL. Kensil pointed out a play in the championship game in which McGee was wide open and Starr did not see him. After acknowledging that such things do happen, Lombardi reportedly said he would like to acquire Meredith—that he would part with any two players on the Green Bay roster to get the young star of the future out of SMU who was ballyhooed as the "best passer from Texas since Sammy Baugh."

In retrospect, Tex Schramm, the long-time president of the Dallas Cowboys, did claim he did not think Lombardi was all that serious. Inquiries about Meredith's availability came in from far and wide to the expansion team that had gone 0-11-1 in their inaugural season. Schramm reportedly never offered the young quarterback to anyone and did not recall Lombardi initiating any deal. Schramm recalled Lombardi as one who would make flippant, impulsive remarks, often intended at eliciting a reaction rather than being an expression of his true intentions.

In any case, the rumor got out. "Perhaps Lombardi was using this rumor as a psychological ploy to motivate me," Starr theorized, perhaps trying to rationalize his hurt. That hardly seems logical. Of all people, Vince Lombardi knew he did not have to threaten Starr's status in order to motivate him. Simply directing him was sufficient. Unfortunately, for the troubled Starr, Ben was of little comfort. "My dad had also been skeptical, however, and I resolved back then to prove him wrong."

In sorting through this, several things become clear. Whether or not Lombardi had his eyes set on Meredith (and Nitschke biographer Gruver states that Lombardi did, in fact, offer Dallas any two players on his roster for Meredith), he was not convinced that he could get to the top with Starr at the controls. Simply observing how different his behavior toward Starr was in 1961 from that of later years confirms this. Also, once again, it was Starr's faith and will that continued to sustain him against the pain of not being believed in by either of the two most significant figures in his life, Vince Lombardi and Ben Starr.

Starr did, however, continue to grow in assertiveness. Lombardi recalled it in his book. "A couple of years ago," Starr said to the coach, when he brought his contract into the office, "I'd have signed anything you gave me, but now you've taught me to be more aggressive and self-assertive and you've given me more confidence, and this is what I want."

"So that's it," Lombardi responded with amusement. "Like Frankenstein, I've created a monster."

As for his status as the No. 1 quarterback in 1961, Starr did not have to wait long. The Meredith rumors died down and soon Lombardi made a bold move. He traded the dyspeptic McHan to Baltimore for a draft choice. The relief for Starr was palpable. If he struggled, he no longer had to look over his shoulder. More important, however, Lombardi had given Bart the one thing Ben Starr had never given him—approval in the form of investing his confidence in Bart. Indeed, Lombardi was putting all his chips on Starr. "He's our No. 1 quarterback," he said. "We rise or fall with him." And Bart was ready. From here on out, it would be Vince and Bart, with Lombardi devoting every ounce of his energy to making the occupant of the team's most important position the best he could possibly be.

"I was proud to be called an extension of him," said Starr of his former coach years later. "I wanted to be one of the best quarterbacks in pro football, and I knew I didn't have the strongest arm in the world. I knew I wasn't the biggest guy (6-1, 200) or the fastest. But Coach Lombardi showed me that, by working hard and using my mind, I could overcome weaknesses to the point where I could be one of the best. I learned many things from him that will help me the rest of my life." But there was more he received from Lombardi, and particularly after the coach's commitment to Starr in 1961. "Most of all," said Starr in retrospect, "he gave me self-confidence."

Life with Ben, an army father, undoubtedly helped Starr here. In addition, he loved to learn, luxuriated in the detail and minutiae, such that Lombardi's exacting methods were far less difficult for him than they might have been for a fun-loving, good ol' boy like Don Meredith. And exacting they would be. It was the only way Lombardi knew how to coach, as his wife described vividly. "And when Vince is challenged to try to make a great one out of a ballplayer," Marie once said, "I can only feel sorry for that player. Vince is just going to make a hole in his head and pour everything in. When it starts the player hasn't any idea what he's in for and he hasn't got a chance. He'll get hammered and hammered until he's what Vince wants him to be. You can't resist this thing. You can't fight it."

Lombardi burned his doctrine of being the best one can be into every one of his players. "But as the years passed, as other careers faded, Bart became the personification of our team, the personification of Vince's coaching," wrote Jerry Kramer. "We all tried to play up to one hundred percent of our ability, and none of us quite made it, but Bart came the closest."

Starr never complained about Lombardi's all-consuming drive for perfection. "From then on," said Starr referring to his statement to Lombardi about being publicly reamed out, "we had a relationship that was just unbelievable. I don't think it had been that bad before, but now it just took off and went to another plane."

Just two years before the Pack was picked for the Western Conference cellar. They were now the team to beat in the NFL. Nothing short of everything would suffice—not for the organization, not for the fans, not for the players, and most certainly not for Lombardi. It is almost impossible to describe the phenomenon that is Green Bay Packer football. The team is a throwback to the old town team days, when grown men would cry if the local high school basketball team lost to its archrival. Or when towns sponsored a fast-pitch softball team in a league of neighboring towns. The battles in these games were incredibly intense, with rivalries often evolving into grudges among these amateur representatives of the village pride. So it is in Green Bay. A Packer, especially in Starr's era although even today, was a visible citizen of Green Bay—inextricably bound to the community. He could not disappear into the anonymity of a Chicago, a New York, or a Los Angeles. Playing for the Packers in the '50s and '60s was an experience unlike any other in the NFL. You played not only for the organization, or even Lombardi, you played for the community, the town, your neighbors.

No matter the size of the metropolis, players are always aware of the fans, even during a game. Jerry Kramer recalled the 56-0 debacle in Baltimore back in '58, when, with a minute to go and the Packers driving, the merciless Baltimore fans began chanting, "Hold 'em, hold 'em."

"You hear the crowd," he stated. "You really do." This sensitivity, however, was perhaps heightened for Packer players, given the cozy size of Green Bay, in which there was nowhere to hide the next day.

The town was bursting with anticipation of the 1961 campaign. Because the NFL had expanded to add Minnesota (coached by newly retired quarterback Norm Van Brocklin), it was one in which each team would play fourteen rather than twelve league games. After sailing through the exhibition season undefeated, the season opener would be played in Milwaukee, where the Pack played three of its seven home games, against the Lions. A crowd of 44,307 piled into County Stadium to witness step one of the Packer march to the title.

They were disappointed. The defensively minded Lions won, 17-13. It was not a good day for Starr. He completed 14 of 26 for just 173 yards and no TDs. He did throw two interceptions. One series stood out. Late in the fourth quarter, down 17-13, the team employed a no-huddle offense and began moving the ball. With but a foot to go for a first down, Starr looked over at the down marker. It read 3, meaning third down. He tried to sneak for the first down. He came up short, only to realize that it had been fourth down—the linesman had forgotten to flip the marker to four. There was no hole for the embarrassed quarterback to burrow into as he left the field, only Lombardi to face. The coach said nothing. Amid this humiliation came an emotional breakthrough for Starr. "If ever there was a perfect occasion to berate me," he wrote, "that would have been it. But Lombardi's decision to let it pass signaled to me a new confidence, a new trust. When he first met me, he wondered whether I was perhaps so polite and modest that I wasn't tough enough to be a leader, to exert authority. He no longer had any doubts."

Starr studied the films perhaps more intensely than ever to ready himself for the games ahead. Lombardi could see how well Starr could translate film and chalkboard drawings into on-the-field reality. "Out on the field," the exacting mentor stated, "he knows what's going on with the other team's defense. He knows it better than any of the coaches." His teammates stood in awe of Starr's intellect. "He could take the game plan," said Willie Davis to ESPN, "and he could kind of commit it to memory. Execution was kind of like second nature to him." "We never called a play in the huddle one year," added Hornung with perhaps a bit of exaggeration. "We just went up to the line of scrimmage, and Bart would look over the defense and call the play." Max McGee marveled at Starr as well. "By the time he took two steps back and he saw what one linebacker did, he'd know the whole scheme of the defense."

The team then hammered the 49ers, Bears, and Colts by a combined 49-17 score, leading to a showdown with the 3-1 Cleveland Browns on the banks of Lake Erie at monstrous Municipal Stadium. Lombardi wanted this one. It would pit him against the legendary Paul Brown. He held a Saturday workout at the stadium and worked at keeping the Pack from being intimidated by the next day's 75,000-plus crowd. It was a blowout. Green Bay destroyed the Cleveland squad, 49-17.

The Italian taskmaster was euphoric. "Every guy that got into the game was at or near his best," he enthused. "They had to be to beat the Browns." Obviously, thinking championship thoughts, he talked about the development of his team. "It takes a couple of years for a team to mature," he observed. "A mature team wins the big ones, so I'm feeling pretty good about our aging process."

The win was especially sweet for defensive ends Bill Quinlan and Willie Davis, former Browns. "I've been looking forward to this game for three years," Quinlan offered. "I would not have asked for a better ending, even if I had written the script myself." It was also sweet for Davis whose family continued to reside in Cleveland. "It was great to win the home town. I have a lot of friends here. Maybe they aren't friends anymore."

Paul Brown was convinced this Packer team was for real. "Our guys knew it would be a rough day—but not that rough," he said in summation.

The huge triumph was followed by back-to-back wins over the expansion Vikings. Now 6-1, the first-place Packers headed for Baltimore to play the Colts. Although they were 3-4, the Colts figured to provide a genuine challenge, because the Packers were now suddenly short-handed. Jerry Kramer broke an ankle in the previous game against the Vikings. Even worse, Paul Hornung, Boyd Dowler, and Ray Nitschke were being called up from the army reserves to active duty owing to the Berlin crisis, placing their availability for the Baltimore game in question.

As it turned out, only Kramer and Nitschke were absent, but the Colts avenged an earlier 45-7 loss to the Packers by grinding them into the Baltimore dust, 45-21. They outgained Green Bay by a 407-225 margin—218-64 in the air. "We didn't do anything different offensively or defensively from the last time we beat them in Green Bay, 45-7," said Lombardi. "And the Colts didn't spring any surprises on us either. The Colts beat us today because they played better football."

The Pack rebounded in Chicago the following week. Starr threw for three scores while permitting no interceptions in a 31-28 squeaker. "I figure we need three more wins to tie for the title, and four more to win it," said Lombardi of his 7-2 squad. George Halas castigated his charges for "playing like girls." One who didn't, however, was future Bear boss, Mike Ditka. The Pittsburgh rookie caught nine passes, three for touchdowns.

Starr threw three more TD strikes the next week in a 35-17 rout of Los Angeles. Despite his team's 8-2 log, the coach was concerned. The loss of Kramer, in addition to the army call-ups, was wreaking havoc with the depth chart. "Now don't make this look like I'm crying," Lombardi said to the press, "but we've lost the best scorer in the league and the best blocking halfback (Paul Hornung)." Now his able replacement, Tom Moore, was also doubtful for the upcoming Thanksgiving battle just four days ahead in Detroit, having sustained a rib injury in the Ram win. In addition, defensive back, Hank Gremminger, who had taken over as the kickoff man in the game, had hurt an ankle. Although losing "the best guard in the league," in Jerry Kramer, the coach was asked if he would acknowledge that the line was doing as well as ever. "I guess I'd have to," he allowed. "We switched (Forrest) Gregg and (Norm) Masters around in there between guard and tackle. They really did the job."

A bruising win in the Detroit mud on Thanksgiving Day, 17-9, left the 9-2 Packers' magic number at one, over the 6-4-1 Lions. The victorious effort was aided by the presence of Hornung, Dowler, and Nitschke, who had been granted passes for the game. Elijah Pitts and Herb Adderley, eventual Packer stalwarts, were beginning to show promise, the latter having intercepted a Detroit pass.

"Packers Western Division Champs," rang the headline ten days later, as Lombardi's charges defeated the Giants in Milwaukee, 20-17. "What a bunch of boys! They're the greatest!" Lombardi exclaimed. "It was our toughest game of the year, but the boys never let down despite the breaks." Although winning the title against his former employers was especially gratifying, the coach was gracious toward the team he was likely to meet for the NFL championship. "We had to play a top game to beat the Giants and we did," he said. "We got off the ball quicker than any time since the Cleveland game in October. This was our best game since then." The coach singled out his quarterback, among others, for praise. "Starr played a great game," he exulted. "He brought the team down to the goal line time after time."

Although Starr was emerging as an aerial marksman, Lombardi valued his engineering skill even more, his bringing "the team down to the goal line time after time." Much of this was done by on-the-spot play alterations—audibles. If, for example, the Packers had called play No. 49 in the huddle and Starr, at the line of scrimmage, could see the defense was set to stop it, he used a signal to change the play right there. Before yelling, "hut," Starr always called out two numbers, a single then a double-digit number. If the single digit number was the same as the snap count, say "two," that meant an audible was being called, and the double-digit number would correspond to the new play number. "Two, 46, hut, hut," means the No. 49 play is now changed to play No. 46, the four back going through the six hole, with corresponding blocking changes.

Green Bay split their final two games to close the season at 11-3, two and a half games better than the 8-5-1 Lions. The team was now one huge win away from going from caterpillar to butterfly in just three seasons, under Lombardi. "I guess, more than anything else, he's a perfectionist, an absolute perfectionist," a retrospective Jerry Kramer wrote of Lombardi some years later. "He demands perfection from everyone, from himself, from the other coaches, from the players, from the equipment manager, from the water boys, even from his wife. Marie Lombardi joined us at a team dinner before one game last year, and the dessert was apple pie. Marie asked the waiter if she could have a scoop of ice cream on her pie, and before the waiter could answer, Vince jumped out of his seat, red in the face, and bellowed, 'When you travel with the team, and you eat, you eat what the team eats.'"

Perfection was expressed in attention to detail, according to Kramer. "He makes us execute the same plays over and over, a hundred times, two hundred times, until we do everything right automatically. He works to make the kickoff return team perfect, the punt return team perfect, the field goal team perfect. He ignores nothing. Technique, technique, technique, over and over and over, until we feel we're going crazy. But we win."

Bart Starr had made some huge strides toward perfection on his own. He completed 172 of 295 passes for 2,418 yards, with 16 TDs to go with his 16 interceptions, for an 80.3 rating. Better yet, he was finally being recognized as a major force in the Packers' success. He was named, with Unitas, to quarterback the West in the Pro-Bowl game. Perhaps even more satisfying, he was selected by a vote of his NFL peers to the second team of the NEA All-Pro squad. He had led his team to dominance. The Packers topped the NFL in scoring with 391 points (a single point short of 28 points per game), and had outscored their opponents by an average of exactly twelve points a game.

By now, Lombardi was well aware of Starr's value. He realized his quarterback's numbers might well have been much stronger were it not for his grittiness. "He's tough enough on that field, too," Lombardi wrote. "In 1961, he played the first half of the season with a torn stomach muscle, and for three games he kept it from me. He was throwing so poorly to one side that I was trying to change his feet and do anything else I could think of until the trainer told me."

On the final day of 1961, it all came together. The Packers destroyed the New York Giants, 37-0 in Green Bay for the NFL championship.

"Hail to Titletown, Packers World Champions, howled the *Milwaukee Sentinel* headline. The mountain had been scaled; it had finally happened. Green Bay went wild. Its citizens engaged in the town's craziest New Year's celebration in 200 years, resulting in a major street-cleaning problem. Adorned in jumpsuits, hunting coats, parkas, snow pants, and ski jackets, and well fortified with flasks of firewater, the fans had eagerly braved a temperature in the teens to cheer on their favorites. Red Smith noted the faithful with elegance: "The poisonous polish of the Packers was equaled only by the fortitude of the natives, who turtled down into their mackinaws and buffalo robes and parkas, and stayed into the bitter dusk, yelping and bawling for blood."

As for the team's trampling of the Giants, the pounding was total.

Green Bay picked up 13 more first downs, 150 more yards rushing, and 45 more passing on 10 fewer attempts. They won the turnover battle 5-0. Paul Hornung, on leave from the army, rolled up 19 points, but had special praise for Titletown's quarterback, Starr. "Give all the credit to our offensive line and our quarterback," he said. "They were the guys that did it."

In "Feeling Unanimous: Starr Was Great," by Ray Doherty of UPI, the writer described Starr's ascendancy in this championship year. "Slowly, he gained respect," Doherty wrote. "And at mid-season, he was the NFL's top passer. And when the season was finished, he was the league's second most accurate thrower. Against the Giants in the playoff game, it would appear he might be outfoxed by the cumulative brains of Y.A. Tittle and Charlie Conerly of the Giants who have each toiled 14 years in the NFL." Doherty then recapped some of Starr's play-calling wizardry, closing the article with a quote from Conerly. "That Starr played a mighty good game."

Characteristically, Starr did nothing to direct the credit toward himself. "We won as a team," he explained in his almost too politically correct style to be true, when asked how it felt to "out-smart" two old pros like Charlie Conerly and Y.A. Tittle. "We have no individual stars in Green Bay. I didn't try to match wits with the Giant quarterbacks. No, sir, the team won the game." Starr understood still another of Bill Russell's leadership rules: Ego $= mc^2$. Starr had invested his ego, not in himself, but in the success of his team. "I want to make one thing clear: ego is about using yourself to your own best advantage," noted Russell, "getting the most out of yourself and your abilities, but only in the context of your team's ability to win." By Russell's leadership definition, Starr had plenty of ego. Russell's statement about a leader's relationship to his team reads like a description of Starr. "To get the most out of being a member of team," Russell stated in his book, "it is absolutely necessary to establish yourself as an integral part of the unit. That is your responsibility, not anyone else's."

Despite being happy simply to be a member of a championship team, the accolades kept coming Starr's way. "This is the greatest team in the history of the National Football League," said the victorious head coach. For his quarterback, Lombardi now doled out the ultimate compliment, the one Bart Starr had wanted ever since his days in Montgomery, Alabama. "He performed like a champion," said Lombardi of Starr, who threw for three TDs on a 10-for-17 day, despite a still sore stomach muscle. "He called the plays and made the changes that were needed, and the score speaks for itself."

It didn't end there for Starr. Resolution could never be complete for him unless it included resolution with his father. "None of the individual awards or team glory equaled the satisfaction I received after the game," he wrote. For years his parents had come to Green Bay for a few games. Over time Ben had changed. "Dad was less harsh than he used to be, patting me on the back, smiling. He never said much, however, and I knew he was thinking about Hilton, still comparing us. On this day, he finally let go." As Starr left the stadium, his mother, father, and Cherry were waiting for him. While the two women rushed to hug him, Bart noticed his father looking at the three of them with tears streaming down his face. "He started to say something," noted Starr, "stopped to gain his composure, then walked up and wrapped his arms around me. He gave me a big hug and softly whispered, 'I was wrong, son.'"

CHAPTER 15

Not Perfection, but Excellence

B Y 1962, Bart Starr was a well-established Pro-Bowl quarterback of an NFL championship team. For Lombardi, quarterback was decidedly the most critical of all positions. He was now a truly accomplished passer. Beyond that, however, was the mental part. "A quarterback must have great poise, too, and he must not be panicked by what the defense does or his own offense fails to do. He must know the characteristic fakes and patterns of his ends and backs and antici-pate the break before the receiver makes it." That poise has a stop-watch on it, because it is all about timing. "'That timing' is that 3.5 seconds your quarterback has to get the ball away. If he doesn't get it off by then, except for those occasions when you can give him the maximum blocking on a try for a long one, his chances of success are minimal." Receivers make their break in 1.5 seconds and that's the length of time the quarterback has to anticipate.

By Lombardi's standards, Starr was almost there, with the coach wanting only to see a bit more of the gambler in this disciple of Tobin Rote, the man who told Starr to hold onto the ball up to the last second, or even beyond, rather than toss it up for grabs. "He is great at picking that defense apart and adjusting, and if I could just get him to be a little more daring, he'd be everything. He kills them with those short ones, those singles and doubles, but he doesn't throw home runs often because, where Unitas or Layne or Tittle will take a chance with an offensive man and a defensive man going down the field together, he has to be more sure that his offensive man has that defensive man beaten."

The mentor's tutorials continued unabated. "I know of no way but to persist," said Lombardi about his relentless commitment to perfection, "and Bart Starr with that analytic mind, retentive memory, and inner toughness can take it." He also pushed himself. "He always wanted to be the best," said Gary Knafelc, "and he never quite felt he was the best."

As Jerry Kramer had said, *perfection* was an important word for the volatile head coach. Everything short of dressing room decorum was evaluated by Lombardi and his staff. The coach described the grading process employed in 1962 after the season's third game against the Bears. "Bill (Austin) and Red Cochran go over the film of our Bears game of Sunday once more. Red takes off the Bears' defenses on each play, the yardage we made and who made the tackle, and Bill starts grading our players for what you might call our Honors Assembly after practice on Friday."

One size did not fit all in Lombardi's customized grading system. "The key to grading players," he noted, "is the recognition of the fact that some positions are more difficult to play than others. On pass plays, for example, your center and your guards and tackles should make 85 percent of their blocks for a passing grade, while your ends have no blocking responsibility. On running plays, 55 percent is a passing grade for your split end, 60 percent qualifies your center, guards, and tight end, while your tackles should make 65 percent. The percentages for backs are 60 percent on runs and 85 percent on passes, and anyone who hits his percentages on both running and passing wins acclaim. You grade your defensive backs on a plus-and-minus point system, and an interception helps a score the most. On a good day, a defensive back will break even, and a plus score means he played an unusually fine game."

Players like Jerry Kramer were understandably suspicious as to the validity of the grading. "The coaches can make the grades come out to almost anything they want," he wrote. "The grading has to be pretty subjective, but even though we all know the grades aren't very accurate, they do accomplish their purpose." By grading player A at 75 percent on runs and 90 on passes, and player B at 65 and 80 percent, respectively, the coaches got their wish: to injure the pride of player B and get a stronger effort. "Actually, it's the coaches' comments that have more effect than the grades themselves," noted Kramer. "Every time you're in a game, an exhibition or a regular season game, you're aware of Tuesday afternoon at the movies. You know that camera is up there taking down every move you make, every single mistake, and if you miss a block, even in the middle of an important game, your first thought normally is, 'How's that going to look in the movies?'"

Kramer was amused at how Lombardi manipulated the players during the movies. "Bob Hyland was the movie star today," wrote Kramer in '67, when Lombardi was attempting to goad his stars to better play by praising a less renowned player. "He was John Wayne, Paul Newman, and Rock Hudson, all wrapped up in one. Everything he did was 'brilliant' or 'terrific' or 'great,' according to Coach Lombardi. Actually, Hyland had played a fair game, but Vince couldn't praise him enough."

As for the team, after demonstrating their dominance at the close of 1961 campaign, the Packers wanted perfection. What just four years earlier had been perhaps the sorriest group ever to play in the modern NFL, had now been transformed into a nearly invincible force. The team was fully loaded. Not only was the roster dotted with All-Pro and Pro Bowl performers, it was filled with players in their prime. Jim Taylor, the backbone of the team's crunching ground game was 26. Paul Hornung, the other half of this Hall of Fame rushing duo and the 1961 league MVP was in just his sixth year. When Hornung was slowed by a knee injury in the team's fifth game, young Tom Moore stepped in and immediately turned in an all-star performance. The offensive line was rock solid with Bob Skoronski and Forrest Gregg at the tackles, and Jerry Kramer and Fuzzy Thurston at guard—every one in his twenties and receiving all-star acclaim. The line was anchored by Jim Ringo, far and away the best center in the league and just 30. Ron Kramer, right behind Mike Ditka as football's top tight end, was only a six-year veteran. The primary pass receivers were slick and quick Boyd Dowler (25) and savvy veteran Max McGee (30). Forrest Gregg and Jim Ringo are enshrined at Canton, with Jerry Kramer arguably the greatest player not yet elected.

On defense it was more of the same. Willie Davis and Bill Quinlan manned the flanks with Dave Hanner and Henry Jordan at the tackles. All except Hanner were under thirty and all were celebrated performers with Davis and Jordan destined for the Hall of Fame. Dan Currie and Bill Forester were the corner linebackers with mighty Ray Nitschke in the middle. Each received post-season acclaim with Nitschke headed for the Hall. Only Forester had reached thirty. Hank Gremminger, Jesse Whittenton, Herb Adderley, and Willie Wood patrolled the secondary—all stars (the latter two Hall of Famers) and none over 28 years of age.

And then there was Bart Starr. For Jerry Kramer, Starr was the key to this all-star cast. He was the man at the controls, the man who called the plays. "Start with the quarterback, Bart Starr," he wrote. "Bart was in his seventh season as a pro; he had just completed his first full season as a starting quarterback. His apprenticeship was over. He had knowledge, skill, confidence, everything, and at twenty-eight, he was the ideal age for a quarterback." By Kramer's standards, Bart Starr was now "the best quarterback in football."

The team did have its characters. Hornung, who with McGee forever tested Lombardi's rules, came to the 1962 pre-season camp at St. Norbert College in nearby De Pere from the army. He was completely out of shape and soon became a Lombardi target. "You look like you're carrying a piano on your back!" the coach bellowed. "You look like you're carrying St. Norbert College on your back!" Soon Hornung, publicly known as the Golden Boy, was "St. Norbert" to his teammates.

His buddy Max McGee never feared the coach. "McGee," ordered Lombardi upon installing him as the punter, "you're not going to run on fourth down." He did, in the championship game against Philadelphia, picking up a first down. Later when asked by the press about the play, Lombardi said, "With veterans like McGee, we give them the option." On another occasion, an exasperated Lombardi told his team it was time to start all over from the very beginning. "This is a football, gentlemen," said the coach sarcastically, holding up the pigskin. "Not so fast, coach," blurted McGee.

Ringo—he of the cut championship ties—of course found Lombardi less than philanthropic when it came to paying the players. At the end of the '63 season Ringo would find out just how tight Lombardi's general managing fists were when he decided to bring an agent with him to negotiate his contract with Lombardi. Perhaps a tad apocryphal, the story goes that Lombardi excused himself for a moment and when he returned, he said to the pair, "You're in the wrong city, Mr. Ringo has been traded to Philadelphia." Jerry Kramer became a renowned author, beginning with his best-selling *Instant Replay*, five years later. Henry Jordan praised the coach's sense of fairness, tongue in cheek. "He treats us all the same;" said the defensive tackle, "like dogs." Jim Taylor had a ready response when Lombardi chided him for running into rather than away from would-be tacklers. "You can't turn a bulldog into a greyhound," said the fullback who loved to sting defenders. The late Ray Nitschke, who was legendary for his love of collisions, was much like Taylor. He simply loved to bump into people, even if they happened to be his own teammates. "I can recall jogging past him after a practice session or something," said Starr, "and he'd hit you with his elbow, hit you in the backside, and kind of push you off stride. He'd say, 'Sorry, didn't mean to do it,' but you knew very well he did mean to do it."

Coming off the '61 title, Lombardi knew, given the quality of the team he had assembled wearing his GM hat, the '62 season could be something special. Right from the outset, the coach reminded them of what was at stake. "Once you're on top," he stated, "everybody wants to knock you off." For Vince Lombardi, there was no championship to be defended, only championships to be won. Furthermore, once to the top proved nothing by his exacting standards. "This is the real test," the coach said. "This year you will find out whether or not you're really champions."

Lombardi always made certain nothing would be left to chance. "He would go over every assignment, showing exactly how each man fitted into the play," said Starr, describing Lombardi's presentation of his patented power sweep. "He would explain how the flanker, whose main assignment was to get the safety, should first try to bump the halfback, to get him off stride. He'd explain how the center and the onside tackle would divide the responsibility for the opposing onside tackle and the middle linebacker. He'd explain how both guards and the offside tackle would pull and how the tight end would handle the outside linebacker and how the onside back would have the key block on the defensive end, and all the time, while he was marking up the blackboard with lines and arrows, he'd be demonstrating blocks, raising his elbows, gritting his teeth, just bursting with enthusiasm."

Once instructed, the team was to run that power sweep until every wrinkle had been removed. The coach's commitment to perfection on this his favorite play was so unrelenting that while other teams closed their practice sessions with wind sprints, the Packers drilled the power sweep.

"Lombardi represented preparation and hard work," explained Nitschke. "Every game was important to him. So when we got to the real important games, we were ready to go, man. Every game was a championship, and that made it easier when we got to the big games because we weren't awed by it, we weren't nervous about it. We were more relaxed than the opponents, and in those years, we all played to our experience. That's how we handled it. That's what you work all season for, to get into the playoff games, and you don't want to blow it."

In fact, not only did Lombardi insist that the Packers play each game all out, he expected the team to give 100 percent on every play. He claimed that very little talent separated NFL teams such that almost any game could go either way. Games, he stated, were determined by about five key plays; but because no one knew when these plays would occur, a team had to dominate over and over again throughout the contest to be certain they would prevail at those critical points.

By the time the Packers had endured a season of Lombardi's grueling mental and physical regimen, they were battle-tested and prepared for any challenge. Once through the school of Lombardi hard knocks, his teams were anxious to take on any comers. "The Lombardi teams wanted to get into the big games," said Nitschke, referring to that preparedness.

But before any playoff games were to be played, there was an exhibition and regular season to be mastered. If anything, Lombardi—perhaps fearing complacency—leaned harder on his squad than ever. He wanted perfection. "I don't suppose any of us will ever forget that scene in the dressing room after our exhibition game against the Cardinals in Jacksonville in 1962" said Starr. "We'd just eaten them alive, 41-14, and still, he chewed the offensive team up and down. Like Fuzzy Thurston said, we thought we were in the Cardinals' dressing room. At the time, most of us thought he was wrong, he was being overly harsh, but when we got home and saw the movies, they bore him out. We had played lousy. The defense had scored all our points, and the offense deserved the criticism he'd given us. He was right, as usual."

With Lombardi cracking the whip, the Packers blew through the exhibition season with six straight wins. And there was no opening game defeat to mar the campaign as was the case in the previous two seasons. After winning their first two games, the Pack faced their arch-rivals from Chicago. It was no contest, as Green Bay de-clawed the Bears to the tune of 49-0. Hammering a team coached by friend, advocate, and legend George Halas troubled the coach. At 3:15 A.M. the following morning Lombardi could not sleep. "Just twelve hours ago, I walked off that field, and we have beaten the Bears 49-0," he wrote. "Now I should be sleeping the satisfied sleep of the contented but I am lying here awake, wide awake, seeing myself walking across that field, seeing myself searching in the crowd for George Halas but really hoping that I would not find him."

The coach described the mental crescendo that attends a single key game for a coach, a similar one to that of a player wanting to "cut the heart out" of his opponent. "All week long there builds up inside of you a competitive animosity toward that other man, that counterpart across the field. All week long he is the symbol, the epitome, of what you must defeat and then, when it is over, when you have looked up to that man for as long as I have looked up to George Halas, you cannot help but be disturbed by a score like this." The Bears had been beaten up coming in, making them more vulnerable than usual. Nonetheless, it would have been self-defeating for the Packers to lighten up, although the outcome was not something of which Lombardi was very proud. "You can't apologize for a score," he explained. "It is up there on that board and nothing can change it now." He had hoped the Chicago magnate was not making more of the rout than was Lombardi.

But there was more. A 49-0 squashing of a key rival might make it more difficult for the team to focus on the game ahead, one against the undefeated Detroit Lions. After the Chicago game, Lombardi warned his team of over-confidence. "All right, let me have your attention," he bellowed. "That was a good effort, a fine effort. That's the way to play this game." There the compliments ended, as he reminded them that the Bears had been wounded and not at the top of their game mentally. "Those people who are coming in here next week will be up," he cautioned his team. "They won again today, so they're just as undefeated as we are. They'll be coming in here to knock your teeth down your throats, so remember that. Have your fun tonight and tomorrow, but remember that."

The coach's words of warning were prescient. Detroit ached to take down the team to which they finished second the previous season. The game was a grinding struggle, one in which the Pack outrushed and outpassed the Lions. Yet, due in part to four turnovers, Detroit led 7-6 with less than a minute left in the contest. "Do you think we will get another shot?" Starr said to Hornung as the Lions came up to the line of scrimmage on third down.

"I hope so. I'm ready," said the man who wanted a chance at least to boot a game-winning field goal.

Matters looked bleak. If Detroit sent fullback Nick Pietrosante rumbling through the Packers' defense for a first down, the game would be sealed. Even if he fell short, they had the NFL's best punter, Yale Lary, ready to boom the ball and the Pack back into their own gridiron kitchen. "Most of our players were standing," Starr recalled, "but the mood was one of disappointment and frustration, not excitement."

Surprise of surprises, Milt Plum, the Lions' quarterback inexplicably went back to pass. The Packer players were sure it was a fake that would eventuate into a quarterback draw. It wasn't. Plum hurled it downfield in the direction of Terry Barr. Barr, however, slipped just enough to give Herb Adderley a shot at an interception. Adderley, a great offensive back at Michigan State, picked it off at the Green Bay 45 and weaved his way down to the Detroit 20.

The Packers' excitement was exceeded only by Alex Karras' rage. The Hall of Fame defensive tackle was screaming epithets at Plum for throwing the ball, as the Lion defense readied itself for a stand against the Pack. Green Bay got the ball down to the 14, and then, with the last seconds ebbing away, Hornung whizzed a strike through the uprights to give Green Bay a 9-7 win.

At that time, both teams left the field through the north tunnel with their respective locker rooms separated by a ten-foot hallway. The doors were thick enough to prevent teams from hearing one another across the space.

Not so on that autumn afternoon. "For the first time since Lombardi joined the Packers, his post-game comments were interrupted," wrote Starr. In the visitors' locker room Karras had ripped off his helmet and hurled it into the chest of Plum. Head Coach George Wilson leaped into the middle of the noisy fray and said falsely, "Look guys, it's my fault. I made the call. Hey, guys, let's shower up and get out of here."

Things only got worse for the visitors from the Motor City. The showers were malfunctioning. The Lions equipment manager was soon pounding on the Packers' door demanding to see Lombardi. When the coach got the word, he consented to have Detroit come in and use the Green Bay facilities. Once dried off, the Lions trudged back to their dressing room. "I expected them to be discouraged," noted Starr. "They were outraged." The last player out turned and said, "See you in Detroit."

With the Lions in the rearview mirror the Packers went on a reign of football terror, racking up six straight wins. Among the victims were the Bears again, the Colts twice, the 49ers, the Vikings, and the Eagles—the latter getting a 49-0 payback for the 1960 title defeat. Green Bay rang up a frightening total of 628 yards against Philadelphia in the rout. Chuck Bednarik, the nemesis of '60, was blown out of play after play. As the Eagles trudged off the field at the half, Bednarik hollered out, "Hey, Tom, when are you going to put in the scrubs?" to Packer assistant Tom Fears.

"Chuck, we don't have any scrubs," Fears replied tersely.

Green Bay now stood at 10-0 heading into their Thanksgiving Day rematch against the Lions. Lombardi despised the holiday date. Given his obsession for organization, discipline, and routine, the coach viewed this Thursday confrontation as a needless interruption.

He liked the disruption even less after the game, as the Lions just plain blew the Packers out. The halftime score was Detroit 23, Green Bay nothing—26-0 after three quarters. It ended 26-14. The Lions flat out mauled Starr, sacking him an unbelievable eleven times. Led by defensive tackles Karras and the behemoth Roger Brown, the Lions went after the Pack with a maniacal zeal. "They came out of the chutes as if they'd gone crazy," recounted Starr. "It looked like there were 50 of them playing us instead of eleven."

The powerful Lion defense simply stopped everything. "We'd do just what we were supposed to do,' said Jerry Kramer, "but one of their defensive players would knock down the intended receiver or tackle him, and Bart'd have no one to pass to. There were millions and millions of people watching on nationwide television, and none of them would realize it was supposed to be a screen pass; all they'd see would be Karras or Brown chasing after Bart, ready to eat him up."

Fuzzy Thurston said that day he and Kramer invented the "look out" block. They would block at the snap of the ball and then yell, "Look out, Bart." Late in the game Starr asked his receivers which of them could get open. "Why don't you throw an incomplete pass and nobody will get hurt," quipped Max McGee, ever ready with a retort. The team cracked up in the huddle, indicating their looseness despite the debacle. Lombardi, taking the loss in stride, put a psychological edge on the experience. "Let it be an example to all of us," he said. "The Green Bay Packers are not better than anyone else when they aren't ready, when they play as individuals and not as one." He followed the object lesson with another of his famous aphorisms. "Our greatest glory is not in never falling, but in rising every time we fall."

Ironically, in this seemingly banner year for the Packers, they were but one game ahead of the Lions. Had Detroit prevailed in Green Bay earlier, rather than handing over a certain victory to the Packers, their records would have been reversed. That is how close this great Packer team came to being just another forgotten contender. Both teams won the following week, leaving two games on the regular season slate. In the early game, the Lions disposed of the Vikings (now in just their second year). Green Bay had to meet the 49ers later on the coast.

The game started badly as the Niners jumped out to a 21-10 halftime lead. One wondered what Lombardi would have to say at the half. The coach was calm and reassuring. "Men," he said, "there is nothing wrong with our game plan, nothing lacking in your effort. The only thing missing is your concentration and execution. Don't worry about the Lions or the standings. Just bear down. Everything will fall into place."

"He occasionally yelled at us at halftime, but never in a panic-stricken manner," wrote Starr of Lombardi. "[That day] he didn't even have to raise his voice. He was at his peak when under pressure. The myth of Lombardi states that he was explosive at halftime and on the sideline, over-emotional, almost out of control. The fact of the matter is that he was all business. His outbursts were serious but never over-blown. He was a master at analyzing an opponent and implementing adjustments."

So was Starr. With the passing game clicking, the team scored on their first two possessions in the third quarter and won 31-21. A 20-17 win over the Rams the following week closed the books on another conference championship, and set up a return date with the mighty New York Giants, this time in New York. The New York Giants were the Buffalo Bills of the late fifties and early sixties. They were now heading into the fourth NFL title game in five years, and were still looking for their first championship.

The game was played on a windy New York day in 15-degree weather. Prior to the game a Giants fan approached Starr, saying, "I'll bet you're delighted with the weather. Boy, what an advantage for you guys."

"He would have lost the bet," noted Starr. The quarterback preferred warm weather because it enabled him to grip the ball more firmly and throw it with greater ease. The weather did give the Pack a mental edge, according to Starr. "Psychologically, we had them right where we wanted them," he said. "The Giants thought we liked to play in weather like that. We never actually enjoyed such adverse conditions, but we were more accustomed to it, and if the Giants wanted to think we liked it, fine. If they had been able to take a closer look at our game plan, however, they would have never given it a second thought."

Believing their line could handle the New York pass rush, and their receivers could beat the Giant defensive backs, the Packer game plan emphasized the pass. The Bronx winds, gusting to 50 mph, obviated all that. When Starr saw team benches being tipped over by the gusts, he took command and changed the offense.

"Coach, I'm going to have to be a little more conservative," he told Lombardi.

"I know, Bart. As long as we keep them off balance. . . ."

Starr directed a conservative ground game balanced off against an occasional pass. Nothing came easily, however, as the wind played havoc with the air game and the field resembled a parking lot; "a slag pile," according to Starr. The great Red Smith captured the conditions as only he could. "Polar gales clawed topseed off the barren playground and whipped it into whirlwinds about the great concrete chasm of Yankee Stadium. The winds snatched up tattered newspapers, more newspapers than people can find in all New York these days, and flung the shreds aloft where they danced and swirled in a Shubert blizzard. . . ."

The high winds made this day the coldest ever in the memory of a number of Packer players, colder even than the Ice Bowl five years later against Dallas. It was so cold that Red Cochran could not chart the game from his position in the uncovered auxiliary press box, owing to a frozen hand. Announcer Ray Scott was so cold his voice began quaking, leaving many listeners to wonder if the venerable broadcaster had been drunk. His partner, Bud Palmer, offered him a few swigs of brandy from Palmer's flask, but froze when he attempted to pour the liquor in Scott's paper coffee cup.

Starr conferred with Lombardi more than in any other game in memory. After the Packers recovered a fumble on the New York 28, he looked at Lombardi, smiled, and said, "How about it, coach?" That he was so relaxed indicates that Starr was now the man in charge and totally transformed from the diffident signal caller of a few short years ago.

"Have at it," replied the coach who now had total confidence in his quarterback.

Starr did. Picking his spot perfectly, he called the only daring play of the game up to that point, an option pass from Paul Hornung. It worked, as Dowler broke off a 21-yard gain down to the seven.

"What would be the reaction of the Giant defense now that they were backed up to their own seven yard line?" asked Starr rhetorically as he gave his readers a window into his brilliant mind. "I decided that they would be extremely aggressive but still somewhat unsure of themselves. As a result, I called for Taylor to run a slant play behind a cross-blocking scheme." It worked for a touchdown. That TD, in addition to three field goals by Jerry Kramer (who took over kicking duties in mid-season when Hornung suffered a knee injury), gave the Pack a 16-7 win. The defense was near perfect. The lone Giant score was on a return of a blocked punt.

Starr exhibited his quiet leadership when, with the game scoreless in the first quarter, Kramer tried to send a field goal through the winds. When Kramer looked up, the ball was past the uprights and well off to the side. Suddenly an unhappy Kramer noticed the referee's arms in the air signaling that it was good. "What's he doing?" he said to Starr, his holder.

"Shut up, and get off the field," was the leader's directive.

Clearly this was a new Bart Starr. Some New York sportswriters mentioned to him that the game might have been different had it been played under more favorable conditions. Though keeping his opinion to himself at the time, he said he agreed with the New York media people in retrospect. It would have been different. The Packers would have beaten the Giants by more than nine points. Indeed the 12-2 Giants were mentally peaked for this game. "Man, that first series of plays, that leather was really poppin'," recalled Hornung to Maraniss. "They were really up. We just had a better football team, that's all."

You strive for perfection, Lombardi would say, and although you may not attain it, you can catch excellence. The Packers missed perfection by a single game in 1962, but they certainly caught excellence. This team for the ages ran up a league-best 415 points (just under 30 a game, and 17 more than runner-up New York, and fully 100 more than the 11-3 Lions). They yielded just 148 (10.6), the lowest in the league. (The Lions were a distant second at 177.) They outscored their foes by an average of 19.1 points a game. "Those Packer teams of '61 and '62 were just fantastic football teams," said Hall of Fame Giant middle linebacker Sam Huff, "if not the greatest of all time. There was no way you could go into Green Bay and beat them." In 1962, half of the team's starters—eleven players—made one or another All-Pro team. Moreover, Taylor, Gregg, Jerry Kramer, Ringo, Currie, and Forester were unanimously named to every All-Pro squad.

Starr was in complete command at quarterback, especially with his play-calling wizardry that controlled the ball and the clock. "The offense made it very easy for us," said Currie, in explaining the team's great defensive statistics. "They'd get the ball and go eight-and-a-half minutes for a touchdown, and when the opposition can't get their hands on the ball, it kills them. It makes it very frustrating for them."

His play calling was so adept that he was being mistaken for a gambler, given his penchant for occasionally going deep on third or fourth down and short. Such plays were not gambles at all for Starr. "In fact," he said, "they are high-percentage plays." In short yardage situations, he reasoned, the defense would be looking to stop Jim Taylor. The linemen would be bunched together, poised to hit Taylor the instant he got to the line of scrimmage. And hit him they did, particularly in the '62 title game. "I never saw a back get such a beating," recalled Starr of the violence the Giant defense visited upon Taylor.

"Taylor was really banged up," reinforced Packer public relations director Lee Remmel to Gruver. "He was bleeding from the mouth, he had a cut tongue, he had bruises all over his arms and I'm sure all over his body. The intensity of Taylor and Huff kind of matched the weather."

Given the various teams' intense focus on Taylor, Starr often saw a perfect opening. "There is no way a defensive lineman can rush the quarterback once he's on all fours with his nose six inches above the ground," noted Starr.

In addition, the linebackers would edge closer to the line of scrimmage wanting to pop Taylor before he got any traction. With the Pack renowned for running high-percentage plays there was all-the-more reason for the defense to look for the run. "Most defensive backs were guilty of reacting too quickly to a run fake," wrote Starr, in explaining the choreography further. "If Taylor came roaring through the line, they had to be prepared to meet him head on, lest he run all the way into the end zone. Our receivers were glancing toward the middle of the field, where Jimmy was to carry the football.

"As I took my position under center, I could see that the defense was pumped up to stop Jimmy." Starr would then take the snap and hand the imaginary football to a raging Jim Taylor charging into the line of scrimmage, the odds now tilted in the Packers' favor. The receivers—Dowler, McGee, and Kramer—were estimable threats under ordinary conditions, but now with the defensive backs on their own, unaided by the linebackers or weak-side safety, all of whom had bitten on the fake, Starr had the mismatch he was looking for.

"My first objective was to find one of our receivers deep downfield," he explained. "They were smart and sure-handed, so I simply had to throw the ball away from the defensive back; they would adjust to the ball and make the catch. In the unlikely event they were covered, I dumped the ball off to an alternate receiver who had run a shorter route." How successful was this ploy? Starr could remember only one time the short yardage play action pass did not work.

Starr had mastered another Russell leadership lesson. He could use his imagination and see the unseeable. "Visualization," said Russell, "is a practical skill that can be sharpened though exercise. Seeing yourself and others in your 'game' brings not only a familiarity, but also the ability to see past the obvious nuance that can be the difference between winning and losing." Starr was now looking for the positive in his imagination. He was visualizing successful plays before he experienced them, and then actualizing his imagination by executing a game-breaking maneuver.

Again, this was a new Starr, one unknown to his teammates in years past. Despite the "yes, sirs" and "no, sirs," any questions about his toughness and leadership had been put to rest. He was, according to Gruver, an "angelic assassin." Polite, respectful, even deferential off the field, the quarterback seemed to undergo a transformation once he lined up behind the center. "On the field," said Zeke Bratkowski, much Starr's superior in their college days but now his understudy, "he'll cut your heart out and show it to you."

CHAPTER 16

Almost

B Y 1963, Starr had no more to prove to anybody. He was at the top of his game. Not only had he led his team to a 13-1 season, Starr had emerged as a major force in his own right. He had completed 178 of 285 passes (62.5 percent) for 2,438 yards and a dozen touchdowns against just nine interceptions, good for a 90.6 rating, outstanding at the time. Yet, unlike other quarterbacks that would compete with their coaches, he had no such ego needs. As a result, he was more a colleague or protégé of Lombardi's than a subordinate. "He and Vince were hand and glove," said Murray Warmath later, who had coached with Lombardi at West Point and visited Vince at practice from Minnesota.

Starr had bridged all the gaps between himself and Lombardi. And again, there had been many: The urban north vs. the rural south, the brash extravert vs. the self-effacing introvert, the Catholic vs. the Protestant, and even the coach vs. the player, given that both needed to be leaders. And it was Starr who had to bridge those gaps because it is for the player to please the coach, all the while having to establish himself in the coach's eyes.

Lombardi, however, had effected a psychological metamorphosis in his quarterback. "With most of us," wrote Jerry Kramer, "he just plain whipped us toward our full potential; with Bart, he used patience and understanding, quiet teaching." "I got to know him, really, in the small meetings we'd have every Wednesday, Thursday, and Friday morning,"

Starr told Jerry Kramer. "We'd get together around quarter to nine, just him and the quarterbacks, and it was kind of casual, more like a father and son discussing something that [they] were going to do over the weekend than a lecturer and a listener. He was much more at ease then than he was in front of the whole team."

Starr did, however, challenge this colleague and father figure. After being selected to the '62 Pro Bowl squad, Starr expected to start, given the year he and the Packers had just had. He didn't. Lombardi chose Johnny Unitas. Starr did not like it and told Lombardi. "What's wrong with starting Unitas?" the coach wondered, all along realizing that it was a blow to his quarterback's pride.

Starr stated that he had earned the right to start. Lombardi did not feel he could start every Packer chosen to the team. Starr couldn't have cared less about how many Green Bay players were on the gridiron at once, he deserved to start and wanted Lombardi to know it. Although the coach did not relent, Starr not only had made his point (something for which Lombardi likely admired him), but had shown a toughness and confidence absent in the past.

Challenge III was the slogan for the 1963 season. The Green Bay Packers were embarking on a quest to become a genuine dynasty by being the first team in NFL history to win three straight league championships. Everything was aimed in that direction, and everyone believed they would do it.

Things started rather inauspiciously in the annual late summer College All-Star game, when the collegians upset the seemingly bulletproof Packers, 20-17, in part on a touchdown pass by Green Bay native Ron VanderKelen to his fellow Wisconsin Badger teammate Pat Richter. Even worse, however, Packer star Paul Hornung would not be contributing to the quest.

On April 17th of 1963, Commissioner Pete Rozelle suspended Hornung and Detroit's Alex Karras indefinitely for betting on NFL games. The NFL had done a gumshoe investigation of the pair and found they had been wagering on league games (although never betting against their own teams). Ever since the Black Sox baseball of scandal of 1919, this has been the unpardonable sin in professional sports. Many fans fail to realize this. When Pete Rose was banished from baseball and made ineligible for the Hall of Fame, many fans leaped to his defense.

"There are adulterers, alcoholics, wife beaters, and perhaps even murderers in the Hall; how can baseball keep Charley Hustle out?" they would ask incredulously. Indeed, some those in the Hall have lived no more honorable a life than has Rose. But the matter is not about relative morality. It is about violating the only rule posted in every baseball clubhouse, a violation that carries with it expulsion. It is fortunate that the NFL penalty is less severe.

Certainly, Hornung and Karras were not the only players using bookies at that time. They were, however, extremely high profile performers and for the young commissioner, in just his fourth year, to take down those two for this misdeed sent a message to every player in the NFL that betting had to stop.

In any case, the news of Hornung's suspension hit the Packer world like a thunderclap. Not since 1919 had any one been fingered for gambling. Moreover, 1963 was not a media-heavy, ESPN-saturated era, replete with investigative coverage of scandals and athlete's misdeeds. The lifestyles of wantonly promiscuous players like Hornung—now open-season subjects for the sports journalist/analyst—were referred to with euphemisms and broad generalities. The sexual mania of President John F. Kennedy, who would be assassinated later in the year, though well known to the White House press corps, was never reported. In that context, it is obvious that there would be no advance warning, even within the Packer organization that their immature though multi-talented halfback was on the brink of expulsion.

Hornung is an interesting case study. Reared without a father in Kentucky, he seemed to find vent for his manhood in sports and sexual conquests. He never tired of trying to assert himself as a national playboy. The title of his jockish autobiography, *Football and the Single Man*, is testimony to this yearning. As the sun set on his football career by the mid-sixties, he seemed to engage in even more attention-getting behavior focused on his sexual prowess. There seemed always in Hornung an adolescent need to draw attention to himself as a masculine icon, perhaps driven by the inner insecure child without a father. Much of his behavior was regarded as fashionably sophisticated at this more innocent time, but, in retrospect, suggests a somewhat childish attempt to make himself larger than life. "He (Paul Hornung) makes a trip to the corner grocery sound like an Arctic expedition," wrote the witty Jimmy Breslin. After his retirement, not surprisingly, he attempted to get into television sportscasting and analysis. Though he managed to put together a minor career in that venue, he was found wanting when compared with other contemporaries like Frank Gifford and Pat Summerall, who established themselves in the sports media. Hornung also dabbled in business, and loved to talk about his savvy. "I'm vice president of a real estate firm in Louisville worth fourteen million in equity," he told Jerry Kramer in *Distant Replay*, still self-aggrandizing almost two decades after the conclusion of his playing days, "and a group of us just bought a soybean refinery that did a hundred million in sales last year. I've also got a manufacturing company, in the aluminum business, and I just got out of the coal business. Got out at just the right time."

For the Pack, the loss of Hornung figured to be more psychological. Tom Moore was a ready replacement, fully capable of filling Hornung's role with brilliance. He was not, however, as charismatic as the Golden Boy, whose confidence in his own athleticism and that of his teammates radiated through the squad and pushed the Packers to championship heights at just the right moments.

Lombardi's new mantra became, "No one person is bigger than this team," a thinly disguised reference to Hornung who, despite Lombardi's unbounded affection for him, had angered the coach by his behavior.

The season opened with a bitter defeat to the hated Bears, 10-3, in Green Bay. Lombardi was beside himself with rage at this, the third opening season loss in the last four years. The game had interesting story lines. Halas had had a bellyful of defeats to his arch-rival, Lombardi—five straight going into the contest. The Bears had been very competitive in '62 with a 9-5 log. Had they reversed their two defeats to Green Bay, they would have matched the Pack at 11-3. In addition, the Bears had picked up Green Bay linebacker Tom Bettis, who had been at odds with Lombardi and so eager to provide any insights he could into the Packer offense. Bettis' reports fell on the ears of Halas— "who picked my brains"—and that of George Allen, the new Chicago defensive coordinator, obsessed about making a name for himself in the NFL.

As for the game itself, Halas had circled it on his calendar. "If we win that game," he told his charges, "we have a chance to go all the way." Scoring was limited to pair of field goals in the first half, leaving the game knotted at 3-3. The Bears got their score on the heels of a Taylor fumble on the Packer 33. When Joe Marconi plunged in from the one in the third quarter, it was over for the Pack.

Starr was horrible. Forced to throw (Taylor gained a puny 33 yards, after rolling up a league-leading 1,474 yards and 19 TDs the previous season), he saw four of his aerials picked off by the confusing defense composed of shifting fronts and zone coverages constructed by Allen. The Bears' defensive coordinator had set an elaborate trap. "He realized that since Green Bay's well-schooled blocking schemes were based on instant recognition of defenses," noted Gruver, "the Bears would seek to confuse them by playing odd-man fronts with a man over center Jim Ringo. Since Starr was an excellent audible quarterback, Allen planned to disguise Chicago's coverage schemes by dropping his linebackers— (Joe) Fortunato, Bill George, and Larry Morris—into short zones."

It was a typically violent Bear-Packer gridiron war. The confrontation between Bears tight end Mike Ditka and Green Bay middle linebacker Ray Nitschke is illustrative. Both luxuriated in the violence of the sport. All-pro outside linebacker Dan Currie enjoyed the science of defensive play. "With me, it's the tackle instead of just belting the other guy."

"Not with me," teammate Nitschke retorted. In this contest, Ditka delivered a low, peel-back block in the second quarter that sent Nitschke head over heels and out of the game. He wasn't finished, however. With his knees taped, the middle linebacker returned to the battlefield shortly thereafter. Nitschke was not himself, however, and when Billy Wade caught Ray and the Pack in a third quarter blitz, he threw a strike to Joe Marconi setting up the game's lone touchdown.

Lombardi drove the team and himself harder than ever. The Packers responded by reeling off eight straight wins. Lombardi, however, was exhausted. He decided to stop smoking. He had been suffering from dizzy spells, and was concerned for his health. Typical of his iron will, and despite gaining twenty pounds while lusting for a puff amid a coaching staff of heavy smokers, Lombardi never smoked again.

Along the way, however, the team hit another major speedbump. In the sixth game of the season—a 30-7 win over the Cardinals, now in St. Louis—Starr broke his right hand. "I dropped back to pass," he explained, "but sensed a heavy rush and ran out of the pocket. As I was going out of bounds, Jim Hill, one of their defensive backs, swung at my head. I ducked but lost my balance, falling awkwardly on my right hand."

Lombardi, now with only John Roach, who had thrown only 16 passes in his two-year NFL career, available wanted to keep the injury as quiet as possible, as he scurried to pick up Zeke Bratkowski, an understudy for the Rams. Packer injuries were always, if anything, under-reported, the coach feeling that such information provided ammunition for opponents. Several years previous, the coach went to almost absurd lengths to conceal a finger injury sustained by his quarterback. According to Maraniss, St. Vincent Hospital X-ray technician Robert Strom received a call from Packer physician James Nellen after a game. Nellen told Strom to be at the back (non-entrance) door in thirty minutes. A half hour later, Vince Lombardi, Nellen, and Bart Starr emerged from a car. "This is not to be recorded," Nellen told Strom, who knew every patient was to have a number and a file.

"So I didn't record it in the book," said Strom. "I took the picture. They waited for it to be developed. And before anyone else saw it, Dr. Nellen took it. Lombardi came along to make sure none of the media saw it. It was a cloak-and-dagger thing."

As they left, Nellen gave one more direction to Strom. "If anyone calls and asks 'Any Packers here?', you know what the answer is."

Keeping the lid on with injuries was only a part of Lombardi's obsession with controlling the flow of information. One of the most prominent signs in the Green Bay locker room was the familiar,

> What You See Here
> What You Say Here
> What You Hear Here
> Let It Stay Here
> When You Leave Here

Given his predilections for secrecy, Lombardi had to have spent some restless nights thinking about what revelations concerning the Packers' offense and defense Bettis may have had for the Bears.

"OK, now we've lost our quarterback; we'll still find a way to win," were the coach's words upon realizing Starr was out.

He was right. Roach led the Pack to the final three wins in the 8-game streak, setting up a rematch with the now also 8-1 Bears in Wrigley Field. Everything was now on the line, and the Packers were ready and confident.

They shouldn't have been. The Bears beat them soundly, 26-7.

Lombardi, ever the savvy psychologist, would not quit. Sullen and silent—"He wouldn't talk," said Ruth McKloskey to Maraniss—on the long bus ride to the airport, the coach willed himself out of the funk when he got on the plane. He left his seat, patted each player on the head, and beers were served.

"They're down enough already," was the coach's response to the question as to what was behind this gesture.

President Kennedy was assassinated five days later.

The team won an emotionless, lackluster game against San Francisco that numb yet painful weekend, one in which new commissioner Rozelle had mandated the games go on, albeit without fanfare, and with Starr now back at the controls, they headed into Detroit for the annual Thanksgiving Day brawl with the Lions. Detroit managed a 13-13 standoff, due much to a blocked extra point against Jerry Kramer who had kicked so reliably in Hornung's absence. Nitschke played part of the game with a broken arm, testimony to both his own intensity and that of the Packers. The season was now essentially over. The Bears tied two of their final five outings, closing the books on a 11-1-2 campaign, but a half game better than the 11-2-1 Packers.

In a vicious, cold weather struggle in 11-degree Wrigley Field, George Halas won his final NFL title, 14-10 over New York. It was the fifth time in six seasons that the Giants had appeared in the title game, only to fall short each time. The Packers were left to play Cleveland in the Playoff Bowl, a brief, ill-conceived NFL experiment matching the second place conference finishers. Green Bay won, 40-23.

Frustrating was perhaps the best word to capture the 1963 campaign for the Packers. The team had played without Hornung, Nitschke, and Starr during the season. With the exception of '62 (when Green Bay went 13-1) the team's 11-2-1 record would have won the Western Conference in every one of Lombardi's years up to that time. Despite coming in second, Green Bay was probably the best team in the NFL again in 1963. The Packers' 369 points against a yield of just 206, both second-best in the NFL, gave them the best net points total (163) in the NFL. Given the adversities, this was a tremendous football team. Both Lombardi and Willie Davis later said the '63 squad was perhaps the best of the era.

For Starr, the year was frustrating, but not dispiriting. "I didn't like losing," Starr said to Tex Maule, reflecting on the '63 season and his own personal growth as a confident leader. "No one does. But by then I had learned to accept defeat with grace if not with pleasure." A loss here or there no longer shook the now established Packer field general. "I learned to forget about defeat the year before when Detroit racked us up on Thanksgiving Day," he explained. "The Bears reminded me of Detroit. No matter what we tried to do, they were a play ahead of us. I remember once, in the Detroit game, I knew they were going to blitz—they did most of the time—and I tried to take advantage of them. They had been sending in their linebackers, so I figured I could hit Ron Kramer, our tight end, with a quick pass in the hole a linebacker leaves when he blitzes. Wayne Walker was their linebacker on that side and he moved up like he was going to rush, but when the ball was snapped, he dropped off into the pass pattern and I couldn't hit Ron." It had been the same with the Bears. "Not enough worked against the Bears. They won and we lost and they deserved the championship."

Individually, he turned in another strong season, completing 132 of his 144 passing attempts for 1,855 yards and 15 touchdowns. He threw only ten interceptions—six after the opener against the Bears—for a solid 82.2 quarterback rating.

Rather than brood about past failings and obsess over trying to prove himself worthy of his role as the quarterback of the Green Bay Packers, the 29-year-old Starr was now philosophical about the "almost" Challenge III season. "You can't waste time going over old losses," he said, perhaps not realizing that that is what he used to do. "You have to look ahead. I knew we had a good ball club and I knew we could win. So I didn't worry about one bad year."

That Starr would refer to an 11-2-1 season as a bad year is just another indication of what a winner he had now become. "Winning is not a sometimes thing. It is an all-the-time thing," Lombardi would say, and Starr had internalized that dictum. Winning had indeed become a habit—another of the coach's proverbs—for Starr and he was confident that the habit would be reinforced with the return of Hornung to a hungry Packer team in 1964.

CHAPTER 17

The Long Road Back

W HILE THIS has been a very frustrating season," Starr said after the near miss of '63, "for many reasons, this team will always have a soft spot in my heart because of the many adversities and the many frustrations it had to meet. The one big lesson it had to learn, which we all have to learn, is that a team, like men, must be brought to their knees before it can rise again."

And Lombardi fully expected the Packers to rise again in 1964. So did the players, the fans, and the rest of the pro football world. The team had learned much in the crucible that was 1963, and now with Hornung reinstated by Rozelle as of March 16th, a Green Bay resurrection to championship status looked more certain than ever.

If appearances are deceiving, they were never more so than in 1964. The Green Bay Packers not only did not rise, they fell, to an 8-5-1 record, after which the team went to Miami and lost the meaningless Playoff Bowl—a game the very existence of which Lombardi detested, regarding it as a game for losers, and renaming the bowl substituting a common slang term usually applied to human excrement for the Playoff—24-17, to the St. Louis Cardinals. It was not a great surprise that Hornung was no longer the same runner he had been in the early sixties. What no one expected, however, was that the usually clutch player would miss fully 26 of his 38 field goal attempts, and so almost singlehandedly ruin the Packer season.

Ever the leader, Starr along with Boyd Dowler had helped Hornung get in shape by running wind sprints—four at a hundred yards, followed by four at fifty—over and over again. For the Starr family, there was much more than an upcoming season to be excited about. On February 1st, Cherry gave birth to the couple's second son, Bret Michael. "The thrill of being with Cherry during the delivery," wrote Starr, "and actually witnessing the miracle of birth quickly put my life back into focus."

"Hornung's back! Hornung's back! The Golden Boy is back," Lombardi had hollered at an earlier practice, jubilant at the return of his triple-threat halfback. Indeed he was, as the regular season opened with a rousing 23-12 revenge triumph over the Chicago Bears, in which the halfback kicked three field goals and rushed for 77 yards. Starr, although overshadowed by the return of No. 5, fired two TD strikes in the contest. From there, however, Hornung and the Packer fortunes headed downhill, as the team dropped three of their next five games, largely due to missed kicks by Hornung.

Some of the losses were particularly galling. Game two went to the eventual conference champion Baltimore Colts, 21-20, with the difference being a missed extra point by Hornung. It was also a painful game for Starr. Late in the second half, and trailing by a 21-20 count, the Packers had the ball. Starr called a timeout and talked strategy with his coach. Lombardi suggested he throw to his big tight end, Ron Kramer. As the play unfolded, Starr could not find Kramer and tried to get the ball to Max McGee. The aerial was picked off, ending the drive. Lombardi chewed into Starr in the dress room after the game. The quarterback had no rejoinder. It was a beastly error, one over which the conscientious Starr wept at home that evening.

The venerable Hank Stram, who coached the powerful Kansas City Chiefs of the seventies, once said the most important attribute an NFL head coach can have is the capacity to slam the door and pull down the shade on a tough loss, and focus on the next game. Starr, Green Bay's coach on the field, had, despite his remorse, developed the winner's capacity. "After I got over kicking myself for blowing the play," Starr recounted to Maule, "I forgot about it. Before that, when I made a mistake, I couldn't stop thinking about it. But I forgot about this one and so did Lombardi and the rest of the team. You can't go back and correct yesterday's mistakes."

Two games later, the up-and-coming Vikings (a team that would also finish 8-5-1) blocked another of Hornung's PAT attempts to register a 24-23 victory. From there, things got even worse. In the sixth game of the season, the 3-2 Packers engaged the Colts in a return match and lost 24-21. Paul Hornung missed four field goals. A 27-17 defeat to the Rams left Green Bay with a sub-.500, 3-4 record at the halfway point.

The Pack closed the season, going 5-1-1 in the second half, salvaging a bit of dignity if nothing else. An extra point here, a successful field goal there, and Green Bay would have won at least three more games, going another 11-2-1 rather than 8-5-1. The team outscored the opposition by nearly 100 points (342-245), trailing only the two conference champions, Baltimore and Cleveland in net points. Nonetheless, it was a disappointing season for a team in transition.

The Packers had been slowly remolded by Lombardi over the past several years. After the '62 campaign, the GM/coach dispatched Bill Quinlan, feeling his play on the field no longer compensated for his off-the-field antics. Jim Ringo was sent to Philadelphia after the '63 season over the contract imbroglio. Long-time defensive tackle Dave Hanner was also replaced. Some changes, however, were not anticipated. Jerry Kramer had felt pain in his abdomen during the opener with the Bears. Physicians were concerned that the great lineman was suffering from cancer. Later they discovered that he had been housing a seven-and-a-half inch sliver of wood since crashing into a fencepost chasing a calf as a teenager in Idaho. The intruded splinter had become infected. Kramer was lost for the season. With Ringo gone and tackle Bob Skoronski moved to center, the loss of Kramer was acutely felt.

If ever Starr emerged as not only the team's offensive leader but one of its top performers, 1964 was the year. With a depleted line and less potent ground attack, the no longer "me too" quarterback took to the air 272 times, hitting on 163 (59.9 percent) of his throws for 2,144 yards. He threw for 15 touchdowns against just four interceptions for an eye-popping 97.1 rating.

Lombardi was always on the alert for signs of a team or player losing the edge. He believed it had a psychological, rather than physical, genesis. "When a ballclub flattens out," he wrote, "it is because they go mentally and psychologically, rather than physically, stale. A well-conditioned athlete may be exhausted by the end of a game but, barring injury, he can come back with twenty-four hours' rest. He does not lose his vigor; he loses his urge. That is why we go to such pains to keep them from becoming bored by this week-after-week routine."

From a team standpoint, a big play was the only hope for a flat team. "When you are flat, you're always looking for that big play or that big man who will bring you out of it," he noted. Maybe the Packers had been a bit stale in '64. Perhaps they had lost their urge. In any case, Lombardi was never more determined to return Green Bay to dominance than in 1965.

"You're better than a second place team," he told them at training camp. "You quit paying the price. This year, you pay the price."

"He nearly killed us," recalled Starr. "He always worked us hard, but he worked us until we dropped. But we knew we had it coming."

For the devout Lombardi, the matter of paying the price was in part theological. "We have God-given talents and are expected to use them to our fullest whenever we play," he said. His view was nearly Calvinistic, that one is placed on the earth with but a single mission statement: to glorify God. The Packers glorified God by exerting maximum effort. Starr was Lombardi's number one disciple. When you give less than your best, he would say with dead seriousness, you are cheating yourself, your team, and God. In fact, Lombardi recited a Henry Hancock poem that captured a portion of his football theology:

> *Out of our beliefs are born deeds;*
> *out of our deeds we form habits;*
> *out of our habits grows our character;*
> *and on our character we build our destiny.*

Starr loved that poem as he did Lombardi. He was often called an extension of Lombardi on the field. He was more than the reader of the coach's mind and therefore the caller of the correct plays. He embraced much of Lombardi's world-view in his personal life, embodying the very values of the coach so temperamentally different from him.

It was more than Lombardi's will that would drive the '65 edition of the Green Bay Packers. The team would be fresh and different, as Lombardi all but completed the roster renovation in which he had engaged over the past several years. Ken Bowman took over at center, with Lionel Aldridge and Ron Kostelnik going to defensive end and tackle, respectively. Bill Forester had retired and Dan Currie traded, opening the doors to Lee Roy Caffey and Dave Robinson at linebacker. Tight end Marv Fleming and wide receiver Bob Long, both draft choices, began playing major roles. Bill Anderson came in from Washington during training camp and eventually grabbed the starting tight end spot. In the defensive secondary, Bob Jeter and Tom Brown now became major figures. Lombardi had also seen enough of Hornung doing double duty as a halfback and placekicker, and brought Don Chandler in from the Giants to do the punting and placekicking.

On September 11, 1965, City Stadium was officially renamed Lambeau Field, in honor of Earl "Curly" Lambeau, who had died the previous June. Although there was strong sentiment in favor of the new name, there was one member of the Packer organization that did not like it at all. It was the man who did not want to finish second in anything. In any case, his Packers bolted out of the gate in '65, winning their first four games, taking down the Steelers, Colts, Bears, and 49ers. Game five was a pivotal contest against the always tough Lions, who with the Colts were just a game back in the standings. At the half, Detroit led 21-3. "Lombardi's halftime speech had a biting edge to it," recalled Starr. He turned to the defensive players and said, "You are capable of shutting them out from here on. You do it, we'll win, because we have made some slight adjustments offensively, and we're going to make some big plays. But you've got to stop them." He also injected a bit of Knute Rockne. "Win, lose, or draw, you are my football team," he concluded. "You are the Green Bay Packers and you have your pride."

One of the adjustments involved Jerry Kramer, who was coming back from his stomach ailment. Dan Grimm had had the unenviable task of taking on Alex Karras in the ballgame. Grimm had played well the previous year against an injured Karras, leaving the Detroit lineman eager with revenge. "Alex just chewed him up and spit him out in the first half," noted Kramer. "Alex tore off Danny's helmet two or three times and got to Bart three or four times."

Karras was jubilant after the first thirty minutes and hollered, "What do you think of that, you big fat wop?" at the Packer coach, as the teams left the field.

Lombardi thought it was time for Jerry Kramer, and started him in the second half.

The defense answered Lombardi's challenge, and the Packers won 31-21, largely on the throwing of Starr who fired three touchdown aerials of 62, 31, and 77 yards in the second half.

After ten games, the good news was that the record stood at 8-2. The bad news was that Baltimore led at 8-1-1.

Game eleven was critical, but the Packers came up short in Los Angeles, losing a one-sided battle, 21-10. Lombardi was in no mood to comfort his troops. Seeing any hopes for a championship slipping away, the following Tuesday he decided to light into them with a vengeance. He addressed the squad in the absence of the rest of his coaching staff. "You guys don't care if you win or lose," he roared at them. "I'm the only one that cares. I'm the only one that puts his blood and guts and his heart into the game! You guys show up, you listen a little bit, you concentrate . . . You've got the concentration of three-year-olds. You're nothing! I'm the only one that cares if we win or lose."

Forrest Gregg took it personally and charged the coach, necessitating the efforts of several teammates to subdue him. He cursed loudly and then quickly apologized "for the profanity," indicating a curious mix of respect for the coach amid a boiling rage toward the same man. "It makes me sick to hear you say something like that," he went on. "We lay it on the line for you every Sunday. We live and die the same way you do, and it hurts." He then continued after Lombardi as his teammates held him back.

"That's right," said an angry Skoronski. "Don't you tell us that we don't care about winning. That makes me sick. Makes me want to puke. We care about it every bit as much as you do. It's our knees and our bodies out there that we're throwing around."

A stone silence followed, with the players wondering where things would go from here. "All right!" exclaimed the coach, picking the perfect tack to turn the disorder to his advantage. "Now that's the kind of attitude I want to see. Who else feels that way?" With that the room came alive and the team decided to salvage what it could of a seemingly lost season.

Shades of '60. The following week the Bears upset the Colts and knocked Unitas out for the rest of the season, while Green Bay prevailed against the Vikings. The schedule-maker must have been guided by divine providence, for game thirteen had Green Bay heading to Baltimore for a showdown against the Colts, now but a half game ahead of them. This is the one the Packers had to have; with a Colt victory, Green Bay would be a game and a half back with one game to play. Baltimore also needed it. A pair of Packers triumphs and they would be heading for the NFL title game.

With Hornung rising from the ashes, after having been benched in the previous game, Green Bay defeated the Colts, 42-27, on a field shrouded in fog. The Golden Boy ran for five touchdowns in the triumph. Starr, in his own quiet way, continued to etch his profile as both a consistent and clutch player. He was en route to another strong 89.0 quarterback rating fashioned around 140 completions in among his 251 throws, for 2,055 yards and 16 TDs against nine interceptions. In this all-or-nothing confrontation, Starr called a brilliant game, exploiting the Baltimore defense with an astute mix of runs and passes, throwing and setting up scores with key completions, especially to Hornung and fleet Boyd Dowler.

Green Bay was now the lead dog with but a single game to play. This, however, was not the Packer team of the early years of the decade—one that had a wildcat's killer instinct. The regular season concluded with a 24-24 tie against a John Brodie–led 49er team. A Colt win knotted the two squads at 10-3-1, necessitating a playoff be held in Green Bay owing to the Pack's having defeated Baltimore both times during the regular campaign.

Beating a team three times in a single season is a formidable feat, and such was the case for Green Bay in this winner-take-all battle. The Colts were short-handed, having lost both Johnny Unitas and ace backup Gary Cuozzo to injury. Option halfback Tom Matte returned to his old college position—quarterback—where he was named All Big Ten for Ohio State. The Packers, however, were not much healthier. Hornung was hobbled and on the very first play from scrimmage, and then additional disaster struck. Starr hit Bill Anderson with a completion in the left flat, but an instant after having possession, he was hammered by defensive back Lenny Lyles, and the ball came loose.

"Colts linebacker Don Shinnick snatched it in midair and headed down the sideline," recalled Starr. "I moved over to cut him off but Jim Welch met me first with a hard block. From the ground, I watched Shinnick cross our goal line." Starr was hurt, and had to be assisted off the field. He was unable to continue. "On the sideline I attempted to throw, only to discover that I could not lift my right arm above my shoulder. The collision with Welch had broken a rib."

With Starr out, trusty Zeke Bratkowski was at the throttle. Throughout his tenure in Green Bay, "Brat" performed brilliantly in Starr's absence. How Starr treated this potential competitor, however, provides another glimpse into Bart's character. "Bart picked me up at the airport the day I arrived (in 1963)," said Zeke, "and took me to his home to watch films." The friendship grew from there. "He's like a brother to me," said Bratkowski. "He just took me under his wing."

The two became so close that their wives became best friends and their children went to school together. "Bart is one of the greatest people I've ever met," said Bratkowski. "Our friendship is so deep, it's like gold. We've never had a fight, never a serious disagreement. Our families took half a dozen vacations together. We spent every Christmas together for twenty years."

In this game, however, Zeke could not perform any magic and the offense sputtered. Green Bay trailed 10-0 at the half. Hornung managed to push over the goal after the Pack took advantage of a botched Baltimore punt. With just under two minutes remaining, Don Chandler kicked what will forever be a disputed field goal to tie the game at 10. Colt fans will never relent on their certitude that the kick was off to the right, and indeed it looked wide even to many Packer players and fans. With his ribs taped tightly, Starr held for Chandler, and described the kick. "As the ball approached the crossbar," he noted, "it began to drift right. Don turned around and waved his hands in dismay, thinking our season was near the end. The backfield judge standing under the crossbar at the goal line, however, shot both arms in the air, signaling three points." For the record, another strategically placed official also called it good in this era of short uprights. The Colts were nonetheless outraged over what they felt was a missed call.

The overtime went 13 minutes and 39 seconds before Chandler hit a 25-yarder to put the Packers into the NFL title game against the Cleveland Browns, champions of the previous season.

The Packers went into the championship game banged up. Jim Taylor had a sore leg, Hornung had a twisted knee, a sprained wrist, and sore ribs. Jerry Kramer, coming off his lost '64 season, ached right up to kickoff. Starr's ribs also ached, but he was ready to go. "Although I was experiencing some pain, I knew that it would be diminished by a flow of adrenaline before kickoff," he wrote. Nevertheless, he was concerned. "But I also realized that one clean blow to my ribs could force me out of the contest. The possibility that I might be unable to lead our team in such an important game troubled me."

His wife, Cherry, seemed even more concerned. "You don't have to play today." "Honey, don't worry about it," he said as he kissed her goodbye. Such a lighthearted attitude is testimony to Starr's burgeoning confidence in his ability now to excel in the face of pressure. No longer was he worried as to *how* he would perform. *It was that he would be able to perform at all.* Conditions were less than ideal. When Starr left with his father for church earlier that morning, they encountered a snowstorm. Five inches blanketed the field by noon. By kickoff, the snow had stopped but the field was mushy and soft. A later rain turned the turf into mud.

The conditions were perhaps worse for the traveling Browns. To rid the team of distractions, Head Coach Blanton Collier housed the squad in the Fox River Valley town of Appleton, about thirty miles from Green Bay. The idea backfired when the team bus got lodged in a brutal traffic snarl due to congestion on the highway and hazardous driving conditions. The Browns did not get to the stadium early enough for more than a brief pre-game warmup. Players are often creatures of ritual and superstition, and many of the Cleveland players were rankled that their usual personal and team preparation patterns were being aborted for this, the most important game of the season.

As for the footing, it was treacherous. "The mud was coming up over our shoelaces," said Brown center John Morrow. "That was a terrible day. Our running game (with the great Jim Brown) was central to our offense, and their field was a quagmire, like soup."

Starr, as usual, went to work beating his opponents from the neck up. He opened the contest by throwing the ball. "Showing once again why he was one of the best big-game quarterbacks ever," wrote Nitschke biographer Gruver, "Starr theorized that since the Browns had only arrived at the stadium a short time ago and had to get dressed quickly and get in a brief workout, he would keep them off balance by throwing early in the elements."

This was exactly the logic of the now go-for-the-throat Packer signal caller. "We knew it had to be bad for them psychologically, so we hit them right away," he said. He nudged the Brown defense in with a series of short passes to Taylor and Hornung. Then he executed a play fake to Hornung and let fly a bomb to Carroll Dale in what turned out to be a fortuitous touchdown connection. "On our first possession," Starr explained, without mentioning that he had played with heavily taped ribs that restricted his throwing motion, "I went deep to Carroll Dale. I slipped just as I released the pass, and it was underthrown. Fortunately, Carroll slid to a stop, came back to the ball, caught it, and waltzed past the Browns' defensive back, who had fallen trying to adjust." Starr's ribs were not only taped, they ached. Nitschke claimed he winced when several times in the first half, he saw Brown defenders taking shots at Starr.

With the Brown defense back on its heels, the ground game kicked in and behind Hornung and Taylor's last hurrah, Green Bay ground out a 23-12 win over the Browns, and with it claimed their third NFL title in five seasons.

It had been a long road back—a near miss in troubled '63, a disappointing '64 marred by missed opportunities, and now a championship that seemed more a testimony to will than excellence. No matter, Bart Starr and the Green Bay Packers were back on top of the football world.

CHAPTER 18

At the Summit

THE HARDEST thing about winning the third title is that you have to win two championships before you can capture a third. Should you fall short, as the Pack did in '63, you are at the minimum three years away from another run at the same distinction.

For Vince Lombardi and the Green Bay Packers, the victory in '65 put the team back on the championship road. Moreover, although no one dared to speak about it publicly, there were a number of players focused on doing what the team had come up just short of doing three years previous—stamping themselves indelibly in the minds of football followers for all time as the greatest of the great, having won three straight NFL titles. Time, however, was running out on much of the Packer nucleus of the past.

Paul Hornung was now paying the physical price of having been hit myriad times for the Packers, turning him into at best a part-time player. He would rush just 76 times in '66. By 1965 Jim Taylor began showing signs of deterioration, amassing over 400 fewer yards rushing (734) from his '64 mark of 1,169, picking up just 3.5 a carry. Max McGee was no longer a first option in the passing offense, Ron Kramer was gone, and Fuzzy Thurston was being supplanted at the guard position by an up-and-coming Gale Gillingham. The defense had seen many changes as well over the past few seasons. Mainstay linebackers Dan Currie and Bill Forester were gone, as were Hank Gremminger and Jesse Whittenton in the secondary, and of course Dave Hanner in the line. All of this was testimony to Lombardi's personnel wizardry. He had gradually revamped the team without ever allowing it to slip out of contention.

One player who had led the team each of its three titles loomed particularly large in 1966, and that was Bart Starr. Starr was operating behind a new group of linemen, throwing to a different set of receivers, handing off to a different pair of running backs, and was now the focal point of the Packer offense.

It was difficult to discern exactly how good the 1966 Green Bay Packers would be. On one hand, there was still a cadre of solid veterans—Starr, Jerry Kramer, Dowler, Gregg, Skoronski, Dale, Davis, Jordan, Caffey, Robinson, Adderley, Wood, and Nitschke—to go with emerging stars like Gillingham, running back Elijah Pitts, defensive tackle Ron Kostelnik, and defensive backs Bob Jeter and Tom Brown. On the other, this was clearly a team in transition built on a '65 championship squad that had been far from a dominant force. Although the Packers led the league in preventing points (224), the team's 316 points scored was a middling eighth in the fourteen-team NFL. Their average winning margin of 6.6 per game left them third, behind Chicago (with two of the best young players in the NFL in Gale Sayers and Dick Butkus) and Baltimore.

There was also controversy. The AFL was doing battle with the NFL by bidding against the more established league for present and future players. The result was a sudden explosion in salaries for prized rookies, all of whom were free agents, able to choose between the two unaffiliated leagues. (The warring leagues announced a merger on June 8, 1966, setting up the first Super Bowl at the conclusion of the season.) Joe Namath had set the football world on its head the previous year when he eschewed the NFL for the bigger dollars of Sonny Werblin's New York Jets. Two of the higher priced first-year men in '66 were running backs Donny Anderson of Texas Tech and Jim Grabowski of Illinois. Lombardi, desperately needing to replace a fading Taylor and an injured Hornung, plunked down around a million dollars in salary and bonuses for the two. Although many of the players welcomed the pair, hoping they would both help the Packers win and drive salaries higher for the rank and file, some players—Jim Taylor in particular—

resented the new economics that so benefited the players being groomed to replace him.

Packer fans need not have worried as the team stormed through the NFL, winning twelve of its fourteen games. Green Bay led the league in fewest points allowed (163) and won its games by an average of 12.3 points a game. Though not as dominant as the 13-1 '62 team (with 19.1 per game net margin) the '66 squad came closer to being undefeated with its two losses being by a total of just four points.

Bart Starr was now at the summit. He had truly become what Bill Russell called a craftsman. "For a player to experience the game on a level where he has to use all of himself," wrote Russell who may as well have been describing the Bart Starr of '66, "where he is, in effect, a problem solver as well as a body, constantly committing himself all out to the possibilities of the moment, creating chances and opportunities for himself and his team, is to experience the game at the highest level of creativity. Craftsmanship at this level is about artistry."

In 1966, everyone finally appreciated Starr's gridiron portraits as a football artist. He was not only the Packers' top player; he towered over the NFL as its MVP by the vote of the league players. Starr's numbers were astonishing. He completed 62.2 percent of his passes (156 of 251) for 2,257 yards. More important, however, he threw 14 TD strikes against just three interceptions, giving the All-Pro signal caller an incredible 104.9 quarterback rating, this in an era prior to the liberalization of pass blocking rules. Moreover, to put those three interceptions in perspective, the Packer defense returned six opposing aerials for touchdowns. The '66 season was not, however, actually the high water mark for Starr in his avoidance of interceptions. Over the course of '64 and '65, he threw 294 consecutive passes without yielding a single "pick."

Starr made the clutch plays. In game two, the Packers trailed the Browns, 14-0. The team faced a fourth-and-one on its own 44. "A field goal was out of the question," noted Starr, "and we needed a first down to continue a drive and keep the game within reach. We went for it. Cleveland was expecting a run all the way as I threw a play-action pass to Hornung, who was wide open down the left sideline. Paul ran untouched to the end zone for a 56-yard touchdown."

Starr's play-calling and execution was put to the test again in the fourth quarter. The Packers, with the ball on the Cleveland nine, were down 20-14 with just over two minutes remaining. Here again, Starr demonstrated his brilliance. "On fourth down, the Browns, knowing that we must pass," wrote Starr, "dropped seven men into the end zone and prevented me from throwing it there. I dumped it off on Taylor, who was flowing to the right at the line of scrimmage. Taylor carried the ball and Browns' defender Erich Barnes into the end zone." Green Bay won, 21-20.

Although Green Bay's 12-2 record sent them into the NFL title game, this time the opponent was not from New York or Cleveland. It was Tom Landry's 10-3-1 Dallas Cowboys. Landry had taken the expansion franchise from an 0-11-1 start in 1960, to the title game in seven seasons. To win three consecutive titles necessitates that you first win two, and there was no surety that the Packers would prevail in this one. The Cowboys—who would be playing host to Green Bay—were the more powerful team if one considered the scoring differentials. Dallas had outscored the Pack by 110 points (445 to 335), and owned a net point margin of 14.7, even better than the Packers' 12.3. In short, the championship game would pit the league's most potent offense (Dallas' 31.8 points per game) against the league's stingiest defense (Green Bay's 11.6 ppg). Lombardi, likely due to his confidence in Starr, laid it all on the quarterbacks. "If Bart Starr has a good day, we'll win. If Don Meredith has a good day, Dallas will take it."

The Packers got out of the gate quickly in Dallas' Cotton Bowl, throbbing with 75,000 fans. "We had a special play to open the game," Starr told Maule. "The Cowboys had great pursuit on defense and we took advantage of it."

With the Cowboys chasing the Pack's apparent ball carrier, Jim Taylor, they were open to a countermove. "We put the counter in to defeat the pursuit," explained Starr. "I faked a handoff to Taylor going one way, and when the Cowboy defense reacted to his movement, I handed the ball to Elijah Pitts, cutting back in the other direction, against the grain of the pursuit. The first play gained 32 yards and we were on our way." Starr hit Pitts with a 17-yard strike a bit later for the opening score. After a Dallas turnover, the Packers struck again, making it 14-0.

The Cowboys, led by quarterback Don Meredith, came roaring

back and the game stood 21-17, Green Bay at the half. Behind Starr's three additional touchdown strikes—to Dale, Dowler, and McGee—the Packers pushed the margin to 34-20 in the fourth quarter. The wily McGee, substituting for Dowler who had been injured on a late hit, snookered the Cowboy defense. "I can beat [Warren] Livingston on a zig-out," he told Starr in the huddle. "Give me a shot."

"Max was always thinking," according to Starr. "In our game preparation, we noticed that Livingston, Dallas' right corner, tended to overplay the middle on a post route. Lombardi and I had discussed taking advantage of it inside the Cowboys' 30. At the snap, Max cut to the middle and then broke to the outside. I couldn't believe how open he was when I threw to him for an easy score, my fourth touchdown pass of the day." A blocked extra point, however, left the Cowboys just two TDs behind in these pre-two point conversion days.

Dallas struck again, and after stopping Green Bay, drove the ball down to the Packer two-yard line with 45 seconds left to play. It was fourth down and the season hung on the next play. Meredith took the snap and rolled to his right. Dave Robinson exploded through and forced Meredith toward the sideline where he was in peril of going out of bounds. With that, he hurled a desperation aerial into the end zone, only to have it picked off by Packer safety Tom Brown. The Green Bay Packers had won their second straight NFL championship, 34-27.

"Coach Lombardi did a brilliant job of getting us ready for every game we played, but I don't think he ever did a better job than he did preparing us for the National Football League championship game against Dallas in 1966," said Starr of Lombardi. "We had the luxury of two weeks to get ready for that game, and with that much time to study the movies, Coach Lombardi cut all the fat out of our offense. Our game plan against Dallas included eight or ten running plays and about eight passing plays, and that was all—no more than eighteen plays. We had only the plays that Coach Lombardi was positive would work against the Dallas defense, and he was right. We opened the game with a running play to Jimmy Taylor, and that worked, and from then on, every play we tried worked." And the man who made it work was Bart Starr. He executed that simplified offense to a level of near perfection. Carrying the Green Bay offense on his shoulders, he scorched the Dallas defense for 304 yards and four touchdowns.

There was joy and relief in the Green Bay dressing room. Winning had indeed become a habit under Lombardi, and success addictive. "It is like a habit-forming drug that, in victory, saps your elation and, in defeat, deepens your despair," wrote Lombardi back in '62. With success now all but taken for granted among the Packers, the media, and their fans, the next game—the first Super Bowl against the AFL champion Kansas City Chiefs—to be played in the Los Angeles Memorial Coliseum, became a psychological mountain.

The Packers stood to gain nothing by defeating the Chiefs, who were 13-point underdogs. They stood to lose everything if they, the representatives of the proud and established NFL, were to fall to the AFL champion. Lombardi was all nerves. "Men, we are the best the NFL has to offer," he told them. "We have won four NFL titles, almost five, in seven years. We cannot afford to let down now."

"He was miserable that week," said Skoronski. "He liked to have killed us." He worked the team so intensely that the veteran tackle feared Lombardi was "going to leave the game on the practice field."

The more you have to lose, the more nervous you become, he would say, and with the Packers representing the NFL in general, Lombardi had everything to lose. He was obsessed about winning the game decisively, leaving no doubt as to the NFL's superiority. A loss here would all but negate everything the team had gained over the past six seasons. Starr confirmed this, noting that, "In addition, he made it perfectly clear that the honor of the NFL was at stake. He treated this like a personal mission, and who could blame him?"

Who could blame him, indeed. He was hearing from his NFL colleagues about the imperative nature of a Packer win. "We were getting all kinds of telegrams and telephone calls from all these millionaires who owned the teams," said Ruth McKloskey to Maraniss. "'Go get it. Go get 'em, Vince!' And over the league Teletype. Everyone giving advice. Watch this. Watch that. Every time something came in, you could see this grim look on Mr. Lombardi's face. The NFL was all uptight about it. So he was very upset." The game, they said with typical hyperbole, was about a way of life. It was a game of survival, a test of manhood, ideas the coach relayed to his team, according to Willie Davis.

"We could feel his sense of urgency as he told us, 'There is no way—NO WAY—the Green Bay Packers are going to lose this football game,'" Starr stated.

Starr was aware of the pressure. "The burden of proof was squarely on our shoulders," he explained, "precisely because many people had dismissed the American Football League as a 'Mickey Mouse' operation."

The films indicated that the Chiefs were not at the Packers' level. "We had them checked," said Willie Wood to Maraniss. "It was just a matter of how emotionally involved we were going to get." Max McGee, who didn't figure to get into the game, knew he could eat the Kansas City secondary alive. "I've been studying film," he said to announcer Ray Scott, "and I've found me a cornerback. I'm going to have him for breakfast, lunch, and dinner." For Starr, preparation required some adjustments. "I know, when I'm watching one of the NFL teams in action against one another how good the individuals are," he said, "because I have played against them. But watching the Chiefs play against other teams in the AFL was like watching strangers. I didn't know how fast the defensive backs were and I couldn't read their defenses very well. So I had to be careful for a while until I could figure them out."

It didn't take him very long, as Starr reached into his bag of tricks early, going for the money on a relatively short yardage third down. It worked, with a major assist from Max McGee subbing for an injured Boyd Dowler. "On third and three from the Chiefs' 37-yard line," he wrote, "I dropped back to pass. Just as I prepared to throw the ball to Max, who was running a short post route, Buck Buchanan crashed through our line. I shuffled to avoid the pressure from Buchanan but he hit me before the ball left my hand. The contact affected the velocity of the ball and caused it to head right at defensive back Willie Mitchell, who was about a yard behind Max. However, in full stride, Max reached back with his right hand, stabbed the ball, pulled it in, and raced untouched into the end zone."

With the game tight early, Starr once again outfoxed Kansas City. "Faced with a third and one from our own 36," he recalled, "I decided to go for the home run. I faked a handoff to Jimmy Taylor and hit Carroll Dale for a 64-yard touchdown. My favorite play, a short yardage bomb, had worked like a charm." Sometimes the breaks even out.

After being bailed out by McGee on the previous score, it was the officials who balanced things out this time, nullifying the score with an illegal procedure infraction. Starr, however, remained clutch, completing four third-and-long passes and engineering another score.

In the third quarter, the Packers recovered a Kansas City fumble on the Chiefs' 5-yard line. "It was an ideal opportunity to cross up the Chiefs' defense," noted Starr, revealing his field general wizardry. "I figured they'd be looking for Jimmy Taylor again, and they were. Elijah Pitts took the handoff and scored easily. The game, for all intents and purposes, was over."

Once again, Starr was the craftsman. It was, as Russell put it, "the result of sincere effort, principled intention, intelligent direction, and skillful execution." Years previous, he had worked to rid himself of the can't-throw-the-bomb tag, and every other rap on him as a quarterback. The craftsman's focus went down to the smallest detail "He used to throw a better turn-in to the left than to the right," Lombardi explained. Starr ironed out that wrinkle. "He used to pull the string a little when he threw to the left," related Lombardi. He tightened up on his throws to the left. "Starr concentrated on his weaknesses," said Lombardi summarizing his perfection-seeking signal caller, "until they became his strengths." And of course, he could see through a defense with what seemed laser vision. "Bart Starr operates like a surgeon when he's out there in the game," said Lombardi complimentarily. "He is a master at diagnosing the opposition's defense, then picking it apart."

And once again, he was the difference in a pressure game. Hitting 16 of 23 passes for 250 yards and 2 touchdowns, the league MVP was also the MVP of the first Super Bowl and the Packer, 35-10, victory. The Green Bay ace converted 11 of 15 third down plays, completing six of seven third down passes. This, according to Nitschke biographer Gruver, lent "weight to his reputation as the best clutch quarterback of his era." Starr had indeed figured the Kansas City defense out. "They played a tough man-to-man," he said being gracious as always, "but once we found out that our receivers could beat them man-to-man, they were dead."

For Starr, the game MVP award did not mean as much as the words of his coach. "I don't know where the story began that Bart couldn't throw the long pass," said Lombardi after the victory. "That's ridiculous . . . he can throw with anyone. He's a fine quarterback, and I'm delighted the he's finally getting the recognition he has long deserved."

The Chiefs were impressed. "Bart picks a weak spot and hits it better than any quarterback I ever saw," confessed a Chiefs defensive back. "He really picked our pass defense to pieces. Every time they had third and long yardage, he made it. You can't beat that."

Starr worked to get the edge he seemed to enjoy so consistently. "Like Nitschke," wrote Gruver, "Starr became a student of the game, endlessly studying films for the smallest advantage." Early in their careers, he and his roommate, tight end Gary Knafelc, devoted hours to reviewing options as they studied opponents' tendencies on film. Lombardi had in his brilliance created a passing game that allowed options within plays. "When Starr called a play in the huddle," said Gruver, "he wasn't calling it for one receiver; he was going to throw to the open man based on the coverage. Starr would read the defense and knew who would be open regardless of whether he was facing a blitz, man coverage, or a zone rotation." While looking simple and conventional on the surface, the Starr-led Packer passing game devastated defenses. "I don't know what you guys are doing," befuddled defenders would say to Dowler. "It doesn't look like you're doing anything but the ball keeps moving down the field."

Bart Starr may well have been the most intelligent quarterback ever to take a snap in the NFL. "Center Ken Bowman said Starr's greatest asset wasn't his throwing arm, it was his brain," reported Gruver. Hornung claimed Starr simply never made a mental mistake, which according to Knafelc, was due to his disciplined preparation. Knafelc and Starr played a game. The tight end would give his roommate a given situation—down, distance, and field position—and ask, "What would you call?" Almost without fail, Starr had the correct answer. By game time, Starr was so thoroughly prepared, absolutely nothing would shake him, irrespective of the defense he was facing. Benny Friedman, former Bear great back in the thirties, reinforced the notion of Starr's brilliance. "Bart Starr adheres to three principles with almost religious fervor," Friedman stated. "He sizes up the defense with an eye to Barnum's rule that 'there's a sucker born every minute.' He disdains the bomb as a weapon of a madman, who may very well blow himself up, to concentrate on short-range, pinpoint passing. He plays for lateral position so as never to be caught penned up against the sidelines."

In the two post-season games after the '66 season, Starr hit on 35 of 51 passing attempts for 554 yards and six TDs. "He had," according to Gruver, "gone from a man who had leaned on his teammates to one who could lead them."

Starr now had real moxie. When he was selected to the Pro Bowl squad, and discovered that he, the league MVP, was not going to start he was not happy. George Allen, with whom Starr was greatly impressed in terms of his preparation, gave the nod to Unitas. "John Unitas was one of the greatest quarterbacks in the history of professional football, and also a friend," Starr explained with typical deference. Nevertheless, Bart was "ticked off," as he put it. "Our record was 12-2, and we came close to going undefeated," said Starr, talking like the winner he had become. "We beat Baltimore twice during the season."

Cherry, Bart's number one advocate did not like it either, according to Starr. On the day of the game, Allen ran into her checking out at the front desk of the hotel. "Cherry, what are you doing?" Allen asked in a friendly way.

"I'm checking out and going home," she responded.

"Why?"

"Because Bart isn't starting and I'm not interested in sitting in the rain to watch someone else play," she said.

"Cherry, I'm not starting Johnny because he had a better year," Allen tried to explain, "I'm starting him because I thought Bart would enjoy not having to worry about the game. He just finished playing the biggest game in years."

Cherry wasn't buying. "Coach, I'm not going to hold a grudge," she said kindly. "I like you very much and so does Bart. But I want you to know, Bart has a memory like an elephant."

The Pro Bowl notwithstanding, for most ordinary players, four NFL championships, a regular season and a Super Bowl MVP award, along with the Byron "Whizzer" White Award for citizenship, would have left no more gridiron worlds to conquer. Bart Starr, however, was not an ordinary player. He was the quarterback of the Green Bay Packers, a team aiming at doing what had, up to then, been impossible— winning three consecutive NFL championships.

CHAPTER 19

Challenge III Redux

L OMBARDI ROARED into 1967, his second opportunity to win three consecutive NFL championships, as intense as ever. "Your whole life is ahead of you," he would yell during pre-season practice. "Most of my life is behind me. My life is now the Green Bay Packers."

In training camp, he laid down the rules as he did every year. Although Hornung was gone, claimed by the New Orleans Saints in the expansion draft after the coach put him on the list, confident the new franchise would not be interested in a veteran nearing the end of his career, Lombardi was very concerned about gamblers.

"You don't sit down and have a drink with somebody if they come up and want to chat," he ordered. "If they say they're from your home town and you don't know them, don't associate with them. As simple as that." Continuing his obsession with information control, he told them, "and don't talk about injuries to anyone, not to your neighbor, not to your father, not to your brother. Don't even tell your wife. Keep your mouth shut."

Conditioning would continue to be a priority. "Fatigue makes cowards of us all," a statement often associated with the man in charge. "When you're tired, you rationalize. You make excuses in your mind. You say, 'I'm too tired, I'm bushed, I can't do this, I'll loaf.' Then you're a coward." He went on to impress the group that in theory, every player was a rookie. Everyone would have to earn his spot. "Of course, you look around the room at people like Bart Starr, our quarterback, who was the Most Valuable Player in NFL last year," wrote Jerry Kramer in testimony to the stature Starr now enjoyed among his teammates, "and you think that's silly. Nobody's going to take his job away from Bart."

As for preventing cowardice, conditioning included agility drills, wind sprints, and the hated grass drills. Although the up-downs usually went on for three to five minutes, the coach had no conscience about continuing them until someone was lying on the ground, unable to get up, owing to exhaustion. On one 90-degree day, Lombardi put his charges through seventy-five or eighty up-downs, such that Leon Crenshaw, a huge lineman, could hardly stand up. Crenshaw, with legs wobbling and his tongue hanging out, would get just enough rest to stabilize himself, before having to resume. The next day, after the morning drills, Crenshaw passed out in the cafeteria line. With his teammates unable to move him, an ambulance was called and he was taken to a hospital. He'd lost 25 pounds since training camp opened.

"If you quit now, during these workouts," Lombardi would holler during an intense practice session, "you'll quit in the middle of the season, during a game. Once you learn to quit, it becomes a habit. We don't want anyone here who'll quit. We want 100 percent out of every individual, and if you don't want to give it, get out. Just get up and get out, right now."

Lombardi's entreaties were apt, because Challenge III in 1967 was no easier than it had been in 1963. Every team would be gunning for them. "I remembered how it was when we were down," Starr told Maule. "We saved the big game for the champion. So every other club was saving their big game for us, even during the exhibitions." There were other, more serious problems. Although the team had Elijah Pitts and the "Gold Dust Twins," Donny Anderson and Jim Grabowski, for the ground game, it wasn't the same. The team would dearly miss Taylor, traded to New Orleans, and Hornung, if not physically, certainly psychologically. They had been the poster children for the mighty Green Bay rushing machine.

"This is a game of abandon and you run with complete abandon," the coach shouted at his running corps, perhaps concerned about losing Hornung's nose for the end zone and Taylor's get-every-yard drive.

"You care nothing for anybody or anything, and when you get close to the goal line, your abandon is intensified. Nothing, not even a tank, not a wall, not a dozen men, can stop you from getting across that goal line. If I ever see one of my backs get stopped a yard from the goal line, I'll come off that bench and kick him right in the can."

Everything was noticed, even the rookies' singing at dinner as a part of their initiation into the Packer family. "The singing absolutely stinks," Lombardi complained. "I don't care what you sing, but I want to hear you. I want to see what kind of a man you are." According to Jerry Kramer, Lombardi judged a player in part on his singing performance. If a man had the stuff to get up in front of nearly sixty people and try to sing on key, particularly with a bad voice, that player would likely handle himself well in a pressure situation. He had poise.

On the field, the ground game was not the only area in question. Starr was hurting. During the pre-season, Starr severely bruised his ribs, slowing down his conditioning. By the time the season opened, not only did his ribs hurt, he added a shoulder injury and a badly sprained right thumb, a far more daunting handicap for a passer. He was unable to grasp the ball effectively, even for handoffs, much less passes.

The impact of the personnel setbacks hurt. "It doesn't take much to hurt even the best clubs," said the great Detroit defensive tackle Alex Karras. "Just lose one of two real quality players. Green Bay lost two, and Starr was hurt. They had a real problem. Their defense was about the same, but they couldn't run when they had to. You have to remember Taylor and Hornung weren't just great runners, they were great blockers, too. With the running shut off and Starr not able to pass as well as usual, they were in deep trouble. The defense can't do it all."

The players felt the tension of this key campaign, well before the regular season began. Before the College All-Star Game—won by the Pack, 27-0—Starr turned to Kramer and said, "It seems like I get more nervous every year."

"Me too," replied Kramer who followed this assent with a Lombardi aphorism. "The more you've got to lose, the more nervous you are about losing it."

Starr was showing the tension. In an exhibition game against the

Steelers, Packer reserve tackle Steve Wright let his man get through to Starr just after he released a pass, slamming the quarterback in the face with an open hand. "Steve Wright, you ought to be ashamed of yourself, letting Lloyd Voss in here," rebuked an angry Starr. "I'll tell you one thing. If I see that guy in here once more tonight, I'm not going to kick him in the can. I'm going to kick you in the can, right in front of 52,000 people." Lloyd Voss did not get through again.

Lombardi was exhibiting the stress as well. "We've made a living here by not making mistakes," he bellowed, unhappy with the penalties he was seeing. "We're a team that's noted for not making mistakes. And we will not make mistakes."

On August 21st, Lombardi said, much to the amazement of his team, that they were starting the "big push." The players could hardly imagine pushing any harder than they had. But Lombardi provided the impetus. "I'm gong to tell you the facts, gentlemen," he stated as the regular season neared, "and the facts are these: At Green Bay, we have winners. We do not have losers. If you're a loser, mister, you're going to get your butt out of here and you're going to get it out of here right now. Gentlemen, we are paid to win. Gentlemen, we will win."

For the players, winning had become internalized. "We go into every game we play knowing we're going to win," said Jerry Kramer. "And we always do. We never lose a game. Sometimes, of course, the clock runs out while the other team still has more points than us, but we know that the game isn't really over, that if we kept playing we'd end up ahead. From our point of view, we haven't lost a game in years."

The coach had no greater tolerance for injuries than he had back in '59. "When are you going to start running, anyhow?" he said to defensive end Lionel Aldridge with an irritated air. "When're you going to stop loafing?" Aldridge had broken his leg less than three weeks previous and had the cast off for four or five days.

Green Bay swept its pre-season games. The last roster cuts were made and training camp closed. "Gentlemen," said Lombardi, "we have our team now. We have the men we're going with, the men who have a chance to bring Green Bay a third consecutive world championship. Gentlemen, no team in the history of the National Football

League has ever won three straight world championships. If you succeed, you will never forget this year for the rest of your lives. Gentlemen, this is the beginning of the big push."

The team, however, was pushing with a hurting quarterback. In the opener, Alex Karras put his performance where his mouth was, flattening Starr four times while attempting to throw. With the sore thumb, Starr was picked off four times, one more interception than he had thrown in all of '66. Despite the miscues, the team managed a 17-17 tie with the always-tough Lions. Lombardi was enraged at Kramer for permitting Karras to get his mitts on Starr. "When Vince chewed me out Tuesday, one of the things he said was that I ought to give Bart my whole pay check this week for the way I got him beat up Sunday," noted the lineman.

Later that day, Starr was standing at Kramer's locker. "Where is it?" he inquired.

"Where's what?"

"Your pay check. I've been looking for the check all week long."

The team relaxed, but the next game was just as difficult. Starr threw five more interceptions in what turned out to be a 13-10 victory over the Bears.

Despite the pain, Starr hung tough, functioning as best he could in the other areas of his life. "One of his greatest characteristics," said Rev. Roger Bourland, impressed with the balance in Starr's life, "is that he does so much for people in a personal way with his time, talent, and money. And most them don't know he is responsible." On the team, he took spiritual leadership. "He has been very influential in bringing many of the Packers to church services," he explained. "And Bart, Bill Curry, and Carroll Dale have been providing devotions for the Protestant members of the team when they are on the road." The informal get-togethers were instituted the previous season. "Four and a half hours before game, half an hour before breakfast, we get together and read from the Bible, and say a few prayers and sometimes have a little discussion, led by Bart Starr or Carroll Dale," said Kramer. About twenty players customarily attended.

In game three, however, won by Green Bay, 23-0, the pain got worse. Atlanta Falcon linebacker Tommy Nobis nailed Starr in the right armpit, numbing the arm and putting him out of the game. The experience called for faith and will. "Until today," noted Kramer, "I didn't realize quite how frustrated Bart was, how intense he was. When he came out of the game, he stood next to me on the sidelines and started kicking the ground. He told me how much he wanted to get back in. He was just so disappointed about being hurt. When Zeke threw his first touchdown pass, Bart was the first to shake his hand, the first to congratulate him, but still, all during the game, he was terribly unhappy. Tears actually came to his eyes on the sidelines. I'd never realized how dedicated he is, how much he wants to win, how much he wants to excel.

"Bart's usually quiet and calm," stated Kramer. "He's got so much character, so much willpower. He's about as complete a person as I've ever known. He admires Lombardi tremendously, and the affection is mutual. When Lombardi bawls Bart out in a meeting, it's always about the receiver he didn't see, or the play he didn't call, never about not putting out enough. I really think the only reason Vince ever criticizes Bart is just to show the rest of the club that he's impartial, that he'll even yell at his favorite."

The team was now concerned about its future without the main man. "We were used to Bart," said Hall of Fame tackle Forrest Gregg. "Zeke Bratkowski did a good job filling in, but he's not Bart. There's a delicate balance in any offense, and when one element is off just a little, it hurts the operation of the machine. We've been lucky because the defense has played so well, because the offense hasn't been doing the job. With Bart back and healthy, I think we will. We know we can move the ball."

Lombardi added to the team's concern two days later. "I don't know if you guys know it or not," he said with emotion filling his voice, "but this guy's been hurt and he's in pain, and he's been playing hurt, and he's been . . ." The coach could not complete the sentence. He motioned to an assistant to turn out the lights and start the movie projector.

Although he was sidelined, Starr was now a Lombardi play-with-pain disciple. "You have to ignore the pain," he said. "It hurts, but if you think about the hurting, you can't think about playing." He also adopted a bit of Lombardi's religious philosophy, as the team devotional before the 27-17 win in Detroit suggests. "Carroll Dale read from the Bible," reported Kramer, "and then Bart gave a little sermon, saying that if a man doesn't use his ability to the fullest, he's cheating on God. The theme of the sermon, of course, came from the Book of Vincent, and Bart did a very nice job."

"Gentlemen, today we start the big push," said Lombardi to the team following the win over the Lions.

By the time Starr could put the play-with-pain doctrine to the test the team was 3-1-1, and heading to Yankee Stadium for a date with the Giants. He had been getting very restless. "Most of the things that have been bothering me have cleared up," he said on Jerry Kramer's show, "and if the shoulder just comes around, I'll be in great shape." Never one to take himself too seriously, he told a story he loved to relate. He claimed he had been extremely irritable one day and upon returning home, yelled at one of his boys, spanked the other, and snapped at Cherry.

"What's wrong with you? I've never seen you so edgy," said his wife.

"I've got a jillion things to do, a jillion things. And I've got to go to a banquet over in Appleton tonight," he said tersely.

"What kind of banquet?"

"I'm receiving a nice guy award," he said.

"You're putting me on," said Cherry.

The story is typical of Starr, who likes to make himself the target of his own humor. "He is humble, but at the same time dynamic and exciting," observed Rev. Bourland.

In that spirit, Starr saved many of his favorite letters. He quoted several in his autobiography. One read: "Our teacher asked our class who was the greatest quarterback in the NFL. I said, 'Bart Starr,' and he just laughed." In another, a young girl wrote, "Please send me two pictures for our school—one with your uniform on and one with it off. Love, Amy, age 9."

As for Cherry, she once sat next to a man on an airline bus in the Denver airport. "Do you live in Denver?" the man asked.

"No," said Cherry. "I live in Green Bay, Wisconsin."

"Green Bay? Have you ever seen Bart Starr?"

"Oh, I've seen him from time to time," she said coyly.

"Have you ever had a chance to talk to him?" asked the now curious passenger.

"Yes, on many occasions." Cherry then leaned over and whispered, "As a matter of fact, I slept with him last night." The man was stunned, until Cherry broke out laughing and identified herself.

Despite the good humor and brave front, pain was a constant for Starr during the season. At practice, he was taking an emperin-codeine compound pill for his shoulder. He would take one or two pills a day, just to get through practice. His throwing was not sharp at all. As the team dressed in New York, the injuries were apparent. Starr taking codeine, Herb Adderley getting a shot of novocaine for his torn right bicep, and Ray Nitschke being taped from hip to ankle. Nitschke was a profile in football courage. Starr believed the middle linebacker fought through more injuries than anyone else. He played with an atrophied leg, and deep purple bruises covering his body from the hip down to the knee. "Ray was a guy who was almost oblivious to pain," said the admiring Packer great Willie Davis. "I saw the guy play with almost every injury imaginable." Starr was also revered for his courage. "A lot of people don't realize how tough he was," says Hornung. "Three or four times during the period I played with him, he really got hit, he really got banged up." Gary Knafelc witnessed Starr taking a shot for some painful broken ribs. "Dr. Nellen comes in," said Knafelc who was there to distract him with talk, "and it looked like a saber and he stuck it right into his stomach, and I was supposed to help him and it was making me sick."

Despite the hurts, and with the Pack trailing 14-10 at the half, Starr took over the game as the Pack exploded for 38 points and a 48-21 triumph. Lombardi was jubilant. "Starr was the difference," he crowed. "He's a long way from a hundred percent, but he gave us a lift. We were down and he picked us up. We ran harder, blocked better, and won."

Even so, Starr had to leave the game in the fourth quarter. "He's still hurt," said the coach. "He had deep receivers open twice and couldn't reach them. But we needed his ability as a leader and a tactician."

"No one was down on Starr in the early games when he played with pain," said Nitschke. "You got to go with a guy like that. He's got pride and he helped us feel pride in ourselves. Sure, the defense had to work a lot harder, but we knew when Bart came around and Grabow- ski and Anderson got a little more experience, the offense would score."

A 31-23 victory over St. Louis followed. Despite the win, it had been a rough day for Starr. When he returned home he was sore, mentally and physically. Starr had a practice of rewarding his sons with a dime for excellent grades in school. When he finally got to bed that night, he found a note from Bart on his pillow. "Dear Dad," the youngster had written, "I thought you played a great game. Love, Bart." Attached to the note were two dimes.

The following week the team fell at Baltimore, 13-10. It was an ex- cruciating defeat. Leading 10-6 late in the fourth quarter, the Colts did what the Packers expected them to do, try an on-side kick. The ball went past the Green Bay front line and rolled between defensive back Doug Hart and linebacker Tommy Joe Crutcher. When Hart overran the ball, Rich Volk of the Colts pounced on it at the Green Bay 34-yard line. Unitas hit a fourth down pass and Baltimore stole the game.

Lombardi was seething, "Stupid high school play, stupid play!" he groused, referring to the team's failure to cover the on-side kick. Crutcher and others did not appreciate being second-guessed. After a cooler Lombardi had completed his custom of patting players on the back and mussing their hair as he walked to the back of the plane, a concerned Starr pulled Kramer and McGee together.

"You know it, Jerry, and you know it, Max," he said, "but perhaps the young guys don't: This man is one great coach. He's got a brilliant mind. He prepares us better for a football game than any other team in the National Football League. Going into the game against St. Louis, we knew exactly what we could do, what we couldn't do, how to do it. The same thing today. I've never seen a more complete book on a team than Coach Lombardi had on Baltimore. It was a really beautiful thing to see."

Despite the injuries, the Packers fought on, grinding through a painful campaign, with Lombardi wringing the last ounce of energy from his charges along the way. "What's going on out there!" he would holler, as he jammed his hands into the pockets of his beige camelhair overcoat. "Everybody's grabbing, nobody's tackling. Grab, grab, grab. Nobody's tackling. Put your shoulders into it out there!"

After a 13-0 win against the 49ers in Green Bay, a game in which Starr was hit in the head with such force that he left the game not knowing what was happening, the team was 7-2-1. "Next week," said Lombardi after the game, "we start the big push."

The Pack now faced a return match with the Bears. The locker room was taut with tension before the game. Once again, Lombardi, the master manipulator, pushed the right button. Instead of offering an inspiring pre-game address, he told a silly joke that snapped the tension. At Chicago, Gale Sayers was all the rage, racing through the Green Bay defense for a 43-yard TD jaunt and total of 117 yards rushing for the game. Despite his heroics, the Packer defense held Chicago to 13 points, while managing 17 of their own as they clinched the Central Division title—the NFL now had four divisions, two in each conference—and a trip to the playoffs. A major bright spot in the season was the play of Travis Williams. The one-year wonder set an NFL standard of four kickoff returns for a touchdown, and averaged an astonishing 41.1 yards per return, smashing the old record by 5.9 yards per attempt.

Winning all but one of the final three games, Green Bay closed the season with a 9-4-1 mark, and a playoff date with the 11-1-2 Los Angeles Rams set for Milwaukee. Just a few weeks previous, the Rams had pulled out a last second 27-24 win on the coast and had boasted that they had broken the Packer magic.

Indeed, the Green Bay Packers were all guts and character. They were no longer physically dominant. They were an aging team and it showed as the season ground on. For the season, the Packers scored 332 points. Eight of the 16 NFL teams had done better. As tough as the defense was, its 209 points allowed was only third best in the NFL. Moreover, the Packers' net point differential of 123 points, although third ranked, trailed the margins of the Rams and Colts (both with 11-1-2 marks) by 79 and 73 points, respectively.

Starr's injuries were reflected in his numbers. He completed just 115 of 210 passes and 1,823 yards. He threw almost twice as many interceptions (17) as touchdown passes (9). His rating was a very unspectacular 64.4.

CHAPTER 20

The Drive to the Top

J E R R Y K R A M E R did not feel good about facing the Rams in the playoffs. "Compare the way we played against Pittsburgh yesterday (in the final game, a 24-17 defeat) with the way Los Angeles played against Baltimore (winning 34-10)," he said in *Instant Replay*, "and you have to believe that the clock, finally, is about to run out on us. I hate to be gloomy. I hate to even think about defeat. I hate the idea that we could come so close to a third straight world championship and miss it. But I have a very bad feeling about this game."

Winning three straight is a simply incredible task. By the end of the millennium no other team achieved that distinction, not Landry's Cowboys, Shula's Dolphins, or Walsh's 49ers. The matchup had the appearance of the old against the young, the past against the present. The Rams were a team on the rise under George Allen, who himself would eventually be inducted into the Pro Football Hall of Fame. The Packers were a team of experience, but possibly more to the point, they were also a team characterized by age and injury.

Perhaps sensing a negativity in his troops, Lombardi, ever the master of surprise, took a new tack. "We may be wounded. We may be in trouble," he told his players. "Some people may be picking Los Angeles over us. But I'll tell you one thing: that Los Angeles team better be ready to play a football game when they come in here because they're going to have a battle. I'll guarantee that. This team has a history of rising to the occasion. This is it. There's no tomorrow." He then finished his speech with a familiar line: "This is really the start of the big push."

Cherry Starr was ready for George Allen, if not the Rams. She had a note for the coach at his Milwaukee hotel. It read: "Dear Coach Allen, Remember what I told you. Bart never forgets. Cherry."

Lombardi took the text for his pre-game address from 1 Corinthians 9:24, and urged his players to "run to win." He told them that many people enter a race and focus simply on finishing, or coming second or third, but that they look for one thing—they run to win. "Vince has a knack," noted the witty Kramer, "for making all the saints sound like they would have been great football coaches."

Starr had planned to attack Los Angeles differently from a few weeks previous in the 27-24 loss. "We played conservative ball in the first game," he said. "A lot of that was because I just couldn't physically handle our whole offense. But this time we'll go for broke. If we lose this one, that's it. The season is over."

The game started inauspiciously. With the Rams up 7-0, Starr threw an interception, and the Rams set up shop on the Packer 10-yard line. Packer pride emerged and the defense held. Then on fourth down, linebacker Dave Robinson broke through and stuffed the Los Angeles field goal attempt. Later Travis Robinson went outside and broke off a 67-yard TD run, because Starr had detected the Ram defense's concern with stopping up the middle. From there, the Packers' veteran savvy kicked in. "Bart, if you can come up the middle with something from a brown right," Kramer said to Starr on the sidelines, "I think it'll go. They're scared to death of the 'seven' hole right now."

The brown right formation had Marvin Fleming, the tight end on the right with Williams behind Bob Skoronski, the left tackle. Starr worked the seven hole several times more, and then called a brown right 41-quick. Actually the team had no such play, but the players knew how to improvise off the 41-quick run from other formations. Williams ripped through for 15 yards and three plays later Starr hit Dale for a touchdown. The Packers led, 14-7.

The team was buoyant at the half, with Lombardi saying, "Magnificent, just magnificent so far."

With Henry Jordan and Ray Nitschke leading the charge, the defense pounded the Rams in the second half, shutting them out. Los

Angeles gained but seven yards in the entire third quarter. Starr made the offense go. "Bart kept mixing up his plays beautifully, exploiting first one hole, then another, taking to the air whenever he felt like loosening up the Rams," recalled Kramer. "He had his finest passing day of the year, and his play calling was even better." The final score was 28-7.

Much of Starr's concern centered on the Rams' great defensive end, David "Deacon" Jones. Jones had cleaned up in the earlier encounter. "We had to do something to slow the Deacon down," related Starr, revealing his incisive sense of the offense versus defense mind game. "If you let him alone, he'll eat you alive. He'll come in like a freight train and you don't have time to get the ball away. So early in the playoff game, we ran right at him. We'd put two blockers on him and ride him out and run over his position until he began to worry about stopping the run first and rushing the passer after that. Once you make a lineman play run first, pass second, you take away most of his rush."

Lombardi was overcome. "Magnificent, just magnificent," he enthused. "I've been very proud of you guys all year long. You've overcome a great deal of adversity. You've hung in there, and when the big games came around . . ." With that he broke down, and with tears trickling down his cheeks, knelt down and led the team in the Lord's Prayer.

The team was jubilant. Nitschke hugged player after player. "I just wish the game hadn't ended," said Jordan, who had been talked out of retiring at the outset of the season. "I could have played another half. I had so much fun. Sure, it was a money game. I'm broke, and I have an expensive wife."

"Hey, Jerry, I don't have to send the coat back," hollered Fuzzy Thurston to Kramer, referring to the mink he had bought his wife for Christmas on an "if" basis.

With the two (AFL and NFL) leagues still not merged, it was fifteen down, one to go for the third straight NFL title. Standing in the way were Tom Landry's Dallas Cowboys. Two days before the game, Lombardi was emphatic. "I want that third championship," he declared, "and I deserve it. We all deserve it." Then he spoke these words that burned into the minds of his players, "Lots of better ballplayers than you guys have won through here, but you're the type of ballplayers I want. You've got character. You've got heart. You've got guts."

On December 31st, NFL Films' Steve Sabol picked up his hotel phone to hear the wake-up message. "Good morning, Mr. Sabol. It is sixteen degrees below zero and the wind is out of the north. Now have a nice day." Paul Mazzoleni of Paul's Standard had to make a stop at Willie Wood's home. "It's just too cold to play," said the shivering Wood as his battery was being brought back to life. "They're going to call this game off. They're not going to play in this." Dick Schaap was driving toward the stadium and noticed a −13 temperature sign on the side of a bank. He thought it was broken. Dave Robinson was eating breakfast with his family. His wife came in, kissed him, and said, "It's twenty below out there."

"Twenty above, you mean," he replied. "Can't be twenty below."

"Man, it's too cold," muttered Wood in the dressing room. "They ain't going to play in this." Gale Gillingham, now Kramer's main running mate at guard, asked him, "You going to wear gloves?" Kramer had never before worn gloves in a game. He decided to break precedent.

Gillingham, Kramer, Gregg, and Bob Skoronski all got gloves from the equipment manager, Dad Braisher. "With this cold," said defensive end Ron Kostelnik to Kramer, "it's going to hamper us on defense. We won't be able to grab, to use our hands too well. You won't have to be afraid of popping people, Jerry. They won't be able to throw you with their hands."

Lombardi would allow long underwear but no gloves for anyone other than linemen. Robinson sought out Braisher. "Give me a pair of those brown gloves," he said, "and he'll never know the difference. I'm the only linebacker with brown hands, anyway."

Many of the Packer faithful were more courageous than their heroes, as hundreds of fans were in the stands two hours before kickoff, despite having reserved seats. By game time, the temperature was a balmy −13, with winds gusting to 15 mph, driving the wind chill down to −38. A standing room only crowd of 50,861—adorned in hunting jackets, parkas, lap robes, and ski masks, many guzzling from flasks—roared as the Packers took the field.

In the bitter cold, Starr was on top of his game. He engineered an

82-yard pilgrimage into the Dallas end zone, completing the effort with an 8-yard TD toss to Boyd Dowler. In the second quarter, he suckered in the Dallas Doomsday Defense on a play-action fake and sent a 46-yard scoring aerial to Carroll Dale. The Cowboys, despising the un-Dallas-like weather conditions, cashed in on two Packer fumbles—one by Starr and the other by Wood—and it was 14-10 at the half.

The third quarter was scoreless. The game was becoming a survival struggle. "Players on both sides breathed steam and spit ice," wrote Gruver, "and officials were forced to call the game without whistles because the small wooden peas inside their whistles had frozen." One official, Joe Connell, had torn half his lower lip off when he tried to yank the whistle from his mouth, not aware that it had frozen to his lip.

On the opening play of the fourth quarter, Landry reached into his bag of tricks and had Dan Reeves fake a sweep and throw an option pass to Lance Rentzel. It worked for a 50-yard score and the Cowboys forged into the lead, 17-14. Defense predominated as the field became more frigid.

With 4:50 left in the contest, the Packers took over on their own 32, for what figured to be the last time. Starr had already been sacked eight times for 76 yards, and with conditions worsening by the moment, the outlook was grim. Nonetheless, it was then that Ray Nitschke, ignoring the frostbite invading six of his toes, had the reassuring thought: "We're losing, but we have the ball. And we have Starr." Starr had reached the zenith of leadership. He had become what Bill Russell called "the invisible man"—a person who now lived in the minds and shaped the thinking of his teammates, much like that of Lombardi.

And if ever the once-tentative son of Ben Starr exuded leadership, this was the moment. "This is it. We're going in," he said firmly in the Packer huddle.

Starr's demeanor had a transforming impact on the team. "You knew who was in charge and you knew if we did what he asked us to, we would get down there, we'd score, and we'd win," recalls Boyd Dowler.

"The feeling I had was that we are going to score," said Chuck Mercein. Mercein had been picked up by Lombardi after being dumped by the Giants. "I felt calm. I felt that everyone in the huddle was calm. I didn't sense any anxiety or desperation. Determination, yes, but not desperation. Bart just said a few words, 'We're going in,' but he had this tremendous presence. He was the on-field personification of Lombardi."

Starr and Lombardi had agreed not to go for the quick score, but to mount a drive. Donny Anderson told Starr that he could pick up eight or ten yards any time the quarterback chose to dump the ball off to him. Starr did just that on the first play, picking up six. Mercein thundered around the end for seven more, and Starr then connected with Dowler for an additional thirteen yards. The ball was resting on the Dallas 42. And it was there what looked like disaster hit. Anderson was dropped nine yards behind the line of scrimmage on a broken end sweep. Starr, ever cool, nibbled away at the yardage deficit, hitting Anderson twice on drop-off tosses that the halfback managed to turn into twelve and nine yard gains for a first down.

The ball was on the Dallas 30. There were two minutes left.

Mercein told Starr he was open on the left if Starr needed him. With 1:35 left, Starr went back to throw. Unable to locate Dowler or Anderson, he threw the ball to an open Mercein. It was a bit behind the fullback and high, but Mercein made a truly clutch catch on the run and wended his way 19 yards down to the 11, where he was pushed out of bounds.

Starr then made the call of the game. Called a GIVE 54, the play had the look of an end sweep. The play was aimed at taking advantage of Hall of Fame Cowboy tackle Bob Lilly's aggressiveness. If the guards pulled, resembling a sweep, and Lilly tried to rush through the hole and finish Anderson off for a loss, there would be daylight through which Mercein could gallop on a draw-like play. If, however, Lilly didn't take the bait, the play would be stuffed.

It worked. Mercein saw a gaping hole as Lilly took off in pursuit, Skoronski banged into the left end, and a linebacker took off in an errant direction. For a moment it appeared that he would score, but the field was now more of a hockey rink. It was like a marble table top, according to Starr, and Mercein stumbled into Forrest Gregg at the three. "I can still hear the sound of his feet clicking on that ice," linesman Jim Huxford said to Maraniss. "You could hear it on the ice. He was slipping but he kept going."

Anderson got one yard for the first down at the 1. From there, it was Anderson again for no gain. There were 20 seconds left. Green Bay used one of its timeouts, after which Anderson was stopped again, this time slipping on the ice and nearly fumbling. There were 16 seconds left when the Packers used their final timeout.

Although a field goal would tie the game—surely the safe call—it never entered Starr's mind. It was "run to win" with Lombardi. Starr told the coach he wanted to go with a wedge play, one in which the runner is tucked between the center and guard. The main concern was whether Jerry Kramer could get sufficient footing to push his man, Jethro Pugh, who stood the tallest on the Dallas front, out of the play. Kramer told Starr to go with it, and Mercein got ready, convinced he was going straight for the end zone on the wedge.

The play was Brown right, 31 wedge; the three back through the one hole. As Starr counted off at the line of scrimmage, every Green Bay player thought Chuck Mercein was going to get his chance to make NFL history. Everyone but one. Starr had had one concern, and kept it to himself. Should Mercein slip on the ice, he would never make it to the end zone, and with no timeouts remaining, the game would be over. Starr also remembered keeping the ball for a score against the 49ers in '66, on an icy Milwaukee field.

Kramer had located a soft spot on the turf and dug in next to center Ken Bowman. The guard bolted at the snap—Pugh thought a tad before the snap—and nailed the Cowboy tackle low, with Bowman knocking him backwards into a linebacker. Mercein took off in anticipation of the handoff that would never be. Starr crouched low and slipped over the goal into the Promised Land of a third consecutive NFL championship. The New Year celebration could not have been sweeter for the Packers or their fans.

"Bart Starr has been in the right place doing the right things for nine years," said Maraniss. "With Hornung no longer in uniform, Starr had to be the one to go in for the winning score." Moreover, while Lombardi had his stamp on every aspect of the Packers' drive, he had nothing directly to do with it. Bart Starr called the plays and scored the touchdown. For Green Bay, this was The Drive. "Of all the games I've done," said announcer Ray Scott, "that final drive was the greatest triumph over adversity I'd ever seen. It was a thing of beauty."

For the Packers, the game against the rival league champions, the Oakland Raiders, was hard to prepare for. The Ice Bowl win had come just eight days after the intense victory over the Rams. The team was drained emotionally and physically. "The previous year we had been taken to the wire by Dallas," said Starr, "and we knew going into the game that they would really be ready for us. We considered it our championship game and didn't give a thought to Super Bowl II. After our frigid victory, the last thing I wanted to do was play another football game."

Nevertheless, after appearing on *The Tonight Show* with three other quarterbacks, Starr had to turn his attention to the Raiders, who had posted a 13-1 record in the AFL's Western Division before swamping Houston, 41-7, for the league title. The powerful Raider offense, led by former Notre Dame great, Daryle Lamonica, had averaged over 33 points a game. The Raiders, already under Al Davis, were not cocky. Coach John Rauch referred to Green Bay as "the very best team in all of football." Lamonica not only kept a copy of Starr's book, *Quarterbacking*, in his locker, he spoke of Starr with awe. "I admire Starr," he said. "I consider it a real privilege to play against the man who is rated top in the business."

One has to assume there was plenty of spinning going on—a Raider defensive end said, "I hope we don't get run off the field," to the press, and Davis himself said, "Imagine the li'l ol' Raiders on the same field with the Green Bay Packers." Nevertheless, there had to be genuine respect and concern after how the Pack had dismantled the 11-2-1 Chiefs, who had also averaged better than 30 a game a year ago.

Playing yet another game was difficult enough for the wounded Packers, but they certainly did not want to practice in Green Bay. That, however, is what they did, rather than head immediately for Miami and the Orange Bowl. On Wednesday, January 3rd, the team worked out in 5-degree temperatures. The following day it was −6. Players were near revolt. Kramer and Nitschke had debilitating colds, with Nitschke limping from the effects of frostbite. He had also lost eight pounds. Others were also suffering. Packer publicist Chuck Lane said that skin was falling off Packer players "by the yard." Lombardi stonewalled when the press began questioning him about the condition of his players.

"Weather," he said, "is a state of mind." It seems Lombardi's own mind was in a less than tolerant state, given that he condensed the frigid Thursday practice to a 45-minute session. Rumors of Lombardi's retirement had been wafting around throughout the season, but now they were everywhere. Starr noticed a change in the coach after the Dallas game. "Lombardi's demeanor in the days preceding the game was our team's most dramatic change from Super Bowl I. He was no longer uptight and ornery, but rather relaxed and cheerful. He even broke a long-standing tradition and allowed our wives to accompany us on the trip. During the 'Five O'Clock Club' cocktail sessions with the media, he was jovial and informative, with one major exception." He would not address the retirement issue. The United Press International did carry a quote from him, saying, "I haven't decided yet. I do know that in pro football today, it is almost impossible to be both coach and general manager if you want to do well at either." He said nothing to the team.

Lombardi tipped his hand to the players on the Thursday before the confrontation. Rubbing his hands together, he said, "Okay, boys, this may be the last time we'll be together. I want . . . I just want to tell you how very proud I am . . . of all of you, so, uh . . ." With that he turned his back, sat down, and ordered the team to break up into offensive and defensive units. In a pre-game meeting, a number of key players urged focus and one more all-out effort at winning. Co-captain Bob Skoronski said, "Let's not waste any time, boys. Let's go out there from the opening play. They're a good football team, boys. If we lose, boys, we've lost everything we ever worked for. Everything. I don't have any intention of losing this ball game, and I don't think anybody else here does."

"Fellas, you know as well as I do that when we went to camp in July, this is what we had in mind," said the other co-captain Willie Davis. "This game. This game is going to determine what's said about the Packers tomorrow. Fellas, in another sixty minutes, we can walk in here with another world championship. Fellas, it's recognition, it's prestige, and, fellas, it's money. So let's go out and have fun. Let's go out and just hit people. Let's just go out and play football the way we can."

"My impression of this ball club," said Forrest Gregg, "is that they're the type of people who like to intimidate you. Watch those linebackers, those linemen, the way they're hitting people late. No sense getting upset about it. They're going to do some pass interference and holding and stuff like that, but let's not get upset about it. Let's go out there and play our brand of football. Let's face it, they're a little bit afraid of us right now. Let's put it to them from the very first whistle and put it to them every play."

Max McGee then added, "It's the last game for some of us, and we sure don't want to go out of here and live the rest of our lives letting these guys beat us."

"Let's play with our hearts," said Nitschke, who never played any other way.

Lombardi then delivered his last pre-game speech. "It's very difficult for me to say anything," he began. "Anything I could say would be repetitious. This is our twenty-third game this year. I don't know of anything else I could tell this team. Boys, I can only say this to you: Boys, you're a good football team. You are a proud football team. You are the world champions. You are the champions of the National Football League for the third time in a row, for the first time in the history of the National Football League. That's a great thing to be proud of. But let me just say this: All the glory, everything that you've had, everything that you've won is going to be small in comparison to winning this one. This is a great thing for you. You're the only team maybe in the history of National Football League to ever have this opportunity to win the Super Bowl twice. Boys. I tell you I'd be so proud of that I just fill up with myself. I just get bigger and bigger and bigger. It's not going to come easy. That is a club that is going to hit you. They're going to try to hit you and you got to take it out of them. You got to be forty tigers out there. That's all. Just hit. Just run. Just block and just tackle. If you do that, there's no question what the answer's going to be in this ball game. Keep your poise. Keep your poise. You've faced them all. There's nothing they can show you out there you haven't faced a number of times. Right?"

"Right!"

"Right!"

"Let's go. Let's go get 'em!"

With that, Lombardi's Packers took the field, and did not waste any time, as Skoronski urged. After two field goals, Starr found Dowler for a 62-yard aerial score and it was 13-0. It was 16-7 at the break. At the half Nitschke, Kramer, Gregg, Skoronski, Davis, Jordan, Thurston, McGee, and Starr committed themselves to play the second half for the coach.

Starr did his share by messing with minds of the Raiders' defense. First he beat the Oakland blitz by sending his fullback Ben Wilson, through the middle for 13, and then pulled Oakland in on a play fake on third and one, and hit McGee for 35 yards. An 11-yard strike to Dale was followed by a 12-yard throw to Anderson, and capped off with a two-yard TD smash by Anderson, for a 23-7 advantage.

Super Bowl II put a sweet cap on Starr's injury-riddled season. He threw for 202 yards and a TD on 13 of 24, with no interceptions. He was the game's MVP in the Packers' 33-14 triumph.

On February 1, 1968, Vince Lombardi, 55, resigned as coach of the Green Bay Packers. He would remain as General Manager. In a little more than two and a half years after that—September 3, 1970—he died.

CHAPTER 21

Transition

D AVID MARANISS quotes a "touching letter" sent to Lombardi upon his retirement. It was from Ben Starr:

"It is with a feeling of deep gratitude that we say 'thank you' for all you have done for Bart since he has been associated with you. He gives you the entire credit for any and all success that he has had and we know he is going to miss the meetings he has shared with you, but we are thankful that you will, at least, still be associated with the Packer organization. I and my wife both feel that Bart will probably rely on you to still offer him advice. It is not only because you are the finest coach in football, but the type of religious man you are also that has made us so happy for Bart to be associated with you. He admires you in so many ways that you have had a far deeper impact on him in more ways than you will probably ever know."

Anyone receiving a letter like this would be moved by the sincerity and kindness behind it. It was a classy thing for Ben Starr to do. On closer look, however, it provides an insight into how he perceived his son. All credit (although Bart himself would endorse Ben's sentiments) goes to Lombardi for his son's success, almost as if Bart would not have succeeded had there been no Lombardi, or that his rise to the pinnacle of NFL success had nothing to do with his own will, faith, and character. It is safe to say that Ben Starr was a man of his generation, an era in which men did not often tell their children—especially their sons—that they were proud of them, or that they had attained adulthood with honor and integrity. Indeed, Lombardi himself was far closer to his own players than he was with either his son, Vincent, Jr., or his daughter, Susan. Nevertheless, in a curious way, the letter is testimony to what Starr had to overcome—the less than confident attitude his father, who loomed so large in his psychological life, had toward him from his childhood forward.

Starr's teammate, safety Tom Brown who had played professional baseball before going to the NFL, once spoke of how so many professional athletes tend to be lazy. "We want to take the easy way out," he explained. "We are so far superior. We've always been better. As nine-year-olds, ten-year-olds, we were always the best athletes on the field. We probably got preferential treatment from youth coaches and all the way up. So we never really had to give one hundred percent effort. Because if we gave seventy-five percent we were better than all the other kids." Indeed, the price for this superiority, as described by Brown, may well be laziness and complacency, but it most certainly is not a lack of confidence. Bart Starr could not have related at all to Brown's description of the model professional athlete. He was not even thought to be the best athlete in his own family. The coaches in his youth had little initial regard for him, either. And, most of all, his father did not encourage him. Bart Starr made it to the top with minimal help from anyone. Even Lombardi, though he continues to be much revered by Starr, did not believe in Bart initially. For Bart Starr, it was faith and will first, and Lombardi second. Luck, it is said, emerges when preparation meets opportunity, making it not luck at all. Starr was not lucky. He was always prepared so that when the door of opportunity opened a crack, he was able demonstrate what he was made of personally and athletically.

Lombardi, though remaining as general manager, turned the team over to his longtime defensive coordinator Phil Bengtson. If Lombardi was north, then Bengtson was south. Whereas the former mentor was an emotional, demanding man with an in-your-face style, the new coach was quiet, controlled, and cerebral. He was an extraordinary defensive mind, every bit as dedicated to perfection as his boss had been, as witnessed by the greatness of the team's defensive play throughout Lombardi's tenure. Moreover, with the offensive "coordinator," Bart Starr, still at the throttle, there was reason to believe the Packers' championship days may well continue.

That Bengtson had Starr at all is testimony to Bart's character. Now 34, and coming off an injury-riddled '67 season in which he gutted his way through and led his team back to the top, capping it off with another MVP Super Bowl, he could easily have retired. Although he continued to say he loved the game, Starr may well have been responding more to a sense of honor as the team's leader. "More important," he acknowledged, "Lombardi's replacement, Phil Bengtson, had been an integral part of our success and I felt that the veteran players owed him their support." Starr would not walk out on a friend who needed him.

Ray Nitschke certainly felt that way. He told *Sports Illustrated*'s Tex Maule in an article entitled, "Green Bay's Greatest Team," that the '68 contingent could well become the franchise's greatest squad. "With Starr healthy for a full season, Grabowski and Pitts back in the lineup (both had injury problems in '67), Marv Fleming at full speed, and with Anderson and Williams carrying another year's experience, we should be more explosive offensively," the middle linebacker said confidently. "I don't anticipate much change in the defense, although we do have some fine young players." Indeed, other than losing Max McGee and kicker Don Chandler to retirement, the club's nucleus was intact.

Jerry Kramer saw it much the same way. He was confident that the Packers could dominate the Central Division, a loop consisting of Detroit, Chicago, and Minnesota, all flawed teams, and each without a quarterback even near the level of Starr. Expectations for a fourth crown were alive and well in the hearts and minds of the Packers and their faithful followers.

There was, at least for some, an added incentive. Certain players would play with special intensity, having become weary of the larger-than-life image of their former coach, one in which all credit for the team's success was accorded to him at the expense of the players whose battered bodies had paid the price and mastered the gridiron during Lombardi's reign. "Yeah, we want to win for Phil," said defensive tackle Jim Weatherwax to Jerry Kramer, "and we also want to win to show everybody that it wasn't just Lombardi these past few years, that it wasn't all him, that we can have a good season without him."

Training camp was delayed due to a players' strike, but the players stayed in shape via workouts conducted by Starr and Weatherwax. Former defensive tackle Dave Hanner, now an assistant coach, urged Bengtson to make the first three days of camp the most punishing in any player's memory, in an effort to rid the team of any notion that they could let up in '68. Bengtson did not take Hanner's advice. Although the camp schedule varied little from previous years, the environment was simply not as rigorous, and the activities not as strenuous as in the past. "We kept telling each other that we were working just as hard as we did under Lombardi, but I don't think any of us really believed it," wrote Kramer. "The obvious difference was the grass drills, the murderous up-down exercises. Under Lombardi, they were the most excruciating torture, and we did sixty or seventy of them at a time, till we were all ready to die. But in training camp in 1968, we did maybe fifteen or sixteen up-downs at a time."

Players were allowed water and Gatorade breaks during practice, and some Packers actually would sneak into a shady area and lie down for awhile, unimaginable under Lombardi. Rule infractions increased in number, with one player actually missing a game bus, and another—a rookie, no less—losing his playbook.

The team lost two exhibition games, no more than they had in '66 when they went on to a sparkling 12-2 championship season. With Kramer kicking three field goals, Green Bay opened the regular season by walloping a weak Philadelphia Eagles team, 30-13. That, however, was as good as it got.

The Minnesota Vikings downed the Pack the next week, 26-13. Lombardi, who stayed away from practice to allow Bengtson the freedom and authority to function without interference, was not happy. He visited the locker room, and seeing his former players looking very contemporary, the always plainly attired general manager muttered, "Too many blue shirts in here. Too many sideburns." Lombardi was obviously referring to the team's loss of focus more than the players' wardrobes or grooming styles. The big three—religion, family, and the Green Bay Packers—were being supplanted by ancillary, often self-aggrandizing concerns. Kramer, Willie Davis, Lionel Aldridge, and Henry Jordan had television shows, while Starr had a radio show.

The edge simply was not there. After going up 10-0 in game three against the Lions, Kramer missed two straight field goals in a 23-17 defeat. Core players were concerned. Davis, Nitschke, and Kramer agreed that they needed to take responsibility for the emotional tenor of the team. "Look," Kramer told them, "we've got to motivate ourselves. We're not going to get motivation from any other source. We've got to be strong enough to do it ourselves."

They all tried. Davis had always been a vocal leader, and Kramer had consistently spoken up as well. Now Nitschke became a holler guy. Despite missing three field goals, the team crushed Atlanta in the next game, 38-7. The team was 2-2, but hurting. Kramer broke his thumb in the game. Jordan's back was so bad throughout the season he went to a chiropractor every day. Ron Kostelnik, the other tackle, was playing with torn ligaments, and Weatherwax, the top reserve, was out for the season with a bad knee. Bob Brown, who might have filled in ably, broke his arm and then his leg. Running back Jim Grabowski had fluid drained from his knee regularly, and worst of all, Starr was knocked out of the Atlanta game after opening the season ablaze, completing nearly 65 percent of his passes.

In the early season he injured the little finger on his throwing hand, pulled a tendon in his bicep, and reinjured his ribs. Though he spoke little about it, Starr spent '68 and '69 suffering from a variety of injuries. "First, I separated the cartilage in my ribs and later broke several of them," he noted. "I also suffered a concussion and was bothered by chronic soreness in my right shoulder." He wound up missing 28 quarters of action in 1968.

The team was incredibly dependent on Starr. He was the incarnation of Lombardi's mind on the field, and now with Hornung and Taylor long gone, he was the lone holdover in the backfield from the glory days. None of this was lost on Bengtson. "I don't want to detract from Zeke Bratkowski," said the coach, reflecting on the season, "but Starr was the leading factor in our attack. Our game was designed around the things he could do, and we didn't have him available for a good share of the time. That's just a fact."

"Zeke Bratkowski took over for the next couple of games," echoed Kramer, "and although Zeke did his usual excellent backup job, it wasn't the same as having Bart."

The team struggled in the next two outings, falling by two to Los Angeles and tying Detroit. Six games into the '68 campaign, the Packers' mark was a very mediocre 2-3-1. They were, however, not out of it as they headed for a Monday night date with the undefeated Dallas Cowboys, because the Central Division had no power team. With the weekend scores in, the Pack knew a win against the Cowboys would place them in a first place 3-3-1 tie with the Lions. The Bears and Vikings were 3-4. It was a critical game, because a loss would be crippling, sending Green Bay to the divisional cellar. Starr carried the offense, firing four TD strikes as Green Bay continued to have the Cowboys' number, this time, 28-17.

Kramer saw only sunshine ahead. "We had shown the mark of champions," he wrote. "We had won the game we had to win. Now we were rolling. There wasn't any doubt in my mind or in the minds of my teammates. We were going to eat up the opposition the rest of the season." He was already handicapping the rest of the schedule. "Our next two games were against Minnesota and Chicago, and we knew that if we won these two, we'd knock them out of contention. Since Detroit figured to (and did) lose its two games against Baltimore and Los Angeles, those two weeks we'd run away from our rivals. We'd practically have the division wrapped up."

Kramer was right. Winning those two games would indeed give Green Bay another championship and its fourth straight trip into the post-season. The problem was that they won neither of them. The Bears beat them by three points on a 40-yard field goal with 36 seconds left and the Vikings won by four, aided by three Packer fumbles.

Through it all, Bengtson remained his stoic self. One of the central differences between him and Lombardi was that the former coach could speak to the hearts of his players. If nothing else, his aphorisms stayed with his charges long after their gridiron careers were over. As it was, it fell largely to co-captains Skoronski and Davis to fire up the troops going into a game. Bengtson would say things like, "Well, we've got to score more points," or "I know you can win if you go out and block and tackle the way you know how to. You're a better team than you've shown so far, and if you block and tackle, you'll win."

The former mentor could also be tough. In fact, he complained that there was no one willing to stand up and be the mean guy, the hard-nose that the team needed. If Bengtson didn't want the role, perhaps one of the assistants could adopt it. No one did. "In the past, Lombardi had had enough meanness for everybody," said Kramer.

The 1968 Green Bay Packers were a study of a team in transition. For nine years the players were bound by a mutual love-hate relationship with Vincent Thomas Lombardi, but now petty dissension ate at the team. The defense griped at the impotence of the offense, with Lee Roy Caffey muttering, "Can't win 'em if you don't score." On defense, frustrations built. Willie Davis, the great defensive end, was finding it harder to get to the quarterback with his fellow linemen at tackle injured and less than effective. With the pass rush slowed, Tom Brown would get beaten in the secondary for a big gainer. "Get that man out of there," Davis yelled without mentioning Brown's name. "What are you waiting for? That man's hurting us. He's hurting us. Get him out of there." Defensive back, Doug Hart, a starter in '65, had made the absolute best out of his role as the top reserve in '66 and '67. In '68, he went to the coaching staff, asking to play or be traded.

Even Starr came in for some criticism. "All of us had always suspected that Bart had a tendency to hold the ball too long before he threw," noted Kramer. "There were times when I'd block my man and block my man and finally release him, feeling I'd given Bart enough time to pass, and then I'd turn around and Bart'd still have the ball. My man'd get to him, and I'd look bad and I'd get angry with Bart, naturally, instead of with myself. But we all knew why Bart held the ball—he hated to throw when there was even the slightest chance of an interception—and as long as we were winning, we realized his reasoning was sound."

Kramer adroitly pointed out how perceptions change when success diminishes. "We knew that Bart was our bread and butter," he went on. "I remember I used to kid around once in a while and refer to Bart as 'the Statue of Liberty,' because he stood still so long, but it was just good-natured kidding, nothing vicious about it at all. But then, in 1968, the kidding by some of the guys lost its good nature. Nobody said anything to Bart directly, of course, but there was more than the usual groaning about his habit of holding the ball. It was ridiculous—Bart had led us to too many championships for anyone to take the groans seriously—but the bloom was off the Packer love in 1968, and a lot of stupid things get said when an affair is ending."

Starr himself tried to regather the team in mid-season. He proposed a team party to be held at his house. The other players decided it would be too much for Cherry to manage, so it was held at Century Bowling Alley in West De Pere. Although the purpose of the bash was to recapture the old magic, the atmosphere was contrived, strained. During the event, Francis Peay, an offensive tackle who had come to the Packers from New York got into it with Marv Fleming. Peay, a serious, non-drinking, cerebral man, who would later be the head coach at Northwestern University, was the object of the looser Fleming's ribbing and had had enough. He threw his Coke on Fleming, saying, "Stay away from me. Stay away from me. Don't bug me. Get away from me."

Any hope for a spirited get-together vanished with Peay's outburst. He apologized to Fleming but told Kramer, "That man just bugs me."

After defeating New Orleans and Washington handily, amazingly the Packers were once again in the middle of the race. At 5-5-1, they trailed the Vikings by just a half game. Game twelve pitted the Pack against the 49ers in San Francisco. Lombardi wanted the game desperately. He broke precedent and came down to the locker room to address the team before they took the field. An emotional Lombardi spoke of glories past and the team was psyched. Starr got hurt again early in the game, but Bratkowski guided Green Bay to a solid 20-7 advantage after three quarters.

Then things collapsed. Bratkowski injured his back and had to leave the game. The team expected Starr to return, knowing he could pull them through in this vital game. "I'd see Bart leave the field under his own power in the first quarter," wrote Kramer, "and I was sure that now I'd see him come running back on the field." He looked at the bench, and saw Starr continuing to stand quietly with his warmup jacket still on. "I suppose he'd discussed the situation with our coaches," commented Kramer, "and they'd decided he wasn't fit to play, but my heart just about broke. I wanted Bart to come running out so badly."

The choice was rookie Billy Stevens from what is now UTEP. He was unable to move the ball at all, and the Niners rallied for 20 points in the final quarter and a 27-20 victory. The atmosphere in the dressing room was funereal. Lombardi's Packers had never folded like this. But with Starr and others out, and many regulars hurting and creaking with age, the end seemed near.

With two games left, there was still hope. The problem was that the Packers were drawing a Baltimore team that had lost only one game all season. Nonetheless, the team was focused. They had, after all, beaten an undefeated Dallas team earlier, with their backs scraping the wall. According to Kramer, before the game, Bob Skoronski rallied the team with an intensely emotional speech. "Fellas," he began, "I'm deeply emotional. I really can't say much. These are the things that come to my mind today. We've dedicated a lot of games over the years to coaches and people. Today, fellas, there's a lot of guys who built the Packers to what they are today who might be playing their last game. I'm asking every guy here to go out and play his level best for the guys who had a lot to do with the Green Bay Packers. Boys, we're wounded, but we're not dead. If you're going to lay down and die out there, you're going to do something I'm not going to do. I may get beat, but it won't be because I want to. Now let's go out there and keep our heads up and do something for the guys who've had a whole lot to do with making the Packers, the green and gold, what they are. A lot of guys have given a whale of a lot . . . We've had a whole lot of memories and a lot of fun, so let's go out there and take it to them. I apologize for my emotion, but that's the way I feel." Ever the gentleman, Bengtson reminded the team that if they blocked and tackled they could win.

With that, the team went out, lost four fumbles, and lost 16-3.

As the Colts ran out the clock, the Green Bay crowd of over 50,000 rose as one and gave their heroes a standing ovation in appreciation for what the Packers had done to bring honor to Titletown. With chills running up and down their spine, the team was both buoyed by the outpouring of affection and depressed at seeing their run come to an end.

The Packers closed the season with 28-27 victory over their arch-rivals from Chicago, leaving them with their first losing record— 6-7-1—in a decade.

On the face of it, the difference between '68 and the glories of the past was in having Phil Bengtson rather than Vince Lombardi at the helm. Undoubtedly, the team missed the fire their former mentor put inside them. They certainly missed his conditioning endeavors. In '68, Green Bay's poorest scoring quarter was the fourth, averaging only four points a game in the final stanza. In '67, the team averaged eight. Had the Packers scored eight points in the fourth quarter of each '68 game, they would have won ten games rather than six. In fact, the Pack lost four games by less than a touchdown, three in the final two minutes. Perhaps fatigue had made cowards of them all. A closer look would also reveal the same problem that had occurred in 1964—poor placekicking. In '67 Don Chandler converted 19 of 26 field goal attempts. A parade of kickers, including Chuck Mercein, hit on just 13 of 29 in '68. Kicking deficiencies resulted in four would-be victories ending in defeats or a tie. Again, a 10-4 finish was within their grasp, more than enough to win the Central Division.

For Bart Starr, the season had pluses and minuses. He proved once and for all that he could be The Man, and carry the team by ringing up a 104.3 quarterback rating. He hit on 109 of 171 passes for 1,617 yards and 15 TDs against just eight interceptions. Regrettably, pain and injury were his constant companions. When he separated his shoulder at the end of the season, Bengston demonstrated his respect for Starr by lamenting, "We have eighty arms on the team, and you have to hurt the only one that counts."

"I guess the good Lord takes care of you in things like that," said Bart. For the dispirited Starr, it was once again faith and will.

"Bart goes to chapel alone each week," said his wife, "and prays for guidance to be a good leader for his club. Each evening before he goes to bed, he reads inspirational material that is based on the Holy Scriptures."

God had certainly answered Starr's prayers. He was far and away the preeminent leader of his team. Unfortunately, it was no longer a team that could lead its league in championship style.

CHAPTER 22

Playing with Pain

THE '69 AND '70 seasons fold into each other in the memories of Packer fans. Vince Lombardi resigned as general manager after the '68 season, and headed for Washington for what would turn out to be a one-year return to coaching. In Green Bay, players continued to retire, and the team continued its mediocre drift. The '69 squad did manage an 8-6 record, but finished well in arrears of the 12-2 Minnesota Vikings. For Starr, it was another year of pain and brilliance. He missed 27 quarters of action, yet fashioned another strong 89.9 rating, by completing more than 62 percent of his passes (92 of 148) for 1,161 yards, delivering nine touchdowns against just six interceptions.

Against Detroit, three gargantuan Lions hit Starr simultaneously, leaving his right arm dangling at his side. It was a shoulder separation, one he found very difficult to overcome. "I had had a shoulder separation before," he said, "and I just had it taped up properly and never missed a game, not even a pre-season game. But this one is more severe. I can't throw the ball."

Despite being severely handicapped by debilitating injuries, Starr had repeatedly hung sparkling numbers over the past few seasons. Clearly, he could still play the game at a peak level. Now he wanted to regain his health.

In the off-season Starr decided to focus on his physical condition. He had experienced injury and reinjury to his arm, shoulder, and ribs over the previous seasons, and he wanted to turn the corner physically.

Under the guidance of Packer trainer Dominic Gentile, he developed a demanding training regimen. He ran six miles daily, lifted weights, and did a series of isometric and isotonic exercises. He had a wheel installed on the wall of the Lambeau Field training room with its height adjusted so that a complete turn of the handle stretched his arm and shoulder muscles. He also worked daily at lobbing the ball and then speeding it up and until he could throw freely and with a proper range of motion.

Hopes were high that the Pack would be back in '70, but they weren't. After being pounded 40-0 by Detroit before more than 56,000 in the season opener at expanded Lambeau Field, the team went on to win only six of its remaining 13 games for a 6-8 final log. The Phil Bengtson era ended after three seasons with a forgettable 20-21-1 record.

For Starr, the season was painful mentally and physically. "I encountered a new experience in the opening game of the '70 season," wrote Starr, "the one we lost to Detroit. I was booed while returning to the sidelines after throwing an incomplete pass on third down." Starr was philosophical about the unsettling event. "As disappointing as the experience was, I could not blame the Green Bay fans," he went on. "They had become accustomed to the Packers' domination in the championship years and were only voicing their displeasure over our more recent mediocre performances."

The season did have its highlights. One occurred on October 18th, when the organization staged Bart Starr Day. The night before, a ceremony in Starr's honor was held at Green Bay's Brown County Arena. Celebrities and dignitaries were on hand, including President Richard Nixon. Rams' head coach, George Allen, showed a measure of class by having his entire team in attendance. They were less gracious the following afternoon, disposing of the Packers and putting a blemish on an otherwise wonderful day for Starr.

Throughout the season, the injuries did not go away, particularly the shoulder pain. Starr's numbers gave indication of physical problems. His 140 completions of 255 attempts for 1,645 yards were at least acceptable, but his 13 interceptions against just eight TDs was atypical of the Starr of recent years. So was his 63.9 rating.

Starr wanted to give it one more shot under new coach Dan Devine, who came to Green Bay after a banner college coaching career at Arizona State and Missouri. The chronic shoulder pain was a concern to the team physicians, and they recommended Starr have a thorough examination at the Mayo Clinic in Rochester, Minnesota. There, a physician named Ed Henderson diagnosed a damaged tendon. He was confident that he could solve the problem by removing the damaged portion. Now 37, Starr was reluctant to undergo a serious operation on his arm so late in his career. Nonetheless, he wanted to play and the soreness continued to increase as training camp approached. He returned to the Mayo Clinic, where Dr. Henderson cut a keyhole-shaped opening in the bone of Starr's upper arm. The incision severed the tendon. It was then knotted, with the knot being inserted in the hole.

Starr got no relief. After three days, his bandages were soaked with blood. Initially, Starr was unconcerned, having been warned that some bleeding would occur but his wife was concerned. The next day Cherry noticed how pale her husband was and how the bleeding seemed to be getting worse.

"I'm calling Dr. (Eugene) Brusky," she said, referring to the team's physician.

Brusky examined Starr's arm and called the Mayo Clinic immediately. "Bart, you need emergency treatment," he told Starr. "The bleeding has broken your sutures."

Two hours later, Starr was in Minnesota and in peril of bleeding to death. When Dr. Henderson examined the quarterback's arm, he was irate. His assistant had not closed off a small artery as the operation was being completed. Starr had been bleeding from that artery for almost a week.

"I was unable to return until the end of the season," wrote Starr, "and performed poorly when I did. There had been some nerve damage as a result of the operation and I had problems gripping the football. A thin leather glove I had specially designed helped some but I could not throw the ball effectively." In '71, he attempted just 45 passes, completing 24 for 286 yards. Worse, he was intercepted three times but did not throw for a single touchdown.

Starr's absence hurt. Devine's inaugural season ended with a dismal 4-8-2 mark.

Faith and will propelled Starr forward. "The Lord takes care of things," he said. He wanted one more chance and rededicated himself to an intense rehab program under Gentile. "We both worked extremely hard during the off-season," noted Starr, "and the chronic soreness in the front of my shoulder faded. I continued to experience severe pain while throwing, however, and realized that I could be only a shadow of the quarterback I once had been."

Shortly before the beginning of the '72 training camp, Bart Starr announced his retirement. The Alabama benchwarmer who had been chosen in the 17th round of the 1956 draft had played sixteen years in the NFL. There he had been an All-Pro, Pro Bowl, and MVP quarterback, and led his team to five NFL championships. Five years later he was elected to the Hall of Fame in his first year of eligibility.

CHAPTER 23

Prayers and Patience

D AN DEVINE knew coaching talent when he saw it. When Starr retired as a player, the Packer coach asked him to remain as the quarterback coach. Green Bay had two young quarterbacks, a former Alabama signal caller Scott Hunter and a local high school star turned Nebraska Cornhusker, Jerry Tagge. For Starr and the Packers, it was an immensely rewarding experience as the team went 10-4. John Brockington and MacArthur Lane made the running game go and Chester Marcol solved the placekicking problems, while Starr guided the untested Hunter as he settled in at quarterback. The season ended with a 16-3 defeat in the playoffs, at the hands of the eventual NFC champion Washington Redskins. "He's like an encyclopedia," said an admiring Hunter of Starr, "We learn something new from him every day."

For Starr, that one year was enough. Claiming he was too busy with some of his business interests in Alabama, along with his speaking engagements, and other activities, Starr moved on. Two losing seasons later, so did Devine. Coaching under intense pressure from legions of disgruntled Packer fans, Devine was tossed what amounted to a life preserver. He was offered (and eagerly accepted) the coveted head coaching position at the University of Notre Dame, succeeding Ara Parseghian.

The Packers were in shambles, with dissension rife. They needed a coach. The team had put together just two winning seasons and one playoff appearance in the seven years following Lombardi's departure as coach. It was an awkward time. On one hand, there had been seven long years since the glory days. On the other, it was not so long ago that the fans could not remember those wonderful seasons and yearn for their return. Moreover, the players from the era, though no longer active, were vital young men, living reminders of what had been and perhaps could be again. In retrospect, it seemed only logical that the organization would turn to one of its own to lead them back to the days of dominance.

In a sense, Phil Bengtson really wasn't a Packer. Indeed, he had been the brains behind the defense throughout Lombardi's tenure. But he had not been a former Packer player whose exploits had thrilled the fans. Dan Devine was a complete outsider, and his time in Green Bay had been marked by discord and controversy. In addition, neither Bengtson nor Devine were compelling personalities. Both were introverted men, men who were uncomfortable with the media demands that attended the celebrity of being the head coach of the NFL's most romantic franchise. Bengtson had been gentlemanly but bland. Devine had occasionally been difficult. Such disabilities may have been tolerable as the media age developed, had the coaches taken the team to an occasional—even divisional—title. But other than 1972, neither had even contended. Especially in the shadow of Lombardi, neither really fit.

In that context, the Green Bay Packers offered Bart Starr a three-year contract to become their head coach and general manager.

According to Starr, his close friends advised him against taking the post. "Bart, you have nothing to gain," Skoronski told him. "Also, you're not prepared for the job. You don't have the experience." Skoronski was half right. Starr did lack experience. He had served a grand total of one year as a coach in the NFL, and that year, 1972, it had not been as head coach, or even offensive coordinator. He had coached the quarterbacks in the context of a ground-oriented offense. He did, however, have much to gain. From nothing, Starr had made himself one of the greatest quarterbacks in NFL history. Now, at just 40, he had the opportunity to make himself into one of the league's greatest coaches. And who could say he wouldn't succeed? Bart Starr had defied the odds from his childhood days in the rural South right up to posting league-leading passing numbers on mediocre, aging teams in the post-Lombardi era. This was the guy who had gone from being a 17th-round draft choice, a player with zero impact on any of his teammates for his first three seasons, to the league MVP in '66 and the MVP in each of the first two Super Bowls. What could be more dramatic, more romantic, more Chip Hilton, than to have this everyman-becomes-superstar, this Mr. Nice Guy, now lead the Packers back to the days of glory?

On Christmas Eve of 1974, Bart Starr accepted the offer.

"I ask for your prayers and your patience," said Starr in his press conference, sounding as if he had responded to a divine call, "we will earn everything else." Bart Starr, faith and will.

Indeed, it was a call to Starr. "I firmly believe," he said, "to every man there comes in his lifetime that special moment when he is figuratively tapped on the shoulder and offered that chance to do a very special thing, unique to him and fitted to his talents. What a tragedy if that moment finds him unprepared or unqualified for that work." Starr knew he was taking over with minimal coaching experience. "I'm not as qualified as I'd like to be," he acknowledged, "but I'm willing."

He didn't see a quick fix. "It may take awhile," he said to the gathered media, "but it is my unequivocal pledge to give this organization a fresh start." Starr had heard from other teams interested in his coaching acumen, but Green Bay was who Starr was. "I have a great love affair with the Packers," he explained. "For one reason or another I could not get excited about going somewhere else. I always felt there would be a time and a place for me at Green Bay."

He wanted to return lost luster. "I've been a little disappointed the last few years in traveling around the country to see that some of the respect for the Green Bay Packers has slipped," he said with almost certain understatement. "I want to restore that prestige, the prestige that has been part of this team for so many years."

Starr, however, had inherited an organization in shambles. The talent level had plummeted over the years. The team was also old, with thirteen players 29 or older. In addition, the team's top player, linebacker Ted Hendricks, tired of losing, refused to return, while Gale Gillingham, the lone holdover from the Lombardi era, decided to take a year off. Moreover, dating back to Lombardi's final years, the organization had not been prepared to replace the quality players that would be retiring. Perhaps the former coach and general manager, knowing he would soon be getting out of the coaching pressure cooker, had taken his eyes off the long-term personnel ball and focused all his

energies on wringing out those last few championships. Whatever, neither Bengtson nor Devine had proven particularly prescient in restock-
ing the franchise. Even worse, there wasn't much immediate hope for
anything approaching a rapid turnaround. In Devine's final season, in
perhaps a high stakes gamble to make a run at contention and keep
his job, he had acquired veteran quarterback John Hadl from the Los
Angeles Rams. On the face of it, the move made sense. Hadl was a
proven star, coming off a strong 1973 season. Unfortunately, the sun
was coming down on the former Kansas Jayhawk's career, and by '74
he was no longer the player he had been. The major problem was not
Hadl's inability to perform as a winner under center, but that the team
had parted with its top two draft choices in '75 (Starr's first draft before
his inaugural season as coach) and their top three in '76 to acquire
him.

With so little room to maneuver, Starr needed first-rate information on players in the college draft. He soon discovered no such thing
existed in the Packer organization. The scouting operation had become
primitive. Not only was information not computerized, it was not even
organized. It was so inept that when Starr inquired about Minnesota's
Rick Upchurch (who went on to a brilliant career in Denver) the Packers' Big Ten scout, a retired high school coach, had nothing for him.

As Starr realized what a morass he had inherited, he also began to
realize his lack of experience as he took over this formidable challenge.
During the league meetings, he pursued other coaches for advice.
Many were very helpful, among them Don Shula, who had suffered so
often from Starr's on-field exploits when he, Shula, coached the mighty
Baltimore Colts. Starr even went to Ohio State to visit Woody Hayes.
He was amazed at how much he picked up from the veteran coach.
The highlight or perhaps lowlight of the visit came when Hayes, out of
respect for Starr, invited him to address the Buckeye team. Starr had
hardly begun before the crusty mentor, a lover of military history,
grabbed him by the back of the collar and chewed him out, saying
"Don't you know that a good field general doesn't address his troops
when they have to look in the sun?"

At training camp, Starr pushed the team hard. "We have no illu-
sions," he told the press. "We have weaknesses to shore up and are
thin in the ranks. We have a lot of work to do."

Sports fans are rarely the most objective of people, so hopes were high now that Bart Starr would now be calling all the signals. When the team won its first pre-season game against the Buffalo Bills, the *Sports Illustrated* people were there for the story. The cover featured an action picture, proclaimed "Dreams of Glory in Green Bay," as the caption.

Starr knew better, and soon, so did the fans. After dropping the opener, with the help of two blocked punts, the Lions cruised by the Pack, 30-16. Three games later Starr was still looking for his first victory as an NFL head coach. The next game was against the powerful Dallas Cowboys, a 4-0 team on its way to the Super Bowl. Once again, playing the Cowboys proved to be the tonic the Packers needed, upsetting the Texas squad, 19-17, with the aid of a fumble by the Cowboy punt returner late in the game. "I am about three feet off the ground," said the excited Packer coach. The now 1-4 Packers hoped this would signal a turn in winning direction. It didn't. The team went 3-6 the rest of the way, closing the books on Starr's maiden voyage as coach, 4-10.

The team was competitive. They yielded just 59 points more than they scored (285 to 226), for a mere −4.2 points per game differential, a very respectable mark for a team six games under .500. The year did have its moments, even if they were off the field. Early in the campaign, Bart Jr. and several of his buddies decided to make their way into one of the city's local strip joints to see one Chesty Morgan strut her rather estimable stuff. Although none of the youths was 18—the legal beer and wine drinking age in Wisconsin at the time—the boys ordered up a few libations and readied themselves for the show. As he was sitting there, Bart spotted Bruce Van Dyke, one of the Packer guards on the other side of the stage. Their eyes met and Van Dyke made his way over to young Starr and said, "I won't tell if you won't." The two howled with laughter and at least Van Dyke was as good as his word.

"Our 4-10 record was shameful," wrote Starr in summarizing the season, "but our effort was Grade A. All we lacked was about ten or fifteen quality football players."

Before the '76 season, Starr started to address that problem. He swung a trade with the Houston Oilers for quarterback Lynn Dickey, a former star at Kansas State. Dickey was available because of inactivity due to a hip injury. He was slated to play backup to Oiler starter Dan Pastorini. Although Dickey proved a valuable addition, Starr was hurt

BART STARR

by some of the subtractions. One of them involved running star Mac-Arthur Lane. Against his better judgment, Starr acceded to members of his coaching staff who complained that Lane was simply too disruptive, and dealt him to Kansas City where he played very well.

The good news in '76 was that the Pack put together a three-game winning streak in mid-season. The bad news is that the team won only two of the other eleven games, giving them a meager one-game improvement over Starr's initial season. Even worse, the team scored fewer points (218) and allowed more (299) than they had in '75. The talent base remained thin in '76. "Because of this lack of talent," noted Starr, "we could move the ball only if we were willing to resort to unusual formations and deceptive plays, gimmicks. Practically every expansion team, starting with the Dallas Cowboys in 1960 resorted to such deception to cover weaknesses in personnel. We were no better than most expansion teams and worse than some."

What Starr wanted and saw that he did not have was a foundation. "If you're going to win in the future," he said early in his coaching tenure, "you have to build a foundation." This took time. "I am very much interested in winning," he explained, sounding like the disciple of Vince Lombardi that he was, "but sometimes you can win with gimmickry. I don't want to do things that way. I want that solid foundation."

Despite the Packers' 9-19 record after Starr's first two years in charge, he was not discouraged. "In many ways the past two seasons were a great deal like I had expected them to be," related Starr. "There was a lot of hard work, long hours, a restructuring of thoughts and ideas. There were a lot of areas in which I had to become familiar in a hurry."

"Cherry tells me that I'm not quite as patient as I used to be," he said, focusing fault on himself. "Maybe she is right."

For Starr it was always faith and will. "There is a lot to be learned in adverse situations," said the man who made a life of turning negatives into positives. "I think you learn a lot about people and about yourself in a losing situation, and that's good. That should help us all in the future."

As for his team, seeing was based on first believing. "I feel that the single most important ingredient to achieving," he said, "is developing and maintaining the proper attitude. Our people were able to overcome a number of handicaps and setbacks because they were able to display this kind of attitude."

No excuses would be made, however. "I think all of us are embarrassed by the record, and incensed," he confessed. "I hope we are. It's going to make us work harder to come out of this the best way we can next year. This record is hanging over our heads. It's something we all have to live with because our names are on it. It's something we have to make up for."

As testimony to the weakness of the '76 team, no less than ten draftees made the squad the following year. Starr has a bitter memory of an August pre-season game against the Patriots that year in Milwaukee. In the process of being routed by New England, playing reserves everywhere, the opponents poured it on, blitzing on down after down. According to Starr, the NFL coaching fraternity has an unwritten doctrine that states, "Thou shalt not intentionally humiliate an opponent once the game has been clearly decided." Chuck Fairbanks was in violation of that credo.

"I'm going to shake your hand," Starr said to him after the game, "but I think you're a first-class jerk. I don't know when, but I'm going to get you for this."

He didn't in '77, as the Packers sputtered their way to a 4-10 mark, scoring a puny 134 points—less than ten per game—though permitting a respectable 219. Far worse, however, late in the week nine game against Los Angeles, Lynn Dickey, the backbone of the offense who had missed time in '76 due to a dislocated shoulder, took a vicious hit from defensive tackle Larry Brooks, shattering his left tibia and fibula. When Starr asked Dr. Brusky for his diagnosis, the news wasn't good. "Bart, this one is really bad," said Brusky. "He might be able to play again, but I can't tell you when." Where would the offense come from now? Dickey did not reappear for two years.

Starr's three-year tenure concluded with an over-all record of 13-29-0. "Had the Packers decided to release me after the 1977 season, I wouldn't have blamed them," wrote Starr. "Our record on the field was the same as it had been in my first year at the helm." Contrast Starr's coach/general manager performance with Lombardi's, and one can understand his sentiments. The year before Lombardi arrived on the Green Bay scene, the Pack had posted a 1-10-1 mark. Lombardi then went 7-5, 8-4, and 11-3 in his first three seasons. Add in his post-season record, 1-1, and the former mentor's three-year log reads 27-13-0, with two conference titles and one NFL crown. Starr had posted a 13-29 mark after taking over a 6-8 squad. In short, Bart Starr had not gotten the job done. He had not rebuilt the team, nor had he focused it well enough in his tenure. Worse, he was being questioned in the most fundamental of ways and he did not like it. After a sportswriter wrote that Starr did not know how to win, the angry coach had all his championship hardware brought before his team and asked, "Does anybody in this room question whether I know what it takes to win?"

"It was a fairly quiet room," recalls offensive lineman Larry Mc-Carren.

The prayers likely had been there, but Starr's teams had earned little. The question now was whether there would be any more patience exhibited by the Packer executive board. "The aura of the Lombardi years sustained me, however," he noted, showing an impressive realism, "and I was given an extension."

With the extension in hand, Starr was ready to press on. He strengthened his coaching staff with the additions of Bill Curry and Ernie McMillan. The scouting operation had been renovated, and the physical plant had also been upgraded, including a now topflight weight room. The off-season conditioning program was really taking off amid improvements in a variety of other areas. A good draft and some player development with the youth currently on the roster, and the Packers may well be on the way.

CHAPTER 24

Hard Times

S TARR OPENED 1978 with a bang. He drafted eventual Hall of Famer James Lofton out of Stanford in the first round. In addition, he snagged linebacking star John Anderson from Michigan with his second first-round pick. Eight more draft choices cut the Green Bay mustard in '78 and Starr felt he may now have the foundation he needed.

The Pack, tired of losing and infused with youth, came roaring out of the blocks, posting a 6-1 record in the early season. In game four, the team played a superior San Diego Charger team in the Southern California heat. At the half, Starr challenged his squad saying, "I know we are in better physical condition than those guys. To win this game, you're going to have to be mentally tougher as well. Someone is going to collapse out there, and it won't be us." It wasn't. The Pack pounded the Chargers, who turned the ball over eleven times, 24-3. The next week San Diego Head Coach Tommy Prothro was replaced by Don "Air" Coryell. On the opening kickoff in the Packer's 45-28 conquest of Seattle, return man Steve Odom made good on a promise to break a kickoff for a score that he had made to a young child dying of cancer in Milwaukee.

The Packers were rolling. It looked as if the Packers had made a wise decision in retaining their coach/general manager.

But not for long. Green Bay went 2-6-0 in their next eight games, setting up a season-ending date with the Minnesota Vikings in Green

Bay. The winner would go to the playoffs. With less than two minutes left, the Packers led, 10-3. With that, Fran Tarkenton took over, completing two fourth-down passes and driving Minnesota into the end zone on a pass to Ahmad Rashad with just six seconds left. The game ended in a 10-10 tie, and the two teams finished the campaign with identical 8-7-1 records. The Vikings, however, went to the post-season, having defeated the Packers earlier in the season in Minnesota.

Starr didn't buy the accusation from the media that his team had "collapsed." "To begin with," he wrote, "we were not a 6-1 team after seven games. Our record was 6-1, but we were only an average team, not a good one. In addition, we were not yet a mature ball club. In fact, many of the major contributors to our success were in their first or second year in the NFL. This factor worked against us once we became the hunted rather than the hunter. We played the second half of the season with little or no chance of sneaking up on opponents." The situation was aggravated by the absence of Lynn Dickey. Starr was correct. The scoring numbers indicate this was at best a middling team. The Packers scored 249 points, placing them tenth in the fourteen-team NFC. They gave up 20 more points than they scored, although their 269 points allowed was good enough for fifth place.

Starr was anxious for the '79 draft. A few good picks could put the team over the top. The Pack chose Georgia Tech's Eddie Lee Ivery with their first choice. Starr reasoned that the addition of Ivery to an attack already featuring a 1000-yard rusher in Terrell Middleton and a big play receiver in Lofton could ignite the offense, especially if Dickey could make it back. It was in that draft, however, that Starr passed on a player he liked out of Notre Dame. His name was Joe Montana. "I blew our next two picks," stated Starr candidly, referring to his choice between Ivery and the availability of Montana, who went to San Francisco in the third round. On the plus side, Starr selected Rich Wingo out of Alabama, much to the delight of his father, Ben. "Son, that boy's a real football player," Ben enthused. "Ol' Bear (Bryant) really taught him well."

"We finished the pre-season with a level of optimism and confidence unlike any we had felt even during our hot streak the previous year," wrote Starr. With Ivery meshing with an offense run by a recovering Dickey, certainly good things were in store. The team opened the campaign in Chicago. In the first quarter, Ivery blew out his knee on Soldier Field's astroturf, and was gone for the season. An overtime loss in Minnesota was typical of the season. The Packers had the ball on their own 25-yard line and the score tied 21-21, with more than a minute left in regulation. Starr chose to freeze the ball and wait for overtime. Green Bay kicked off and never saw the ball again as the Vikings scored a winning TD for a 27-21 triumph. James Lofton was furious. Firing his helmet into his locker he attacked Starr's strategy. "We weren't playing to win," he raged. "We were just playing not to lose."

"Knock it off," the Starr retorted. "You play. I'll coach."

Starr coached Lofton and his mates to a dismal 5-11 record. They scored 246 points, about the same as in '78 (249), but gave up 319.

Among the few bright spots in the season was a Monday night payback win against New England. After falling back 7-0 to the favored Patriots, the Pack turned it on and defeated the New Englanders, 27-14.

With the disappointment of '79, the 1980 season, with the return of Ivery and a now healed Lynn Dickey, seemed certain to be the turnaround year. The team did improve—by a half a game, finishing 5-10-1. In some respects, the team did not improve. They parted with 140 more points than they scored (371-231), for a −8.8 points per game margin. Moreover, their 231 points scored was the lowest in the NFC, while only three other NFC squads gave up more than 371 points.

As is almost always the case in the NFL, there were some tough losses. One of them occurred in Cleveland where Brian Sipe completed a game-winning underthrown touchdown pass in the final seconds because Packer secondary man Mark Lee slipped. In Pittsburgh, the team fell, 22-20, largely due to nine points yielded on bad snaps to the punter. In a 14-14 tie, Green Bay rolled up 569 yards of total offense, only to fall short of victory by missing two easy field goals.

After five years as coach and general manager, Starr had compiled a 31-57-2 record. Moreover, the press was now really on him such that his relations with the media were becoming a "war," according to Paul Attner of the *Sporting News.* At one point, Starr banned Cliff Christl of the *Green Bay Press-Gazette* from riding on the team charter until "the coverage changed and was more positive."

"He suggested that I was out to damage him and out to damage the Green Bay Packers," recalls Dave Begal, then of the *Milwaukee Journal.*

"It was the first time in his life that he was associated with losing," says sportscaster Tom Sutton in summation, "and he hated it."

The executive board decided an alteration was in order. They removed Starr's general manager role and hired Tom Braatz, formerly of the Atlanta Falcons, for that job. Starr did not like it. "I was extremely disappointed in their decision," he noted. "The logical move, in my opinion, would have been to retain me as the general manager and select a new coach. Our progress in areas most influenced through the general manager's role had been significant, for we were now a solidly structured organization." Moreover, if Starr was to be replaced as general manager, he had hoped it would be by someone with extensive football knowledge, a person in the George Young or Jim Finks tradition. Braatz's football roots did not go that deep.

The 1981 draft was another one Starr—still very much in charge of the picks—regretted. In the first round, he favored Ronnie Lott out of USC, but the team needed a quarterback to groom behind Dickey— who was now north of 30 and banged up—and Starr's people urged him to consider Rich Campbell. "Everyone in our organization who was specifically assigned to evaluate Campbell, including me, gave him high marks ranging from good to great," Starr stated. "However, I was very concerned with a flaw in his delivery, which was best described as 'short-armed' and prevented him from throwing the ball very hard. When I reviewed the film of the workout we put him through, I was even more concerned."

Unfortunately, he was not concerned enough to go with his own intuitions and take Lott. Rich Campbell was the Green Bay Packers' first round draft choice in 1981. The Packers opened the season against divisional rival Chicago in the Windy City. It was a near instant replay of the sickening experience of two years previous. Once again, Eddie Lee Ivery planted his foot to make a cut, and once again, his knee gave way, this time tearing a different ligament. The team did manage to prevail against the Bears, but by mid-season Green Bay was a sorry 2-6. Rumors were rife of Starr's being on the way out, but the team stayed focused.

After week three of the '81 campaign, the Packers swung a major deal with San Diego, acquiring wide receiver John Jefferson for three high draft choices. With Dickey's throwing acumen, Lofton already a major force as deep receiving threat, and tight end Paul Coffman emerging as a solid receiver as well, the acquisition of the speedy Jefferson completed the air game. Within a month the quartet was making sweet gridiron music such that, despite the loss of Ivery, the Pack's second half mark was 6-2, the exact opposite of the first. In fact, Green Bay went into the final game of the season against the New York Jets with an 8-7 record. Had they won that one, the Packers would have been back in the playoffs for the first time in nine seasons. The difference from '80 was almost entirely on the offensive side of the ball as the Pack scored 324 points, 93 more than the previous year. They continued to allow too many points, however, as their 361 opposition points was the eleventh worst mark in the NFC.

It had now been seven painful years for the new coach, but Starr, being a man of faith and will, prepared himself for what figured to be the corner-turning year of 1982. The team opened poorly, falling behind the Rams, 23-0, at the half. Starr was livid. He cleared the locker room of all but the coaches and players, and proceeded to tear into the squad. "That was the most disgraceful effort I have ever seen," he raged. "If you don't have any more pride than what's on display in the first half, then go take your showers now."

The showers remained dry and the team called up some pride, as the Pack blasted their way through the second half by scoring five TDs and outscoring Los Angeles 35-0 in the final thirty minutes to post a 35-23 victory. The early season also included a stirring Monday Night Football win against the New York Giants in the Meadowlands. Trailing 19-7, the offense kicked in. A huge play unfolded on the Packers' 17-yard line, when James Lofton took the ball on a reverse and sprinted for an 83-yard score. Green Bay prevailed, 27-19. This appeared to be the year for Green Bay, until the players went on strike.

"You have to assume you'll be playing again soon, even though it doesn't look like you will," Starr told his squad as they readied to part ways. "The team that stays in the best condition will be the one that gets off to a fast start when you return. We'll get information to the captains tomorrow regarding the availability of St. Norbert College's facilities for your use."

With that, the strike was on. It lasted 57 days and lopped six games off the schedule. The Packers won their first game back from the sabbatical, 26-7, at the expense of the Vikings and finished the season with a 5-3-1 mark. It had been a solid albeit abbreviated season. Their 226 points tied them with Dallas as the NFC's top scoring team. They yielded 169 points, leaving them at a +57 in point differential, or 6.5 points per game.

More important, the Packers were in the playoffs. The NFL scrapped its usual format in '82 for a 16-team Super Bowl tournament. Eight teams from each conference, NFC and AFC, were in the playoff mix, and they were seeded within each conference to determine pairings. Green Bay opened against a 5-4 St. Louis Cardinal team in Green Bay. Happy days were here again as the Pack simply pounded the Cardinals, 41-16, setting them up for a date with the Cowboys. The men of Landry had gone 6-3 and so the game was played in Dallas. The Cowboys pounced on Starr's bunch early and jumped out to 20-7 lead. Given that the Dallas defense yielded barely more than 15 points a game during the season, the sky looked dark for Green Bay. Late in the game, however, the Packers closed to 30-26 margin, and the battle was on. The Cowboys emerged with a 37-26 victory.

The 1982 season had marked a major step forward for the Packers and the fans knew it, as a throng of Packer backers enthusiastically welcomed their heroes upon their arrival from Dallas. For Starr, the future looked much brighter, although the Packer president, former circuit court judge Robert Parins, was not rejoicing, and grudgingly gave his coach a two-year extension.

The 1983 season could not come soon enough for Bart Starr and the Green Bay fans. As the season approached, two concerns arose. J.J. Jefferson was not in top shape, owing in part to less than spartan off-season conditioning habits, and Green Bay, despite the assurances of Parins, did not sign free agent defensive back Mike Butler. The failure to sign Butler was of particular import to Starr, who now felt he had plenty of firepower on offense, but needed to fortify his defense.

Starr proved correct. The 1983 Green Bay Packers scored a hefty 429 points (26.8 per game). Only four of the other thirteen NFC teams did better. Regrettably, they allowed 439 points, and no NFC squad did worse. The result was an 8-8 mark.

Not only did the already spotty Green Bay defense have to go into action without Butler in the secondary, in the season opener against the Oilers at Houston, the Pack lost nose tackle Terry Jones with a torn Achilles tendon. (Five games later Jones' backup, Richard Turner was gone for the season with a knee injury.) "It quickly became apparent that we were going to have substantial difficulty stopping anybody," wrote Starr, "as Houston nearly ran the ball down our throats, despite the fact that Earl Campbell was clearly past his prime." Somehow, Lynn Dickey, despite a migraine, hit on 27 of 31 throws for 333 yards and five scores, giving the Pack a rousing 41-38 win.

A loss to Pittsburgh at home was followed with a 27-24 win over the Rams, on one of the great Jan Stenerud's last-second field goals in a game in which the Pack lost another defender, linebacker Randy Scott. The team was 3-3 when the Super Bowl champion Washington swaggered into Green Bay for a nationally televised Monday Night confrontation. The final score was typical of the Packers' season: Green Bay 48, Washington 47. This was followed by a crushing 20-17 overtime loss to the Vikings, and later a 47-41 defeat in Atlanta, where the Falcons, an ordinary team at best, feasted on the crippled Green Bay defense. Still another of Jan Stenerud's last-second field goals pulled the Pack through against Mike Ditka's rapidly improving Bears, 31-28, at Lambeau Field.

Two weeks later, the Packers were in Soldier Field with an 8-7 record, and in a familiar position. A win would put them into the playoffs and a loss would eliminate them. On a bitterly cold day, Green Bay clung to 21-20 lead with a few minutes left. If the Pack's depleted but game defense could stop the Bears, Green Bay would be headed back to the post-season, but the Bears moved the ball down the field and kicked a game-winning field goal. Despite the agonizing defeat, Starr felt good about Green Bay Packer football. The team's last losing campaign was four seasons back. Moreover, he now had a potent offense, and with a return to health on the defensive side of the ball and an additional player or two, the team was on the brink of becoming a consistent contender. "We were no longer a losing ball club," he noted, "and, more important, we were on the verge of long-term respectability. We had rekindled the emotions between the Packer fans and the team. We played exciting, hard-hitting football, and we did so with class."

On Monday, the day after the season, Judge Parins walked into Starr's office as the coach was preparing for his planning and review session with his assistants.

"I want to talk to you, Bart," said Parins.

"The coaches are waiting for me," Starr replied. "Is it going to take long?"

"Not long at all," said Parins. "You don't have to worry about your meeting, because as of this moment I am relieving you of your coaching position."

The Green Bay icon's 26-year relationship with his beloved Packers ended with Judge Parins' final eight words.

Starr closed the door of his office and wept.

CHAPTER 25

What Have I Done with My Life?

I WASN'T QUALIFIED to be the coach when I got the job," Bart told Jerry Kramer, "but I worked very hard for nine years, gave them every ounce of energy I had and was becoming a pretty good coach when they fired me." No one questioned Bart Starr's commitment. "The man gave his entire life to the Green Bay Packers," said former teammate Fuzzy Thurston at the Packer reunion in 1984, less than a year after Starr was fired. "I'll always cherish him for that. He's beautiful."

And it was painful. "I'd never been fired from anything before," he told Jerry Kramer, "and it really hurt. When you've coached your heart out, when you know you've given it your best shot, and you get fired, you'd be less than normal if you didn't resent that. You feel angry. You feel torn up inside." Yet he remained faithful to the green and gold. "I will be the Packers' number one fan. No one has more heart and soul in this organization than I do."

It is difficult, however, to argue with Judge Parins' decision. Although Starr did go 21-19-1 in his last three seasons, it took six bleak seasons to put together that modest run. His over-all mark was 52-76-3. Indeed his lack of experience showed in the early going. Although a brilliant offensive mind, in Starr's first five years, his teams never ranked above 23rd in total offense (yardage); none were placed in the upper half in total defense, either.

It was not until his sixth season, 1980, that he was able to put together a defense that placed above the league middle, and that one ranked 14th in a 28-team NFL. Although they slipped to 22nd the following year, Starr's offenses clicked in his final two seasons, placing 10th and then 1st in his final campaign, 1983. Only once did the team rank above 21st in rushing—'82 when they finished 12th. Although 2nd in the league in passing in '83, they cut the top ten only one other time when they placed 8th in '80.

Similarly, it was not until his seventh season, 1981, that Starr was able to assemble a defense that placed above the league middle (eighth) a ranking they repeated the following season. They dropped to dead last in Starr's final season, sealing his coaching doom. All in all, Starr really had only one good year, the strike-shortened '82 season when the team ranked 10th on offense and 8th on defense. In no other season did the team rank in the upper half of the league on both sides of the ball.

But leadership does not show only in success. Starr never gave up hope, never lost his optimism, and a strong case can be made that he certainly was in the process of turning the Pack around in his final years. Moreover, his successor, Forrest Gregg—who had brought the Cincinnati Bengals to the Super Bowl in '81 season—really did no better than his former teammate. The man who said, "I didn't take this job to field a losing football team. I took this job to field a winning team. That will happen," was unable to keep his pledge. After putting together two .500 seasons in '84 and '85 with the team he inherited from Starr, Gregg went 9-23 in his final two campaigns.

To lose his job was agonizing for Starr. He certainly had given his life to the Green Bay Packers. In fact, losing of any kind had become difficult after those clutch performances in championship seasons. He had learned the lesson of winning from the master's psychology book. "I wasn't mentally tough before I met Coach Lombardi," Starr told Jerry Kramer. "I hadn't reached the point where I refused to accept second best. I was too nice at times. I don't believe that nice guys necessarily finish last. I think what Leo Durocher really meant was that nice guys don't finish first. To win, you have to have a certain mental toughness. Coach Lombardi gave me that. He taught me that you must have a flaming desire to win. It's got to dominate all your waking hours. It can't ever wane. It's got to glow in you all the time." As such,

Starr—faith and will—did not feel he was through with coaching after leaving Green Bay. He had learned the coaching ropes and had made a lifetime habit out of turning failure into success. As such, he worked with a group of Arizona businessmen to bring an expansion team, the Phoenix Thunderbirds, to the desert, where he would once again be coach and general manager. It wasn't to be.

Starr moved back to Alabama after his dismissal in Green Bay, but it was not the end of his heartaches. Although his son, Bart Jr., got married and established a wonderful family, his younger son, Bret, struggled through life. An able musician, the younger Starr learned the guitar and invested his energy in rock music, motorcycles, and reptiles, according his father. He began associating with a drug crowd. "Looking back, there were definite signs," wrote Starr. "Bret was experimenting with drugs, but Cherry and I were in a denial stage, unable to believe our young son could possibly be involved in anything so ugly. Unbeknownst to us, by the time Bret graduated from high school, he was well on his way to cocaine addiction."

He blew out at the University of Wisconsin at Madison. In fact, Bart dropped everything and he and Cherry drove down to Madison to confront Bret after a disturbing telephone call he had with his mother. When they reached his dorm room, he would not let them in. He was afraid to open the door because he owed money to drug dealers. Finally, he gave in and the Starrs were in for the shock of their lives. "The son we adored so much was standing before us, looking like a frightened, hunted animal," wrote Bart. "Cherry and I had never experienced such pain as we felt at that moment."

They sent their son to the renowned Hazelden Clinic in Minneapolis. He did not cooperate there and begged to return home, agreeing to help himself. He improved and, believing he had his problem under control, moved to Tampa to open an exotic animal import business with a friend, financed in part by Bart and Cherry. He was soon back into drugs with his partner, who was also chemically dependent. Tired of the life he had been living, and aware of the pain it caused others, he quit using cold turkey. He used body-building as his new outlet, and put his faith in God and embraced a life of gratitude. He called home regularly, receiving support from his family. In 1986 he spent his first Christmas with his family in three years. The story, however, does not have a happy ending. Two years later, Bret's problems with substance abuse took his life. He was 24. Bart found his son's body as he looked through the window of Bret's locked Tampa, Florida, apartment in July of 1988. "I slid down the side of the house and began to cry," recalls Starr sadly. "That, I think, came as close to killing Bart as anything I know," says Knafelc.

"I could never appreciate what my parents went through when my brother died until years later when we lost our younger son, Bret, at the age of 24," Bart told the *Birmingham Christian Family*, in 2001. "Only then could I appreciate the pain and agony they went through."

"You cannot come out of a tragic situation unless your attitude will allow you," said the man who embraced faith and will. "Your attitude will get you out of it. It worked for us. I think 'attitude' is the most powerful word, other than love, in our vocabulary. You have the choice. God gives you the strength, the power, the courage, the assets with which to do it. It is up to you what you do with them."

Family became even more important after the loss of Bret. "We came out of that with an even greater appreciation for our older son, Bart Jr.," Starr explained. "Out of tragedy can come healing and strengthening that are difficult to describe unless you have been through them. It is tough when we have a death in the family, but I think if we are truly faithful we come to appreciate the strengths that remain with us or they become more evident."

And Starr demonstrated those strengths. When former teammate and then Alabama Head Coach Bill Curry asked Starr if he would someday address his team on the topic of drugs. "You can count on it," said Starr. Curry recalled Starr's stirring presentation on ESPN. "They talked about the real stuff. They talked about what the drugs were, what the chemical reaction was, what kind of person Bret was." Starr then said, "Some of you in this room have these issues and may not know it."

Afterward an emotional Curry said, "You just saved, I don't know, how many."

Starr began working with his now only son in two different companies. "What a joy it has been to be near our son and be able to spend so much time with him, his wife, and our three granddaughters." As for his wife, Cherry, Starr has nothing but superlatives for a woman who has cared for a dying woman, a foreign student who was in danger of being deported, a lonely Packer player, and a homeless child. "She is a marvelous lady, the most caring, concerned, loving person you will ever meet."

"What have I done with my life?" Jerry Kramer courageously asked himself in his book, *Distant Replay*. He remarked at how his father, an Idaho businessman, had forgiven the debts of a number people who had bought television sets from him. His father had walked the walk of honest, decency, and fairness. Kramer himself had gone through a failed marriage and regretted neglecting his children from that union.

In the early eighties Kramer lost his father to cancer, something he wondered if he would ever get over. "Dad was a very religious man," wrote Kramer, "and he was ready to go. He had his faith and he said he was locked in the arms of the Lord." Kramer admired his father, a man similar to Starr. When asked what his greatest accomplishment was, Starr replied, "Attempting to live my life with the priorities of God, family, and others."

When one asks what has Bart Starr done with his life, it is easy to give positive answers. "Bart always said the right thing," wrote Jerry Kramer, "always did the right thing. All the years we played together, I looked for a flaw, waited for a slip, an inconsistency, a contradiction in his nature. I never spotted one."

"He was a superstar," says Donny Anderson, "and his name was Starr. He's always been an idol to a lot of us guys."

Perhaps another of his former teammates, Fuzzy Thurston, said it best at the '84 Packer reunion. "I love every one of my teammates," said an emotional Thurston, "but none of them's higher on the list as a human being than Bart Starr."

BIBLIOGRAPHY

Among the many sources consulted in this biography were the following books:
Barron, Bill, ed. *The Official NFL Encyclopedia of Pro Football* (New York: New American Library, 1982).
ESPN *Sports Century,* "Bart Starr."
————, "Vince Lombardi."
Gruver, Edward. *Nitschke* (Lanham, MD: Taylor, 2002).
Kramer, Jerry. *Distant Replay* (New York: Jove, 1986).
————. *Instant Replay* (New York: World Publishing, 1968).
————. *Jerry Kramer's Farewell to Football* (New York: Bantam, 1970).
————, ed. *Lombardi: Winning Is the Only Thing* (New York: Pocket, 1971).
Lombardi, Vince. *Run to Daylight* (Englewood Cliffs, NJ: Prentice-Hall, 1963).
Maraniss, David. *When Pride Still Mattered* (New York: Simon & Schuster, 1999).
Maule, Tex. *Bart Starr: Professional Quarterback* (New York: F. Watts, 1973).
Parcells, Bill. *The Final Season* (New York: Morrow, 2000).
Russell, Bill. *Russell Rules* (New York: Dutton, 2001).
Schoor, Gene. *Bart Starr: A Biography* (Garden City, NY: Doubleday, 1977).
Starr, Bart. *Starr: My Life in Football* (New York: Morrow, 1987).

INDEX

101–2, 105–6, 118, 131, 133, 144–45, 147, 152, 157, 175, 180, 198; 1970s, 217, 218, 221
Chicago Cardinals, 67, 77, 92
Civil Rights movement, 2
Clay, Cassius, 4
Cleveland Browns, 61, 118, 147, 159–60, 163–64, 217
Cochran, Red, 82, 126, 136
Coffman, Paul, 218
Collier, Blanton, 159
Cone, Fred, 56
Conerly, Charlie, 122
Connell, Joe, 185
Coryell, Don "Air", 215
Cosell, Howard, 4
Crenshaw, Leon, 172
The Crimson-White, 37–38
Crutcher, Tommy Joe, 179
Cuozzo, Gary, 157
Currie, Dan, 65, 91, 128, 138, 145, 155, 161; player high jinks, 82; professional accolades, 137
Curry, Bill, 175, 214, 226
Curtis, Joe, 38

Dale, Carroll: 1965 NFL title game, 160, 162; 1966 NFL title game, 165; 1967 NFL title game, 185; spiritual leadership, 175, 176–77; Super Bowl I, 167; Super Bowl II, 191
Daley, Art, 71
Dallas Cowboys, 9, 105, 164–65, 185–87, 198, 211, 220
Davis, Al, 188
Davis, Willie, 7, 110, 117–18, 128, 162, 196, 199; on Nitschke, 178; on Super Bowl I, 166; Super Bowl II, 189, 191; as a team leader, 197, 198
Dee, Johnny, 45–46, 47, 51
Detroit Lions: 1950s, 61, 65, 66, 67, 95, 97; 1960s, 105, 117, 119, 132–33, 133–34, 147, 155, 175, 197, 198; 1970s, 204, 211
Devine, Dan, 204–5, 207, 208, 210
Devore, Hugh, 48
Dickey, Lynn, 211–12, 213, 216, 221
Dick the Bruiser, 56
Dietzel, Paul, 46
Dillon, Bobby, 57
DiMaggio, Joe, 23–24
discrimination. See racism
Distant Replay (Kramer), 13, 144, 227
Ditka, Mike, 119, 145, 221

Dittrich, John, 92
Doherty, Ray, 95, 122
Dowler, Boyd, 7, 92, 97, 151, 157, 162; military duty, 119; 1962 NFL title game, 136; 1966 NFL title game, 165; 1967 NFL title game, 185; 1960 season, 102, 103, 108, 127; Super Bowl II, 190
Drew, Rod, 35, 39, 41

Eisenhower, Dwight, 1
Elway, John, 10
ESPN Sports Century, 92
Evashevski, Forrest, 85

Fairbanks, Chuck, 213
Farewell to Football (Kramer), 73, 95
Favre, Brett, 10
Fears, Tom, 133
"Feeling Unanimous: Starr Was Great" (Doherty), 122
The Feminine Mystique (Friedan), 2
feminism, 1–2
Ferguson, Howie, 55, 81–82
Fleming, Marv, 155, 195, 200
Football and the Single Man (Hornung), 143
Forester, Bill, 57, 94, 128, 137, 155, 161
Fortunato, Joe, 145
Francis, Joe, 71–72, 93, 96
Freeman, Bobby, 92
Friedan, Betty, 2
Friedman, Benny, 169

gambling scandals, 142–43
Gentile, Dominic, 204, 206
George, Bill, 106, 145
Germanos, Nick, 28, 32, 34, 35, 40
Gifford, Frank, 99, 144
Gillingham, Gale, 161, 162, 184, 209
Gilmer, Harry, 24, 38–39
Goode, Bud, 11
Grabowski, Jim, 162, 172, 195, 197
Green Bay Packers, 4–6, 52–53, 174; Lombardi, signing of, 86; player high jinks, 55–56, 68, 69, 98, 104, 111, 128, 134; racism within organization, 49, 60, 103; religion and, 175, 176–77, 183; scouting operations, 210, 214; 1956 season, 57; 1957 season, 62–63; 1958 season, 65–70; 1959 season, 94–98; 1960 season, 101–12; 1961 season, 117–21; 1962 season, 131–37; 1963 season, 144–47; 1964 season, 151–53; 1965 season, 155–60; 1966 season, 163–68; 1967 season, 175–80,